Paul Schalow



December 22, 1999

Tokyo – from Oba Minako

# Gender Is Fair Game

## (Re)Thinking the (Fe)Male in the Works of Ōba Minako

**A Series edited by**
**Michiko Niikuni Wilson**

**Japanese Women Writing**, devoted to works by and about Japanese literary women, celebrates the resurgence of women's writings in a country that gave women a voice and a room of their own as early as A.D. 900. Despite a long hiatus in the female literary tradition between 1190 and 1868, and another during the Pacific War, Japanese female writers have been able to reclaim what is their due. Introducing a wide range of writing since the early 1900s—fiction, poetry, critical essays, and biographies—**Japanese Women Writing** attempts to redefine the modern Japanese literary canon and highlight a female perspective that intersects with the notions of gender, power, and sexuality.

Japanese
Women
Writing

# Gender Is Fair Game

## (Re)Thinking the (Fe)Male in the Works of Ōba Minako

Michiko Niikuni Wilson

AN EAST GATE BOOK

M.E. Sharpe
Armonk, New York
London, England

**Library of Congress Cataloging-in-Publication Data**

Wilson, Michiko N.
Gender is fair game : (re)thinking the (fe)male in the works of Ōba Minako /
by Michiko Niikuni Wilson.
p. cm.—(Japanese women writing)
"An East Gate book."
Includes bibliographical references and index.
ISBN 0-7656-0313-6 (alk. paper).
1. Ōba, Minako—Criticism and interpretation. I. Title. II. Series.
PL858.B3Z95 1998
895.6′35—dc21
98-18947
CIP

Printed in the United States of America

The paper used in this publication meets the minimum requirements of
American National Standard for Information Sciences—
Permanence of Paper for Printed Library Materials,
ANSI Z 39.48-1984.

BM (c) 10 9 8 7 6 5 4 3 2 1

*For my little girl within*

**Ōba Minako**

# Contents

# Preface

"Gender" (*jendaa*) and "feminism" (*feminizumu*) belong to a group of loan words such as "privacy" and "priority" that have no Japanese equivalents. A feminist perspective has been slow to develop in Japanese literary studies, so much so that it may sound naive (or worse yet, essentialist*) to those feminists engaged in Anglo-American studies, for whom gender has been fair game over the past three decades.

At the height of academe's preoccupation with postmodernism in the 1980s and early 1990s, it seemed that Japanese studies had bypassed *jendaa* altogether. Postmodernists pronounced that "we are beyond gender," that gender is no longer an issue. But others contested this assertion and pointed out that gender as an integral part of feminist studies remains relevant. I concur with Temma Kaplan's affirmation in the foreword to *Who's Afraid of Feminism? Seeing Through the Backlash*: "Since the seventies, critics have been pronouncing the end of feminism. Judging from the backlash, . . . I'd say that feminism was here to stay. . . . Feminism is anything but monolithic. . . [it] is alive and well, free floating and free spirited."** And, I would add, it has finally, and

*Essentialism glorifies female biological destiny. It also sees gender "as rooted in biological sex differences." See "A Gender Diary" by Ann Snitow in *Conflicts in Feminism*, ed. Marianne Hirsch and Evelyn For Keller (New York: Routledge, 1990), pp. 15–16.

**Edited by Ann Oakly and Juliet Mitchell (New York: New Press, 1997), pp. xiii and xviii.

rather dramatically, floated towards Japanese studies.

Nineteen eighty-eight marked the first feminist panel ever held at the annual meeting of the Association for Asian Studies (AAS).* As recently as 1994, if memory serves me, there was still only one panel title on Japan that mentioned feminism.** (The organizer of both panels was Chieko Ariga.) However, in the 1998 AAS program, the word "gender" appears in almost 20 percent of the titles of papers on Japan, and if one includes the words "woman," "female," and "feminine," the percentage increases to 35 percent. Nineteen nintey-six saw the publication of the groundbreaking work, *The Woman's Hand: Gender and Theory in Japanese Women's Writing*, a "collection of essays that takes women's writing as its primary subject," assuming "a link between gender and discursive practice" and recognizing that "the project of describing how the sex/gender system affects Japanese women's and men's writing has only just begun in North American scholarship."†

My encounter with feminism and Ōba Minako's work dates back to the mid-1980s when Chieko I. Mulhern asked me to contribute to another collaborative effort, *Japanese Women Writers: A Bio-Critical Sourcebook.*†† Ōba Minako was one of the four writers assigned to me, at a time when writing about women's lives and works was not even on my agenda. My evolution was gradual.

It was several years before I connected the concept of marginality in Ōe Kenzaburo's work along with Mikhail Bahktin's political message of grotesque realism with female outsiderhood and women's subversive writings—issues that had nonetheless been percolating in my subconscious. With my present work—one attempt to apply the poetics of gender and feminist criticism

---

*"Constructing the Feminine: The Significance of Gender in Japanese Literature."

**A two-part panel entitled "Feminist Criticism and Japan Studies."

† Edited by Paul Gordon Schalow and Janet A. Walker (Stanford, CA: Stanford University Press, 1996), p. 1.

††(Westport, Connecticut: Greenwood Press, 1994).

to engender an alternative reading of Japanese literary texts—the mind has finally found its significant other, the body, in what Adrienne Rich called "personal grounding."

It is a revelation that, I am well aware, comes rather late to many female writers, readers, and scholars. I am such a latecomer. For those who have it early, it is truly a privilege. Women know that integrating the mind and body into an original whole is by no means just a spiritual journey, but an intellectual one as well. To recognize the mind-body split is to pose the question: Does gender have anything to do with what I am, as a reader, scholar, and a woman? The answer is a resounding yes. Needless to say, I have benefited greatly from American feminist scholarship, without which I would never have found my true voice nor appreciated fully the richness of Japanese women's writings.

The University of Virginia provided me a Sesquicentennial sabbatical in the spring of 1996 that allowed me to complete a draft of this project. The East Asian Center of the university made the visit of Ōba Minako and her husband, Toshio, possible in the spring of 1993, when Ōba gave a public lecture at the university. Jamie and Mary McConnell graciously hosted the Ōbas at their estate. The Women's Center and the Women's Studies Program, with Sharon Davie and Ann J. Lane as directors, have been instrumental in creating an environment that recognizes feminist scholarship at the university.

Over the years I have nurtured and carried this project toward a safe delivery, many people have supported me in ways that I could never repay. My special thanks go to Doug Merwin who showed interest and confidence in my project when I first approached him. I wish to thank Kojima Junko who has tirelessly replenished my emotional energy by showing what Japan is not. I have had the great fortune of knowing Keiko I. McDonald, a visiting professor at the University of Texas at Austin in 1974–75, who initiated me into the world of critical writing. I thank Mary B. McKinley for her constant support and generosity, and for a birthday gift in 1989 of a copy of Writing Women's Life by Carolyn G. Heilbrun that began the whole process of my re-awakening. Janice Brown, who read the entire manuscript twice over and validated my undertaking, has cheered me on with a great sense of humor and a vision. I owe Becky Thomas for her intellectuality and ever-ready editorial pen, precise and resourceful, which guided me in the rewriting and reshaping of the manuscript.

Chapter 3, "Becoming and (Un)Becoming: The Female Destiny Reconsidered," is a revised version of an essay that appeared in *The Woman's Hand: Gender and Theory in Japanese Women's Writing*. I would like to thank Susan Fraiman—whose work on Victorian female "unbecoming" writers inspired me tremendously—for her comments on and enthusiasm for my manuscript. I also received encouragement from Bella DePaul who kindly read the entire manuscript. The acknowledgment is not complete without expressing my indebtedness to Michael K. Wilson, my best companion in every possible way, who is and has been always there.

M.N.W.

# Gender Is Fair Game

## (Re)Thinking the (Fe)Male in the Works of Ōba Minako

# 1

# Introduction

"She [is], explicitly, not a feminist; but her life might be an example for many who are."[1]

Ōba Minako (1930– ) began her writing career as an ordinary homemaker in a tiny Alaskan fishing town, Sitka, where she lived with her husband for eleven years. However, her Alaskan life between 1959 and 1971, which coincided with Japan's postwar reconstruction and the ensuing swift economic growth, was anything but ordinary. Minako[2] took full advantage of the status of being a voyager abroad to enjoy traveling by car and painting, two avocations which were almost impossible for her to pursue in Japan at that time. Her wanderlust took her on the road across the North American continent many times over. In 1962 at the age of thirty-one, she took up painting as a graduate student in the art department at the University of Wisconsin at Madison. Four years later, she chose to continue painting lessons in the summer graduate art program at the University of Washington at Seattle, where she was able to audit many literature classes as well.[3] It was soon after her return to Sitka that she produced the award-winning short story "Sanbiki no kani" (The Three Crabs, 1967), for which she won the Akutagawa Prize that launched her career.[4]

---

*Note:* All Japanese names are cited according to the native custom of giving the family names first, the given name second.

Her experience of geographical displacement from Japan indicated a profound intellectual development in the making of a superbly gifted writer, a far cry from the status enhancement, romanticism, and escapism that Japanese male writers often associated with sojourning in the West during the Meiji–Taishō periods (1868–1926).[5] Living in an alien land has always been a trauma for Japanese people. Cut off from the comfortable womb of an unambiguous motherland, often plagued with an inability to speak the host language, and handicapped by an aesthetic of minimalist verbal communication, Japanese are often the victims of their own inarticulate culture, one that is also less interested in logic and reason. First described in the journals written by the samurai bureaucrats sent to the United States in 1860,[6] the admixture of discomfort, bewilderment, anxiety, alienation, and, in the end, distaste seemed to be the summation of experience abroad by Japanese men of that time.[7]

For the overwhelming majority of Japanese who are directly exposed to Western culture, their immediate concern is to prove how little the West has tainted them, how swiftly they can reintegrate themselves back into Japanese society. Minako, refreshingly free from this preoccupation, regards it as a counterproductive fanning of the "new kindling of patriotic sentiments and nationalism" in Japanese men. Instead of liberating them as individuals, these nationalistic feelings reinforce a rigid mind-set, the reestablishment of their psychological footing and their place in Japanese society in preparation for their return home.[8]

Minako's intellectual fortitude and fertile imagination notwithstanding, there is a crucial gender factor involved in her overwhelming sense of release while abroad, a liberation based upon individual reflection. Being a woman requires a particular kind of sensitivity to environment and to social interactions. Being a female and an intellectual compounds the issue.[9]

For Minako and other Japanese female writers, cognizant of their ambiguous status as marginals in their own country, this daunting venture carries with it a reward. As cultural anthropologists have argued,[10] women's status of outsiderhood and marginality also opens up an avenue of opportunity, a freedom that allows leeway for independent behavior and alternative thinking. Minako's is the case of an outsider in her own country living as an outsider in a foreign country. Living in the United States was more than a material blessing for Minako. It was also therapeutic and emancipatory. The alien land led to a discovery of her own voice and the articulation of thoughts she had suppressed for the first thirty years of her life.

Her "marginal" position as a woman intellectual, writer, and sociocultural critic with a not-so-fragile impulse to dissent is a constant in Japan's modernization process that began in 1868 with the Meiji Restoration. For Japanese leaders, the nation's Westernization unwittingly signaled the beginning of the decoding of a masculinist text of quite a different sort, that is, the text of power projected by a formidable and irresistible West. As one critic has pointed out, "Rapid social change . . . can give rise to extensive problems of identity crisis—more for males than for females."[11] These women intellectuals in the Meiji (1868–1911), Taishō (1912–1926), and early Shōwa (1926–1945) periods were "party crashers" in the eyes of the policymakers. The problems of power, gender, and sexuality, issues that prewar women had to face, still remain basically the same for women in today's Japan.[12]

On the surface at least, the encounter with the West was for the Japanese leaders a case of one able master ceding for the moment to another, a foreign master, with Japan assuming that the equalizing factor of male gender, regardless of race, was still intact.[13] Building on the strength of samurai feudalism and the patriarchy[14] of the premodern "Sinicization," Japan's modernization eagerly adopted yet another form of patriarchy, that was "imposed by modern industrial capitalism."[15] In other words, beginning in the Meiji Period, when Japan set itself on a course to modern constitutional statehood, Japanese society "has been rigidly administered under the patriarchal principles of the West."[16]

If, as Karatani Kōjin points out, premodern "Confucian thought can be characterized as patriarchal" and if "the same is true of those (i.e., the disinherited samurai) who opposed the authority of the Meiji state,"[17] then the combined forces of these and the patriarchy of the West the Meiji government enthusiastically adopted have had a staggering cumulative effect upon Japanese women's lives. Japanese female writers therefore need to unlearn the deeply ingrained habit of reading as "truth" the male text that has been written for women by men over the centuries, reinstitutionalized since Japan's modernization, and embraced by most women as their own.

The period of modernization, with its power relations in patriarchy intact, proved to be an exciting time for Japanese women, however, a time to decode for the first time the male-gendered text of the "prevailing economies of power."[18] It was also a chance for them to unlearn the script and find their own female text. Despite the setback of the Pacific War, this process of decipherment was revived by Japanese female writers, Minako among them, after the second wave of modernization triggered by Japan's involuntary acceptance of the United States as model, and once again master, in 1945.

The issues that male writers were forced to face, whether of individuality, self-identity, manhood, or sexuality, are linked with the domination of, and their fascination with, Western power. Ambivalent and yet in awe, male writers also felt threatened by "feminization" in the face of Japan's political goal of assimilating Western culture, a culture which, as Sandra M. Gilbert and Susan Gubar have argued, operated in a masculine mode vis-à-vis non-Western nations: "when we consider the European imperialist consciousness in the context of these equations [of hierarchical oppositions], it becomes clear that . . . women = 'outlanders'/'barbarians' = colonized peoples, and hence colonized peoples = women."[19] There was very little need for Japanese men to question their own "masculinity" before Japan opened up to the West. Motoori Norinaga's definition of Heian femininity (*taoyameburi*) as the essence of literature had been neither questioned nor challenged.

The most symbolic example of the "feminine" Japan came

from the young Emperor Meiji,[20] with his powdered face and long hair tied in back, dressed in an elegant Heian ceremonial robe, almost invisible and always inarticulate, who "spoke" through only an intermediary in audiences he granted to foreign diplomats. One of the most urgent tasks of the Meiji leaders was to transform this feminine image of the "inactive" emperor into that of a ferocious bearded monarch of the West.[21] Japan's exposure to the West unexpectedly ran afoul of the line of demarcation between masculinity and femininity defined by Tokugawa neo-Confucian, feudal sociopolitical structure.

Furthermore, Japan's phenomenal economic success, which followed the withdrawal of the Allied Occupation forces in 1952 created more politically sensitive problems to which Japanese writers and intellectuals were attracted: the role of the emperor system and Japan's codependent relationship with the United States, its status now reduced from master to "big brother." As Sharalyn Orbaugh has pointed out, these issues became the basis of many stories written by male writers such as Ōe Kenzaburo (1935– ) and Nosaka Akiyuki (1930– ), "making the political nature of their literary activity abundantly clear." However, Orbaugh poses a question concerning history and gender:

> Less clear is the relationship of women's writing to the prominent elements of the sociopolitical milieu. I would suggest that this is because the designation of which issues were of importance at the time as well as in the subsequent historical assessments of the period is an essentially male-centered view of what constitutes "politics" and "history." Women were writing, *as always,* "against" this background, not necessarily actively opposing it, but writing about the "physical" and "private" areas of life which for them constituted the "politics" and "history" of the time.[22]

Japanese literary women were essentially gate crashers during the two stages of the modernization process—one in the Meiji Period and the other in post-1945 times—reading Japan's Westernization as an "invitation" to reexamine and question the patriarchal notion of gender, power, and sexuality. As Adrienne Rich has eloquently phrased it, writing was a "re-vision" that became an "act of survival" for them: "Re-vision—the act of looking back, of seeing with fresh eyes, of entering an old text from a new critical direction—is for women more than a chapter in cultural history: it is an act of survival."[23]

Modern Japanese women's literature demonstrates the continual struggle of woman to find her own script, her own text. This quest inevitably entails the activity of what Orbaugh calls "writing *against* the prevailing economies of power . . . [which] includes all writing by women who live in a patriarchal society. Even those women who claim to accept their roles in the economy of power would be implicitly challenging it by the very act of writing."[24] Japanese literary women know, as all women know, that the woman's role is to be seen, but not heard. "Snow White" is not just a Western fairy tale, but a story of all women, castigating a speaking and questioning woman (the evil stepmother) and glorifying a speechless woman (the good queen/Snow White). "'To speak' is not the woman's role, even if what she speaks is the language of patriarchy. . . . [To] write *against a background of* patriarchal control, even if one is not writing 'contra,' is still an act of 'writing against.'"[25]

In this feminist posture of "talking back,"[26] Minako adopts and negotiates three alternative strategies, which are the basic characteristics of satire and parody: describing the "current configurations of power" and exposing their negative impact upon women's lives, turning the "hierarchy of value" upside down in an effort to "valorize the object/passive side of the equation," and reversing the "*gender coding* of the hierarchical power roles."[27] In all three, Minako instinctively "uses and abuses"[28] artistic and social conventions to make her point.

A Japanese female writer, whose status is ambiguous at best in a society where the parodic and the satiric have not enjoyed the status of high culture, finds herself in an interesting position to be able to observe a nation in an ambiguously gendered relationship with the West.[29] To laugh at oneself, to lay bare and pull oneself apart, whether as an individual or as a nation, requires considerable aesthetic distance. Minako, nurtured by her eleven-year sojourn in the United States, possesses this gift, the ability to step back.

A rethinking of the issues of gender, female destiny, and selfhood, themes that dominate Minako's works, has been vigorously investigated by feminist scholars in Japan in the past decade.[30] Thanks to their collective challenge to the Japanese literary canon, "gender" is finally fair game in Japanese literary studies. The problematization of the issue of gender is crucial in light of the lack of interest in, worse yet, the dismissal of, gender politics as a proper subject, even among the "most radical social critics," who "always fail to expand their analysis or critique of a problem into the area of gender."[31] My use of feminist literary criticism throughout this book is a deliberate one, a most pertinent and logical response to the challenge posed by Minako's complex and gender-oriented texts. I hope my study shows that her literary, intellectual, and personal concern for women's (and men's) gendered role offers a refreshing, revisionist perspective on Japanese literature.

* * *

In addition to the "outsiderhood" and gender awareness that mark Minako's unshakable sense of self and unrepenting spirit, there are other factors that have shaped the mind of this imaginative writer: Japan's militaristic past, her education, her unconventional marriage, and her unique family lineage.[32] As a mobilized fourteen-year-old student, she was an eyewitness to the terrifyingly disfigured Hiroshima atomic bomb victims making their way to the neighboring city of Seijō. For two whole weeks she and other mobilized schoolchildren were forced to stay with the victims. The hellish scene created by the refined destructive power of humankind has been haunting Minako ever since and is replayed again and again in various forms in her writings. "Those of us who had this horrible experience of the atomic bomb," Minako once wrote, "had to rethink what had been thrust on us about nations and peoples. What other nations had to do is also our concern. We could no longer afford to feign ignorance, thinking that they had nothing to do with us."[33]

The course of Minako's education was not always smooth. One episode demonstrates how this assertion of ego—something still to be avoided even among men—was displayed by Minako unwittingly as a young teenager. During World War II in the midst of the fanatic fervor of war, she was perceived to be a constant threat by her schoolteachers not because of her open confrontation with authority, but because of her subversive, unspoken, unshakable sense of individuality. Corporal punishment being the daily routine during the war, she was slapped in the face for merely looking, not acting, defiant: she simply forgot to lower her eyes, as a youngster was required to do, in front of a government inspector.

In 1949, four years after the end of the Pacific War, Minako entered Tsuda College in Tokyo, probably the most progressive women's academic institution in postwar Japan. Freed from the effects of war propaganda and the prewar feudalistic environment, for four "glorious" years in the dormitory Minako had a space of her own for the first time, a space in which to nurture the dormant seed of self-expression. Already something of a free spirit, Minako was a perfect match for Tsuda College,[34] one of the earliest women's colleges in Japan founded by Tsuda Umeko (1864–1929). Tsuda had been one of five girls sent to the United States in 1871 during the height of educational reform as part of the Iwakura mission to modernize Japan.[35]

The absence of male students at Tsuda was something Minako took completely for granted, but which she later counted as a blessing. In the aftermath of the Pacific War, Tsuda's all-female environment offered young women the autonomy of managing dormitory life and negotiating with the outside, that is, the masculine, world for various club activities. This freedom extended to debating sociocultural, political, and interpersonal issues without male scrutiny or the heterosexual gaze.[36] This experience was the closest to female bonding that Minako was to experience, and is one that she still cherishes.[37] The Tsuda life fostered the growth of an unusual female writer who is free of the guilt and anxiety typical of those culturally conditioned feminine disadvantages, exclusion and inadequacy.

That Minako remained her own self in marriage attests to the extraordinary relationship she has developed with a very unconventional man. She met her future husband, Ōba Toshio, in 1949. She was eighteen years old, Toshio twenty. She married him in December 1955, two years after she graduated from Tsuda College, on the condition that she be allowed to continue fiction writing. This "conditional" marriage was not by any means an indication of Toshio's potenial sexism, but of the still conservative environment in postwar Japan. Minako felt the need to express clearly where she stood as a literary woman in the form of requesting from him full understanding and support of her position not only in marriage, but also in society. In 1959 Toshio, an engineer at a company in Japan, was selected to be the Japan-Alaska Pulp Company representative in Sitka. He, Minako, and their daughter Yū[38] lived in Sitka for the next eleven years.

If Minako had made the right choice in marriage, it was because the spirit of individualism and humanism, two Western concepts, which her liberal education at Tsuda reinforced, were, remarkably, part and parcel of her upbringing. Behind her rather innocent yet indomitable spirit lie two generations of extraordinary people. To become acquainted with her grandparents and her parents is to gain insight into Minako's inner workings as artist, thinker, woman, daughter, and mother. One might say that it is almost impossible to speak of Ōba Minako without referring to her humane, whimsical, eccentric grandparents, her parents, and their children, upon whom she has often modeled her fictional characters.[39]

It was her maternal kin who provided Minako with an intellectual environment in which a continual supply of literary works were within easy reach. One of her vivid memories as a young girl was the excitement of visiting her maternal aunt's house, where literature was a family affair. Copies of the literary magazines *Shinchō* and *Bungakukai* (considered the top literary journals then and now) were always available there, as well as in her own home and that of her maternal grandfather.[40] Minako's mother, Mutsuko, a self-taught literary woman and a discriminating reader, often astonished Minako with her knowledge and appreciation of Japanese and European literature.

Born one year after the Meiji Restoration, Mutsuko's father, Morita Yoshikazu, was the embodiment of the new government's slogan, *bunmei kaika*[41] ("civilization and enlightenment"). He was at once an intellectual, a progressive thinker, a romanticist, a reformer, and an entrepreneur. At fourteen, he entered a mission school in his hometown in Niigata, where the majority of teachers were Westerners. At seventeen, he abruptly left home for Tokyo, where he studied under Ōkuma Shigenobu (1838–1922), one of the Meiji's most powerful politicians, at his newly founded university (the current Waseda University). Because of this connection, Yoshikazu briefly served in the new government.[42]

However, he became weary of the increasingly rigid, institutionalized world of the bureaucracy, and at the news of his father's death he returned to his native village. He eventually also became bored with the typical country gentleman's life: visiting teahouses and dabbling in business, activities that almost bankrupted the family. To save the dwindling family fortune, Yoshikazu married his oldest daughter to an adopted son and transferred all his assets to them.[43]

A good storyteller and a clown, Yoshikazu possessed none of the tyrannical and misogynistic characteristics of the stereotypical Meiji patriarch. If he had an arrogant side, he compensated for it with an almost feminine sensitivity and sensibility.[44] What characterized him most was his tendency to hold two opposing views simultaneously: he would in one breath pontificate on the virtues of Confucian morality and praise the modern Western ego. By way of outrageous sophistry he would entertain the listener by linking the two contradictory views.[45] If he was cornered, instead of defending himself with logic, he would first play possum, then wake up, and, winking, smooth things over with rhetorical wordplay. He excelled at laying a smoke screen around what he had to say.

In the final analysis, no matter what others said, he did what he set out to do.[46] One striking example involved the arranged marriage forced upon him. In order to extricate himself, immediately after the wedding he went to a warehouse, where he hid for a month, until his bride had no choice but to return to her parents. For a wife, he chose an outsider, Kisa, a sophisticated "new woman" with strong opinions. Although he respected her superior mind, he eventually found her samurai-like propriety unbearable. His solution was to put her on a pedestal and abandon her there.[47] A firm believer in education, he sent his three daughters to a women's school and his two sons to university. At the age of fifty, however, he left the village again. Leaving his morally superior wife behind, he moved into the house of his mistress, who lived with their child and her older sister. Thirty years later, he returned to his native village to die.[48]

Minako's paternal grandparents, Shiina Tadaharu and Kuma, were as atypical as Yoshikazu and Kisa. Born twelve years before the Meiji Restoration, Tadaharu was also very much a product of *bunmei kaika.* He pursued almost everything that smacked of modern, that is to say, Western, enterprise, including rice refining, flour milling, and green tea export. The first in the region to purchase and ride a bicycle, he also brought in agricultural machines for his tenant farmers and had Kuma make Western clothes for one of their daughters. In Minako's recollection, Kuma seemed "sentimental, hard-nosed, and a nagger,"[49] not necessarily because she was, but because, Minako concluded, her behavior was a way of protesting against Tadaharu's eccentric lifestyle and behavior.[50]

Like Yoshikazu, Tadaharu had no gift for business matters. As one venture after another failed, he squandered almost all the family fortune. A self-proclaimed admirer of Tolstoy, he also launched land reform measures and took up Catholicism. That was the last straw for the Shiina clan who banded together and forced him to step down as head of the clan. Tadaharu rebelled: he abandoned his family. Missing for three years, he was found working at a port in Yokohama. He explained that he was trying to earn enough money to go to the United States, a land of liberty and equality.[51]

Despite his three-year stint of roving and his eccentric behavior—the only time he abandoned his family—Tadaharu was a perfect gentleman to his wife to the end of his life. He took care of the bedding (the usual practice of setting out the futon at night and reversing the process in the morning), helped hang laundry (a chore the majority of men still refuse to do in today's Japan), and volunteered to massage Kuma's sore shoulders with tender loving care. He would "serve tea" and "listen with perfect composure to her nag and complain as if he were hearing his favorite music."[52] She once told Tadaharu, in reference to his Christianity: "When I die, I don't want to go to heaven. I don't know anything about it. I want to go to a paradise where lotus is in bloom and join my parents and brothers and sisters." Tadaharu reassured her by saying, "All right. I'll accompany you. I don't want you to be lonely up there. Whether it's heaven or paradise, it can't be that different. Must be just the difference between lilies and lotus."[53] At the age of eighty-six Kuma had her wish come true: her funeral was carried out according to the customs of the Pure Land sect of Buddhism. Tadaharu joined her in paradise six months later at the age of eighty-seven.

Tadaharu was also a caring father: When his son, Saburō, faced with the bride that the clan had picked for him, began to talk about marrying someone else from outside, Tadaharu faced off clan opposition and personally met with the young woman, Morita Takiko. After a satisfactory inspection, he gave his son permission to go ahead with the wedding.[54] Saburō had also profited from Tadaharu's flexible and liberal outlook on life on an earlier occasion. A bit unmotivated and often too easygoing, he failed a middle-school entrance examination. After he was finally admitted to another middle school, he failed the first year and had to transfer to a private school in Tokyo. The father's response to the academic failure of his only son was: "Whether you do it in a hurry or take your time, life is the same. The worst you can do is not to do what you really want to do."[55]

True to the spirit of her progressive father, Tadaharu's youngest daughter, Hisano, a graduate of a women's vocational school and the wife of an army officer, persuaded her husband to retire early so that the two could found a private women's school. Tadaharu, who had always been interested in medical science, found for his oldest daughter, Kei, the fifth son of a physician as a husband. His father had once studied under the famous German physician Phillipp Franz von Siebold (1796–1866), who opened the first clinic of Western medicine in Nagasaki.[56]

Saburō also inherited Tadaharu's spiritual and cultural legacy. He was born in 1894, a quarter of a century after the Meiji Restoration. It has already been shown that he, like his father, did not compromise when it came to making choices as an individual. At a time when the concept of individuality was simply an imported idea, when sexuality was something to be repressed and romantic love in marriage was still an impossible dream for the vast majority, Saburō proved to be a radical.

Three years of persistant courtship earned Saburō the fair-skinned Takiko, the second daughter of Morita Yoshikazu, the young woman to whom his father personally gave a blessing. Cheerful, vivacious, and sociable, regal as a queen, she was also a wonderful conversationist and taught Sunday school.[57] Once engaged to Takiko, Saburō was instantly transformed from a rather intellectually aimless, unfocused young man into a model student at the Niigata University medical school. He graduated *summa cum laude,* a remarkable feat considering that he had been admitted to the school after two failed attempts. His choice of medicine as a career (one which later took him as a navy doctor around the world) seemed to echo his grandfather's desire to cross the Pacific in order to explore alternative worlds outside Japan, which he found too rigid and stifling.[58]

Saburō's love marriage to Takiko abruptly came to an end with her death at the age of twenty-five. He honored the request in her will that he marry her younger sister Mutsuko, who let three years go by before she accepted his proposal. Even more fair-skinned than Takiko, Mutsuko wore her hair in curls when an elaborate classical Japanese coiffure was still the norm for women. She looked so much like a Westerner that, in growing up, her Caucasian features had invited jeers from neighborhood children who called her, "Ijin-san" (literally Ms. Westerner).[59] As husband and wife, Saburō and Mutsuko turned out to be more than a good match. However, as parents, they were something of an oddity, certainly by the standards of the early Showa period, but even by today's norms.

Emotionally compatible, they were able to fulfill each other's needs without viewing their children as "a symbolic credential, a sentimental object," or "a badge of self-righteousness."[60] In fact, Saburō regarded his children as nuisances that would come automatically attached to the woman he loved, something he would have to put up with. All he needed was the company of his wife, or so it seemed to the young Minako: "Except for a couple of hours after a meal when the children enjoyed conversations with their parents, they were not allowed any intimate contact with them; I learned to enjoy reading in solitude relatively early on."[61] Mutsuko's preoccupation with her husband was also out of the ordinary. They were not afraid of displaying affection for each other in front of their children, and always called each other Saa-chan and Mutchan at home,[62] diminutives usually reserved for small children (a practice only used among young newlyweds in today's Japan).

Mutsuko also loved literature. One of her first purchases after her marriage was a newly published multivolume set of Japanese literature and European literature in translation. As was appropriate for upper-middle-class women of Taishō Japan, she also took classes at a dressmaking school and attended a newly opened English-language school. She became so proficient in English that she began to read English and American literature in the original. Minako, as an English major at Tsuda College, would turn to Mutsuko for help in deciphering difficult passages in

English. She became Minako's "best and only friend" with whom she could discuss literature intelligently.[63]

However, if Mutsuko fulfilled Minako's intellectual needs, something very few mothers were prepared to do at that time, she was incapable of giving her daughter emotional love and support. Motherhood did not suit her well, and she left child care to a nursemaid, while she steeped herself in reading during the months her husband was on assignment as a navy doctor, and later when she took up dressmaking and English classes. Her upper middle-class conservatism and her emotional disequilibirum were also a source of constant frustration and puzzlement to her daughter. At one moment Mutsuko would exhibit every sign of being avant garde and even decadent, but then in the next moment, without warning, she would turn suspicious of anything new and declare that a profession is not for a woman from a good family.[64] What Minako saw in her mother's sudden change of moods and views was what feminist critics call a "self-division": the public/tame self *(tatemae)* "designed to please others" and the private/wild self *(honne),* those impulses driven to "secrecy where they seethe and increase."[65]

For Minako, Mutsuko's duality and her unconventional marriage to Saburō proved to be valuable material for understanding the complexity of the human mind. For example, she learned that the secret of their successful marriage was Mutsuko's complete lack of jealousy toward her sister, Saburō's first love, and his paradoxical display of resentment that she did not show any jealousy. "Saburō was a strange man who was exasperated by the fact that his wife was not jealous of any woman. He was paranoiac—in fact very jealous and possessive of his wife."[66] As if reading his mind, Mutsuko would show no inhibition, and would bring up the subject of Saburō's first wife Takiko, sometimes teasingly, sometimes affectionately. In fact, bringing up the topic became her favorite pastime and even her obsession.

Mutsuko's often-repeated recollections about Takiko, as well as about her oldest sister, Matsue, a classic beauty, were so familiar to Minako that the three sisters became heroines in many of her works. Saburō never interfered with Mutsuko's obsession. On the contrary, he obviously delighted in her repeated assertion, despite his contrary feelings: "I didn't choose your father. She [the dead sister] pushed him onto me."[67] A variation was, "I was begged to marry him. Nothing to do with my free will. I wished I could at least choose my own husband."[68]

Mutsuko had still another pet phrase: "No one can prohibit people from thinking what they want to think," to which she would add chuckling, in front of Saburō, "Of course, I only have you and the children on my mind, you know."[69] After Mutsuko's death at sixty-two, Saburō gave up his practice as a country doctor, saying, "I don't want to do anything anymore."[70] He outlived her by eight years.

Among Minako's grandmothers and grandfathers, great aunts and uncles, aunts and uncles, and parents, there is neither a single male who would lay the back of his hand to a woman, nor a female who would stifle her own voice or exercise self-effacement. It is women who speak up in Minako's stories, men who listen and delight in female self-assertion, no matter how outrageous it is or how strident the women are. At the center of her literary world is the image of the "undomesticated woman" who "refuses to hide her sexuality, abnegate her maternity, silence her hungers and angers."[71] Also in this undomesticated, unrepentant woman is the refusal to "impose male ownership upon a complex realm of human experience,"[72] which the power of her gaze penetrates with unrelenting precision.

## Notes

1. Godfrey Hodgson, "Mysteries, Sacred and Profane," a review of *Dorothy Sayers: Her Life and Soul* by Barbara Reynolds (London, Sydney and Auckland: Hodder & Stoughton, 1993), *Book World, Washington Post,* August 22, 1993, p. 6.

2. I have chosen to call Ōba Minako by her given name rather than her married name in the main text of this work because of my desire as a woman to relate to her. The practice of referring to authors by their given names is widely used among recent feminist scholars in Japan. See Numazawa Kazuko, *Miyamoto Yuriko ron* (Discussion on Miyamoto Yuriko) (Musashino Shobō,

43. Ibid., p. 29.
44. Ibid., p. 91.
45. Ibid., p. 79.
46. Ibid., p. 92.
47. Ibid., p. 90.
48. Ibid., p. 82.
49. Ibid., p. 130.
50. Ibid., p. 131.
51. Ibid., p. 132.
52. Ibid., p. 133.
53. Ibid., p. 130.
54. Ibid., pp. 49, 139–140.
55. Ibid., p. 137.
56. Ibid., p. 137.
57. Ibid., p. 54.
58. Ibid., p. 171.
59. Ibid., p. 50.
60. Rich, *Of Women Born: Motherhood as Experience and Institution* (New York: W.W. Norton, 1976), p. xxiv.
61. Ibid., p. 189.
62. Ibid., pp. 55, 63.
63. Ibid., p. 33.
64. Ibid., p. 177.
65. Alicia Suskin Ostriker, *Stealing the Language: The Emergence of Women's Poetry in America* (Boston: Beacon Press, 1986), p. 83.
66. Ibid., p. 171.
67. Ibid., p. 63.
68. Ibid., p. 63.
69. Ibid., p. 112.
70. Ibid., p. 69.
71. Adrienne Rich, *What Is Found There: Notebooks on Poetry and Politics* (New York: W. W. Norton, 1993), p. 158.
72. Adrienne Munich, "Notorious Signs, Feminist Criticism and Literary Tradition," in *Making a Difference: Feminist Literary Criticism,* eds. Gayle Greene and Coppelia Kahn (London: Routledge, 1988), p. 239.

# — 2 —

# The Lyric Mode: To Write Like a Woman

Although Minako's principal literary mode changed from poetry to prose early in her career, she has always been a poet at heart.[1] Prose and poetry coexist and blend seamlessly in a continuous point and counterpoint in her stories.[2] Impregnating the textual fiber with a poetic perspective that is at the same time full of psychological nuance, she relies heavily on the lyric mode, with its associative connection of events, images, scenes, or memories, and a "feminine" style that is "discursive, fluid, sensual."[3]

Along with the associative feature of the lyric mode, the plotless, open-ended, and nonlinear pattern of the Heian feminine literary tradition dominant in her work has also been identified as a major characteristic of the modern Japanese prose narrative, *shōsetsu.* We find in Minako's writings many of its formal characteristics, as defined by Masao Miyoshi:[4] like *shōsetsu,* her fiction strives neither for formal coherence—as understood in the West—nor a central event. Consisting of episodes and anecdotes, her work defies the "formation of a center and structure."[5] In addition to the "plot" being "sequential, but hardly consequential," we see "no preparation" being made by the author "toward a climax or denouement," because "causality. . . is not a focus of concern." What determines the direction of events and actions is the "association and juxtaposition on the surface of the text."[6] The narrative point of view, which often multiplies, is always fluid, and several points of view shift and merge in a continuous flow.

With these characteristics of the Japanese prose narrative in mind, it is very useful here to compare them to what the American science fiction writer Joanna Russ defines as the lyric mode: It is "*the organization of discrete elements* (images, events, scenes, passages, words, . . .) *around an unspoken thematic or emotional center.*"[7] The main concern is not with the connection of events "by the *chronological order*" as in the narrative mode, or with "*voluntary human actions* . . . connected both by *chronology and causation*" as in the dramatic mode. Rather, the lyric mode exists

> without chronology or causation; its principle of connection is *associative.* . . . A writer who employs the lyric structure is setting various images, events, scenes, or memories to circling round an unspoken, invisible center. The invisible center is what the novel or poem is about; . . .there is no action possible to the central character and no series of events that will embody in clear, unequivocal, immediately graspable terms what the artist means.[8]

Russ's analysis of the lyric mode exactly describes the content and structure of most Japanese masterpieces. From *Tales of Ise* (c. 907), *The Gossamer Years* (c. 974), *The Pillow Book* (c. 992), *The Tale of Genji* (c. 1010), *As I Crossed the Bridge of Dreams* (c. 1059), to *Kokoro* (1914), *Some Prefer Nettles* (1928), *A Dark Night's Passing* (1921–37),[9] and *Snow Country* (1934–47), the supremacy of the lyric mode is unmistakable in the Japanese literary canon. Certainly, nothing really happens to the central character in any of these stories except that she or he *feels.* We do not expect any clear, unequivocal, immediately graspable meanings to be derived from characters or events in the story. We also take it for granted that there is an unspoken, invisible center, which the reader is to sense rather than discover. Both the reader and the author tacitly accept the assumption that what is left unsaid carries more significance, that what is invisible, indeterminate, and equivocal heightens the emotional message of the story.

All the above-mentioned modern works, as well as the overwhelming majority of those which compose the modern Japanese literary canon, were written by men. The paradox of this interesting historical case of appropriation is best expressed by Janice Brown: It is not so much modern female writers as male writers who "have eagerly appropriated [these] elements of the feminine tradition. . . . [T]he ancient feminine literary 'voice' speaks, even in mainstream Japanese fiction, a haunting echo in the works of major male literary figures."[10]

The irony of Japanese women writers' status in the face of this appropriation of the feminine literary tradition has not been well understood by either Japanese or American critics. Since Japan's opening to the West in 1868, women's sensibility and perspective in the Heian female tradition, which inspired Motoori Norinaga (1730–1801) to claim the quality of *taoyameburi* (femininity) as the "essence of literature,"[11] have been transformed into male prerogatives. The question that immediately comes to mind, then, is why the lyric structure of Heian sensibility and perspective in modern Japanese women's writings is no longer the right stuff for literary production and inquiry.

Chieko Ariga, in her discussion of the practice of writing "commentaries" *(kaisetsu)* at the end of a paperback edition of a literary work, articulates her frustration over how male critics' readings naturalize and domesticate female texts into "textual moments of erasure and displacement."[12] This is also a point of contention for Janice Brown, who points out that studies of Japanese women's literary works "on par with male writers as part of major literary trends or movements . . . are non-existent."[13] In her analysis of Tsushima Yūko's "Fusehime," Livia Monnet joins Ariga and Brown in raising the issue of gender politics implicit in the current Japanese literary establishment, still very much a male jurisdiction:[14]

> There seems to be consensus in the critical literature . . . that her texts dramatize narrow, self-contained worlds of typically female experiences. . . , and that many of her stories are autobiographical,

> reflecting her unusual family history, as well as her experience as a divorcee and single mother. . . .
>
> The present study . . . arose out of a need to express my dissatisfaction, not only with the prevailing critical view of Tsushima's work, but with the methodologies of orthodox literary criticism as practiced in Japanese academia (*kokubungaku kenkyū:* Japanese scholarship of the indigenous literature) and journalism (*bungei hihyō*), as well as with our own interpretative and theorizing practices used when dealing with Japanese women's texts.[15]

What baffles Brown, Ariga, Monnet, and female readers is that the Japanese literary establishment (called *bundan*), which considers the lyric mode to be a Japanese literary staple, simultaneously thinks that this mode somehow ceases to be a viable property in the hands of modern Japanese women writers. Brown goes so far as to say that "the very fact that Japanese women writers have a literature of their own seems due as much to the hegemonic strategies of a male-dominated literary elite as to classical tradition."[16] By the same token, prevented by a "gentlemen's agreement" from reading women's works from a woman's perspective, Japanese female scholars have not until recently taken into account the possibility of a feminist challenge to both the literary canon and women's texts.

It is doubly ironic that Joanna Russ's definition of the lyric mode is directed against the Anglo-American male criticism of women's writings. She points out that "[According to a male reading of Virginia Woolf's work] there is nothing the female characters can *do*—except exist, except think, except feel."[17] This situation is very similar to what Japanese feminist scholars have often encountered: "[C]ritics (mostly male) employ the usual vocabulary of denigration: these novels [by women writers] lack important events; they are hermetically sealed; they are too full of sensibility; they are trivial; they lack action; they are feminine."[18]

Even though Japan, part of the mysterious Orient, was forcibly opened by the United States in 1852 and unwittingly played the feminine role in face of the masculinist or imperialist West, Japan's literature has very little to do with the problem of Western domination. As Russ's comments indicate, the Japanese literary canon has a great deal in common with women's writings in the West because the "feminization" or the lyric mode of Japanese literature is native to Japanese culture. "Feminine" in this case is indeed a relative term in today's Japan.

It is not my intention here to lay out detailed theoretical arguments regarding the Japanese modern prose narrative form, *shōsetsu,*[19] in relation to its most orthodox and "feminized" form, *shishōsetsu* (I-fiction, I-narrative, I-novel). However, what is relevant for our discussion of Minako's literary strategy is that her fiction has often been dismissed by *bundan* critics on the basis of what I consider to be her "typical" *shōsetsu* style. To add insult to injury, her autobiographical fiction has been harshly treated by Japanese male critics[20] who, when faced with female texts, seem to suffer from a chronic *shōsetsu-shishōsetsu* amnesia.

If there is anything other than sheer gender bias that prompts this male criticism, it is not the style but the content and approach Minako and other Japanese women writers take concerning the concept of the privileged individual, as well as their adoption of irony and satire and the sociopolitical implications of the stories they tell. Because of the rejection of individualism by Japanese society, the *shishōsetsu* has become the medium for expressing the "I" in its most private and ego-dominant form.[21] A product of Japanese intellectuals' conscious attempt to claim the private self, an import of Western capitalism, the autobiographical *shishōsetsu* in particular (described by Janet Walker as the "process of self-definition") is the narrative of the individual given a privileged status in search of "sexuality as a major aspect of selfhood."[22] Keeping in mind that both selfhood and sexuality are the main concerns of female writers, it is not surprising that *shishōsetsu* has something in common with what American feminist scholars call women's literary autobiography.[23]

Despite detractors who long for originality and imagination, the confessional *shishōsetsu,* devoid of irony, humor, and satire, nurtured and defended by the *bundan*[24] since the development of the form in the early 1900s, has not lost its popularity or influence and "has remained essentially unchanged and continues to dominate present-day thinking."[25] *Shishōsetsu*'s indebtedness to the Heian female tradition, which created a *nikki bungaku* (poetic diary) form that not only is confessional but also is mainly concerned with the private sphere of the author's life, is unmistakable. In Karatani Kōjin's words, "*shishōsetsu* deals with the space of concrete family ties rather than with society as a homogeneous space and depicts *a precognitive realm of feelings and perceptions* rather than the 'I' as defined in relation to such a society [as in the West]."[26] The nature of this lyric form is not to construct, but to fragment and decenter, to rebel against "the configuration of linear perspective [as in Western painting]" imported into Japan by its encounter with the West and Christianity, and it envisions a narrative form "as a centerless interrelationship of fragments."[27] Strangely, however, the *shishōsetsu* hero often remains both a recluse and a conformist.

Its close resemblance to women's writings in the West and in Japan notwithstanding, what is missing in *shishōsetsu* is the notion of gender, any female perspective. This glaring omission is still hardly noticed either by the practitioners or the critics of the form.[28] Instead, they exhibit an overriding concern for what may be conceived as the male-defined master narrative[29] in the early twentieth-century *shishōsetsu.*[30] For example, this narrative of what Cody Poulton calls the "melodramatic subjectivity and idealism of adolescence"[31] has for a protagonist one dominant type: overtly identified with the author, he is a middle-class male intellectual, sexually engaged with different women but unengaged with his job, emotionally and sexually unfulfilled, and totally self-preoccupied.[32] Through this protagonist, a *shishōsetsu* writer invests all his emotional capital in what Edward Fowler calls the "ideology of sincerity," considered the most essential aspect of this nonfiction form.[33] This posture of truthfulness—that is, confession—extends to the detailed description of every mood, every grudge, every foible and hostile thought he exposes to the male reader, who is expected to be familiar with the author's life.[34] Out of this intimate, self-flagellating act the protagonist emerges as a sage-hero, particularly in the mind of an unresisting reader.[35]

The hero, however, is neither an outsider nor a marginal individual, even though he may resist or despise the world he lives in. As Sidonie Smith writes, apropos of women writers in the West: "Even the rebel whose text projects a hostile society against which he struggles to define himself, if he is male, takes himself seriously because he and his public assume his significance within the dominant order: Only in the fullness of that membership can the fullness of his rebellion unfold."[36]

That membership in this club is not extended to modern Japanese women writers is a fact of life. One of the reasons female autobiographical fiction in Japan fails to rank with its male counterpart, Saegusa Kazuko speculates, lies in the most obvious factor: the protagonist's gender. It allows a *shishōsetsu* hero to expose his ego to public scrutiny. With his role and status as a writer protected and sanctioned by society, he can afford to conduct a "self-excavation" (jiko tekketsu), which is considered a strength in Japanese society, into the darkest depths of his personality. Saegusa's argument is supported by Karatani Kōjin, who suggests that "confession is itself a manifestation in twisted form of a will to power. Confession does not necessarily imply remorse. Behind a facade of weakness, the one who confesses seeks to become a master, to dominate. . . . The 'truth' . . . is an assertion of authority which precludes disagreement."[37]

For a female, however, the act of self-exposure has no intrinsic social value. If this is the case, there can be no true female *shishōsetsu,* Saegusa argues. In other words, who would wish to identify with someone who is intellectually and emotionally inferior on the gender scale? There is surely no appeal or value, except as a bit of humor, for the reader to learn about "a woman who has been abandoned by a man." Japanese society is not quite ready for this type of "humorous" story, Saegusa concludes.[38]

✻ ✻ ✻

Contrary to Saegusa's pessimistic views on female *shishōsetsu,* Minako is one of many Japanese women writers who have successfully appropriated the autobiographical narrative form for their own use.[39] But, of course, one might wonder whether the *shishōsetsu* as fostered by the *bundan,* with its traditionally antisocial and egocentric perspective revolving around one dominant alienated protagonist, is something women writers should aspire to at all. The answer is "no," and the fact is that they have not.

While Minako's writings bear the clear signature of the *shōsetsu-shishōsetsu* features, she also diverges from them in crucial ways. She "uses and abuses"[40] the basic lyric structure of both forms with sophistication and humor.[41] The most prominent deviation involves the very notion of the privileged self, which, in its reclusive and misogynistic manifestation of individuality, relentlessly advances the male protagonist's "causes" and desires, making of the *shishōsetsu* a Japanized version of *Bildungsroman* in the sense that it is "focused on one character, the hero, and his development, with the other characters individualized only so far as they need to be to affect the hero, *appearing* when needed by the hero and *dropping out* when the hero has absorbed their teaching."[42] This analysis of *A Dark Night's Passing* by Janet Walker indicates that the focus is indisputably on the protagonist's well-being, not on the interrelationship of characters. In other words, despite its refusal to offer a unified subject or voice, and its abandonment of the "implicit claims of omniscience or objectivity, claims that have authorized the hegemonic position of [Western] realist approaches to textual studies,"[43] *shishōsetsu*'s foremost preoccupation is to secure the individuality denied the protagonist by his own country. Those characters who come in contact with him are secondary, nothing more than temporary advisors in his drive to achieve the ego's desire.[44]

Minako's stories on the other hand, aggressively pursue a different course: the exploration of the interrelationship of characters, often through earthy and humorous dialogues. She exercises fully the "need to complicate the notion of power, regarding it as something that is not given or static but negotiated differently in the multiple contexts of women's lives."[45] Additionally, Minako's narratives thrive on psychological observation and analysis, which are of a secondary matter in *shōsetsu.* Yet another point of deviation for Minako concerns what Masao Miyoshi calls the "worrying self," an alienated modern individual who "is usually worried about his or her relationship to groups and models . . . [and is in the end] subsumed by the preponderance of the collective consciousness."[46] If the "worrying self" appears at all in Minako's narratives, it is there to highlight or satirize the dominance of the collective consciousness that restricts imagination and independent thinking.

✳ ✳ ✳

Reminding one of collections of thematically united short stories, Minako's major narratives employ an episodic and anecdotal structure.[47] I will focus on four of her works that illustrate the main characteristics of this distinctive approach. In *Yōbaidō monogatari* (Tales of Yōbaidō, 1984),[48] for example, the invisible center is a negotiation among different tales governed by multiple narrative points of views. The narratives in each chapter are independent of one another yet are interconnected through the agency of characters as neighbors, friends, acquaintances, or relatives. The unnumbered chapters, eleven in all, with titles taken from flowers, a vegetable, a poetic phrase, characters' names, and so on, demonstrate that the narrative world is literally an open book, an open invitation to step into any chapter of the reader's choice.

Minako brings together individuals who try to remove themselves from the constraints of the collective consciousness by a physical move to Yōbaidō, a place partially developed but still secluded from urban life. For these neighbors, moving to a new environment and building a house in a new neighborhood mean more than material improvement.

For the fifty-seven-year-old Chiyoko, the move, solely initiated and executed by her, signifies a revolutionary change in lifestyle, a complete break with the role that society and her husband's family have thrust upon her for thirty-five years. For the first time she speaks up to her husband, Tōru, and proposes the sale of their old house: "If you don't want to go ahead with the sale, I want a divorce. You're welcome to stay here in Tokyo with your mother and sisters. . . . Also, I want full payment on all the domestic service I have rendered for the past thirty-five years" (p. 94).[49]

Chiyoko's radical change stuns Tōru's family but remarkably also ends their complacency, especially Tōru's:[50] "When she suddenly began to plan the sale of the house and carry out all the business on her own, he realized for the first time that she was an individual entirely different from him" (p. 94). In an ironic twist, Chiyoko feels a little chagrined in the end: "*Why didn't I speak up much earlier!* She began to feel angry at the stupidity of enduring everything so much so long" (p. 98).

Unlike Chiyoko, Keiichiro, the "originating" character in *Tales of Yōbaidō,* decides to leave Tokyo because of his wife, Matsuko, who has become paranoiac soon after their son's death. Exhausted from coping with her condition, he seeks a change of environment that may be beneficial for both of them. As the first couple to settle at Yōbaidō, they either directly or indirectly initiate the development of a story in each chapter. Interactions among neighbors, sometimes very brief and superficial, sometimes illuminating, produce an unexpectedly positive change in the relationship of Keiichiro and Matsuko. Her possessiveness toward Keiichiro gradually diminishes as she discovers female friendship, while he experiences an alternative outlook on reality: "During her illness, he took it for granted that he had the exclusive attention of his wife and had never bothered to think about her interests in other people. Now that her obsessive behavior had eased up, he unexpectedly re-discovered his imagination. He used to put the blame totally on Matsuko for her mental illness, but, he said to himself, it is entirely possible that my own lack of imagination might have driven her to it" (p. 153).

*Tsuga no yume* (The Dream of a Hemlock, 1971) is a more daring example of Minako's innovative application of *shōsetsu* and her deviation from it. With its emotionally wobbling center a housewife-mother whose only available means of self-expression is madness, the work revels in disorienting the reader with tales that seem to have no clear agenda. Once the originating character is introduced, a story moves forward not chronologically or by causation, but associatively.

Many of the secondary characters in *The Dream of a Hemlock* reappear as "main actors" to take center stage with their own narrative space and voice. Nobue, the paranoid wife-mother, narrates in the first chapter the frightening experience of losing her mind in a claustrophobic, dark restaurant where she goes with her husband Ryō and their teenage daughter Sae. The voice of the daughter takes over in the second chapter, to critique the world of grown-ups. The third chapter, which opens with "Today, my wife looks very calm" (p. 84),[51] introduces the husband's view of their marital relationship. Sae reappears as the central character in Chapter 4, her brother Shirō in Chapter 7, each articulating views of the peculiar family situation. While an interaction between the mother and the daughter is the focus of the sixth chapter, the last three chapters describe the details of the steady deterioration of Nobue's condition. Ironically, *The Dream of a Hemlock* ends with the father and son communicating for the first time over Sae's disappearance and Nobue's hospitalization. Each episode dovetails with the next; each character plays both major and secondary roles in a story of a family in turmoil.

For Minako, a story is not about a single dominant character, but about its own spawning of other stories. As in Kurosawa Akira's "Rashōmon," the cinematization of "In a Grove" by Akutagawa Ryūnosuke (1892–1927), the center is not univocal, but is equally claimed by different facets of an incident or of its characters' experiences. Through the use of dreams, memories, and recollections, Minako the author hovers around an unspoken thematic or emotional center, invisible also for the narrator, the reader, and perhaps even for the author herself.

By keeping "the multiplicity of movement and experience concrete," and "without organizing these into a shape," Minako "lets a narrative run on."[52] Often unplanned and spontaneous, it has a life of its own. However, the author's own presence, which sometimes takes over from the narrator, is evident everywhere. The best and most humorous example of how the authorial voice is conscious of its "own performance in disjunction with the drift of the narrated events"[53] is found in *Naku tori no* (Birds Crying, 1985). The narrative first goes out of its way to inform the reader of the female protagonist's circular style:

> This is the way Yurie's talks almost always end, with one thing leading to another, just like in one of *Mother Goose*'s nursery rhymes, you know the one that goes like this: "This is the House that Jack built, etc., etc." Jack builds a house and makes the Malt, the Rat eats the Malt, the Cat kills the Rat, the Dog worries the Cat, the Cow with the crumpled horn tosses the Dog, the Maiden milks the Cow, the Man who's dazzled by the Maiden marries her and builds the House, and, so the cycle begins all over again (pp. 164–165).[54]

That this circular style also happens to be both the narrator's and the author's becomes clear at this point in the story because a different voice then speaks up, that of the author who is penning the narrative:

> Surely, that's how a story-spark takes off. Well, let me see, when did Nastasha's tale come into our story? Wait a minute. That's not necessarily the beginning of a story, is it. I[55] can start with Nastasha, or the cat, or the dog, the cow, the maiden, or the rat, for that matter. In other words, Nastasha's tale can come in at any time and that would make no difference.
>
> A tale that unfolded on a drowsy, lazy early spring evening lasted till dawn, while the gentle, intermittent murmur of a drizzling rain penetrated the walls and tatami floor.
>
> Now that the long rainy season's just around the corner, the cuckoos will soon come to call. Mizuki remembered that was what an old female neighbor said this very morning (p. 165).

The last two short paragraphs plant in the reader's mind a seed of uncertainty. Is it the same narrator (perhaps the author) or someone else who breaks in? Who is describing the drowsy spring evening that seems to stretch into infinity? The uncertainty is gently dispelled as the narration seamlessly blends into the familiar voice of Mizuki, the overall narrator of *Birds Crying,* who happens to be the originating character, the first one to appear in the opening chapter, and later the last in the closing paragraph of the work.

The most liberal and sophisticated use of the formal features of *shōsetsu* is found in the award-winning *Katachi mo naku* (Amorphous, 1982).[56] This sensuous tale of two brothers and their neighbor and girlfriend is literally "shapeless." The title, echoing Minako's affinity with the mystery of the cosmos, comes from Chapter 25 in *Tao-te Ching* (The Book of Tao):

> There was a chaotic something, yet lacking nothing
> Born before Heaven and Earth.
> *Alone.*
> Still.[57]
> Standing alone, unchanging.
> Revolving, endlessly.
> *It can be thought of as Mother of the World.*
>
> I do not know its name,
> *One can call it 'Tao.'*[58]

All the main characters' names indicate Minako's intention of keeping this sense of ambiguity and paradox intact. The older brother is called Ton, which means the "state of being dim and weak like a fool"; his younger brother is Haku, "not knowing where one is, like a newborn babe before it learns to smile"; and the name of Mayuko, their childhood girlfriend, means the "ten thousands things of the universe."

What underlies the interrelationship of these characters is the awareness of sexuality as the self,[59] or in Niwa Fumio's words, the "absence of the word shame (shūchi)."[60] According to the Western definition, shame is a "disturbed or painful feeling of guilt, incompetence, indecency, or blameworthiness," while in Japanese the word is also predominantly linked with sexuality.[61] *Amorphous* dismisses the notion of *shūchi,* which plagued the early *shishōsetsu* writers[62] and continues to influence gender relations in today's Japan. The unabashed exploration of the sexual awakening of the adolescent in *Amorphous,* its graphically erotic pursuit of sexuality, and the insertion of an unfinished soft-core pornographic story written by Haku in the middle of the narrative, make the work a daring challenge to the Japanese literary canon.[63]

*Amorphous* also resists the concept of prose. It is an experimentation with what Masao Miyoshi calls "orality," in opposition to "literacy," a letting go of the constraints of intellect, reason, and self-awareness. Minako, calling the work "a piece born out of the conscious subconscious"[64] via a writing process seen as a series of constructions and deconstructions, further explains: "When a writer spends an inordinate amount of time and effort to try to connect things together so that they make sense, the finished product is often boring. It is a bit like trying to dance while being constantly preoccupied with which steps to take next. You can't call that dancing. Dance happens when legs move on their own. . . . What I probably want to say is that *Amorphous* is a continuation of all the other works I've written so far, and this particular part of the process has caught the special attention of the award's selection committee."[65] Poetic, surrealistic, shapeless, almost cubist, yet sober, *Amorphous*, which is divided into twenty-five short chapters, begins with a dream and abruptly ends with a mundane scene of everyday life. There is no indication of any attempt on the part of the author to make sense out of a narrative form.

It is well to recall here Joanna Russ's assertion concerning the lyric mode, a style devised by women writers in the West: that there is no possible action or series of events that will embody in clear, unequivocal, immediately graspable terms what the artist means. In Minako's hands, the lyric mode of the *shōsetsu* as we have known it has been revitalized and transformed into something the Japanese modern literary canon had not thought possible. Armed with humor and sophistication, Minako is a witness both to Japan's female literary tradition and to the arrival of women who are reclaiming their rightful voice and place in a country that gave birth to the world's first women's literature, speaking to readers and writers alike beyond cultural and gender boundaries.

## Notes

1. The only critical essay on Ōba Minako's poetry that I am aware of is Janice Brown's " 'Once There Was a Woman': Revisioning Gender in the Poetic Writings of Ōba Minako," a paper presented at the 1996 Annual Meeting of the Association for Asian Studies in Honolulu, Hawaii.

2. Ōba Minakō is the recipient of the Kawabata Yasunari Prize, named after one of the most lyrical writers in Japan, not once but twice: for *"Umi ni yuragu ito"* (A Thread Swaying in the Sea, 1989) and for *"Akai mangetsu"* (A Blood-Red Moon, 1996). Both are short stories. I thank Gretchen Jones for providing me with a copy of the latter story.

3. See Janice Brown, "Reconstructing the Female Subject: Japanese Women Writers and the *Shishōsetsu,*" *British Columbia Asian Review,* no. 7 (Winter 1993–1994): 18–19.

4. For a critical discussion and analysis of the Japanese prose narrative form, *shōsetsu,* in comparison to the Western definition of the novel, see Masao Miyoshi, "Against the Native Grain," pp. 17–36, and "The 'Great Divide' Once Again," pp. 45–50, *Off Center: Power and Culture Relations Between Japan and the United States* (Cambridge and London: Harvard University Press, 1991).

5. Ibid., p. 46.

6. Ibid., p. 47.

7. Joanna Russ, *To Write Like a Woman: Essays in Feminism and Science Fiction* (Bloomington: Indiana University Press, 1995), p. 87.

8. Ibid.

9. For an excellent collection of critical essays on this narrative, see Kinya Tsurutu, ed., *Shiga Naoya's A Dark Night's Passing* (Singapore: Department of Asian Studies, National University of Singapore, 1996). I thank Janet Walker for providing me with a copy of this book.

10. Brown, "Reconstructing the Female Subject," p. 19.

11. Cited in Karatani Kōjin, *Origins of Modern Japanese Literature,* ed. and trans. Brett de Bary, with an introduction (Durham, NC, and London: Duke University Press, 1993), pp. 170–171. Well known for his interpretation of *The Tale of Genji,* Motoori Noringa almost single-handedly initiated the process of appropriation for male writers and scholars. This process has been so consistent and thorough for centuries that Masao Miyoshi, "Women's Short Stories in Japan," *Manoa: A Pacific Journal of International Writing,* vol. 3, no. 2 (Fall 1991): 37, writes: "During the same long period there were very few female writers of any kind. By the time modern Japanese women began their practice in the late nineteenth century, they were as deprived of tutors of

their gender as their Euro-American sisters of the eighteenth century. They had to start from scratch and wrench their space from a male-dominated literary world."

12. Chieko Ariga, "Text Versus Commentary: Struggles over the Cultural Meanings of 'Women,' " in *The Woman's Hand: Gender and Theory in Japanese Women's Writing,* eds. Paul Gordon Schalow and Janet A. Walker (Stanford, CA: Stanford University Press, 1996), p. 355.

13. Brown, "Reconstructing the Female Subject," p. 19.

14. Masao Miyoshi seems to be the exception to the rule. See his brief treatment of Tsushima Yūko's narratives in "Gathering Voices: Japanese Women and Women Writers," *Off Center,* pp. 212–216.

15. Livia Monnet, "The Politics of Miscegenation: The Discourse of Fantasy in 'Fusehime,' " *Japan Forum,* vol. 5, no. 1 (April 1993): 53. See also her *"Connaissance delicieuse,* or the Science of Jealousy: Tsushima Yūko's 'The Chrysanthemum Beetle,' " in *The Woman's Hand,* pp. 382–424. I thank James Fujii for bringing my attention to "The Politics of Miscegenation," and also for providing me with a copy.

16. Brown, "Reconstructing the Female Subject," p. 19.

17. Take, for example, the most revered *shishōsetsu* writer, Shiga Naoya (1883–1971): according to Karatani Kōjin, "When Shiga writes, in Japanese, *'to omou,''* this should not be translated as it usually is into English 'I think,' but rather as 'I feel,' or, even more accurately, as 'It thinks in me,' or 'It feels in me' " (p. 96).

18. Russ, pp. 87–88.

19. Janice Brown, "Reconstructing the Female Subject," would concur with Miyoshi on the idea that *shōsetsu* (which she calls 'prose fiction narrative'), a form created by Japanese male writers in response to Japan's Westernization, is a "fairly mixed bag, including fiction (both novels and short stories), diaries, essays, memoirs—in short, almost any other type of prose writing that one might care to toss in" (p. 20).

20. One such example comes from Miki Taku, "Dokusho teidan" (A Three-Person Roundtable Discussion on Reading Literature), *Bungei* (March 1981): 272–286, who attacked Ōba for "inconsistency" and "lack of logic," in *A Journey Through the Mist.* For a detailed discussion of the narrative, see chapter 4 of this book.

21. Masao Miyoshi, *Off Center,* points out that "the rejection of individualism in Japan is thus compensated for by the dominance of the first person. What makes the *shōsetsu* fascinating is this complex negotiation between the formal insistence on the 'I' and the ideological suppression of the self" (p. 23). While Miyoshi seems to differentiate *shōsetsu* and *shishōsetsu* in terms of degree, James Fujii focuses on the analysis of the former as an independent entity in *Complicit Fictions: The Subject in the Modern Japanese Prose Narrative* (Berkeley: University of California Press, 1993). The 1996 study by Tomi Suzuki, *Narrating the Self: Fictions of Japanese Modernity* (Stanford: Stanford University Press, 1996), suggests a different approach to *shishōsetsu.* Arguing that "the I-novel critical discourse . . . became from the mid-1920s the

dominant paradigm and meta-narrative by which almost all literary works . . . were described, judged and interpreted," she regards *shishōsetsu* as something determined by the reader. It is not the "results of a contract proposed by the author," she continues, but it is the "reader's expectations concerning, and belief in, the single identity of the protagonist, the narrator, and the author of a given text [that] makes a text an I-novel" (pp. 3, 6).

22. Janet Walker, "A Naturalist Quest for the Sexual Self," in Kinya Tsurutu, ed., pp. 159, 160. For a comprehensive and vigorous study available in English on the subject of *shishōsetsu,* see Edward Fowler's *The Rhetoric of Confession: shishōsetsu in Early Twentieth-Century Japanese Fiction* (Berkeley: University of California Press, 1988). Arguing that modern Japanese literature probably came into existence together with the confessional literary form, Karatani Kōjin views confession as a system; for example, he says that Tayama Katai (1871–1930), whose *Quilt* (1907) is commonly accepted as the first *shishōsetsu,* discovered "sexuality" through the system of confession that "gives rise to the need to conceal" (pp. 76, 77).

23. See Sidonie Smith, *A Poetics of Women's Autobiography: Marginality and the Fictions of Self-Representation* (Bloomington: Indiana University Press, 1987).

24. Marvin Marcus, *Paragons of the Ordinary: The Biographical Literature of Mori Ogai* (Honolulu: University of Hawaii Press, 1993), gives the following definition of *bundan:* "The network of writers, intellectuals, critics, literary coteries, periodicals, journalists, and publishers that came to dominate the Japanese literary scene beginning in the late-Meiji period [1890s]" (p. 345; also see pp. 32–38).

25. Fowler, p. 69.

26. Karatani, p. 154. Emphasis added.

27. Ibid., pp. 155, 158.

28. Cody Poulton, *"Ecce Homo:* The Cult of Selfhood in *A Dark Night's Passing,"* ed. Kinya Tsuruta, pp. 13–49, seems to be the first male critic to openly discuss this lack of gender perspective in *shishōsetsu.* In his analysis of *A Dark Night's Passing,* he focuses on Shiga Naoya's portrayal of women, female characters portrayed as the "vessels of a sin whose seed is carried by men like Kensaku from one generation to another . . . shift[ing] responsibility from the protagonist onto others [women] in an almost karmic conception of fate" (p. 30). Poulton agrees with Donald Keene that "there is nothing feminine about the language of Naoko's [the protagonist Kensaku's wife] soliloquy. . . . It is of course possible that Shiga, like Kensaku, simply could not write from a woman's point of view. . . . Naoko's promise to Kensaku sounds more as if it has been dictated to her by Kensaku; it is what he wants to hear from her." On this similar point in Shiga's work, also see my article: Michiko Niikani Wilson, "Re-Visioning Japanese Literary Studies Through a Feminist Perspective," in *Revisionism in Japanese Literary Studies, PMAJLS* (Proceedings of the Midwest Association for Japanese Literary Studies), vol. 2 (Summer 1996): 119–137. I thank Janice Brown for bringing my attention to Poulton's article, and also for providing me with a copy of it.

29. Sidonie Smith, *A Poetics of Women's Autobiography: Marginality and the Fictions of Self-Representation* (Bloomington: Indiana University Press, 1987), points out what Western female writers are up against: "master discourses of the West that privilege the word and thus the logical argumentation and causal narrative characterized as 'masculine' writing" (p. 13).

30. Not only is there no mention of the women's movement, which was at its height during the Taishō era (1912–1926) in Tokyo, the center of intellectual activity and of the *bundan,* but there is no sign in the *shishōsetsu* of any sociopolitical awareness of such an unprecedented historical moment. That the institution of the *bundan* was able to ignore what the Taishō feminists had to offer is amazing.

31. Poulton, p. 23.

32. Tokitō Kensaku in *A Dark Night's Passing* is the exception to the rule on one score: he tries to remain chaste. His visits to brothels as a single man do not count. Kensaku is still considered chaste by critics.

33. Fowler, pp. 69–70.

34. This familiarity is the key to the success of this narrative form: Fujii writes that "without an audience of like-minded estranged figures (members of [the] *bundan*), confessional novels would not have become the defining form of serious modern prose narratives" (p. 79).

35. *Snow Country,* although it is not regarded as a *shishōsetsu,* gives an excellent example of a perfect blend of the *shōsetsu* and *shishōsetsu* forms, as manifested in the Japanese literary canon. Shimamura, the protagonist, a lost soul in a lyrical fantasyland, lives only from image to image, from memory to memory, from event to event. In all this, he is a disengaged, emotionally immature dreamer. Far from being an alienated modern man, here is a man who wants female attention, pure and passionate, a re-creation of an unconditional maternal love that demands no reciprocity. I do not think any male critics have yet paid attention to what the narrative might say to female readers. Besides responding to the *universal* quality of lyricism in the story, are women supposed to deny their gender and identify momentarily with Shimamura as he revels in the voluptuous body of Komako? Women readers have done that for centuries, identifying with Odysseus, Prince Genji, Tokitō Kensaku, Tom Sawyer, and even the most misogynistic protagonists in Norman Mailer's works.

In a feminist reading of *Snow Country,* Tajima Yōko, "A Rereading of *Snow Country* from Komako's Point of View," *U.S.-Japan Women's Journal,* English Supplement, no. 4 (January 1993), says it is a "sanatorium for male self-recovery" (p. 33), and calls Komako "a sexually liberated, unpaid nurse" (p. 33). Tajima shows that the protagonist Shimamura, far from being an "example of the meaninglessness, isolation, and futile love of modern man" (p. 42) who brings himself closer to "modern enlightenment" (p. 47), is nothing more than an immature man who is totally incapable of developing an equal relationship with a woman. Tajima's article originally appeared in Egusa Mitsuko and Urushida Yazuyo, eds., *Onna ga yomu Nihon kindai bungaku* (Women Reading the Modern Japanese Narrative) (Shin'yōsha, 1992), pp. 149–180.

36. Smith, *A Poetics of Women's Autobiography,* p. 9. Karatani clarifies the connection between the *shishōsetsu* writer and modern literature as defined in the West, and his close relation to Japan's modernization as a whole: "[N]either what is *shishōsetsu*-like nor what is *monogatari*-like [ancient/Heian tales] ever served to subvert the institution of modern literature, but on the contrary, existed within an apparatus which supplemented and revitalized that institution" (p. 163).

37. Ibid., p. 86. Karatani also traces the origin of the practice of confession in modern Japan to those disinherited samurai who became converts to Christianity.

38. See Saegusa Kazuko, *Sayonara otoko no jidai* (Goodbye, the Era of Men), (Kyoto: Jinmon Shoin, 1984), pp. 128–132.

39. See chapter 4 in this book for an extensive discussion of Ōba Minako's major *"shishōsetsu," Birds Crying.* What Saegusa has failed to mention is that both Hayashi Fumiko (1903–1951) and Uno Chiyo (1897– ) have written sensational autobiographical and picaresque works. Hayashi's *Hōrōki* (Diary of a Vagabond, 1928) and Uno's *Aru hitori no onna no hanashi* (The Story of a Single Woman, 1971), propose heroines who never regret, never give in to the female destiny prescribed by Japan's male-centered sociopolitical codes. Also, Miyamoto Yuriko (1899–1951) published *Nobuko,* a literary autobiography par excellence. However, Saegusa is right in doubting the existence of a true female *shishōsetsu,* because all three female writers' works, including Minako's, are not regarded as such by the *bundan.*

40. Linda Hutcheon, *A Poetics of Postmodernism: History, Theory, Fiction* (New York: Routledge, 1988), pp. 3, 20.

41. Poulton points out the "unrelievedly humourless" portrait of Kensaku (p. 26).

42. Walker, p. 192.

43. Fujii, p. 13.

44. Poulton remarks on how clever the protagonist in *A Dark Night's Passing* is "in avoiding responsibilities and in getting others to do his dirty work, or in blaming others when his desires are rebuffed" (p. 25).

45. Sandra Buckley on Ide Sachiko, in *Broken Silence: Voices of Japanese Feminism* (Berkeley: University of California Press, 1997), p. 34.

46. Masao Miyoshi, *Off Center,* p. 47.

47. *Ūmi ni yuragu ito* (A Thread Swaying in the Sea, 1989), is one such example. The title of the book comes from one of the seven short stories collected in the work. All the stories are narrated by Yuri, the female protagonist in the 1985 autobiographical fiction, *Naku tori no* (Birds Crying). It is as if Ōba Minako, unable to put aside *Birds Crying,* revisits Yurie's world filled with memories of those people she encountered in Alaska.

48. For works which have not yet been translated into English, I have added an English title, rather than citing only the original Japanese title, to help those who are uninitiated in Japanese language.

49. The passage is from the 1984 Chūō Kōronsha edition.

50. The husband and the mother-in-law together assume part of the cook-

ing chores, and the married sisters alternate weekends taking care of their mother.

51. The passage is from the 1971 Bungei Shunjū edition.

52. Miyoshi, *Off Center,* p. 23.

53. Ibid., p. 48.

54. These quotations are from the Kōdansha edition.

55. This tour de force of style does create a problem for the translator. Because Japanese language does not require one to indicate the personal pronoun in every sentence, we are uncertain whether "I" should be used or "It" here. The fact that Japanese can remain ambiguous is the charm of *shōsetsu.*

56. A Tanizaki Junichirō Prize.

57. These two words in this translation, "alone" and "still," represent an expression that gave rise to the title *Katachi mo naku.* In the modern Japanese rendition, the four-character title means "lonely and desolate"; yet Ōba Minako assigned her own *hurigana* (phonetic scripts) to read it, "without a shape." Another, and more traditional, rendition of the original four-character phrase goes: "Soundless and formless." See *A Source Book in Chinese Philosophy,* trans. and compiled by Wing-Tsuit Chan (Princeton: Princeton University Press, 1969), p. 152.

58. The translation is from *The Tao of the Tao Te Ching,* trans. Michael LaFargue, with commentary (NY: State University of New York, 1992), p. 84.

59. See Walker, p. 160.

60. In his comment, "Watashi no kansō" (My Thoughts), as a selection committee member on voting for *Amorphous,* in "The Announcement of the 1982 Tanizaki Junichirō Prize," *Chūō Kōronsha* (November 1982): 359.

61. For example, the medical term for pubis in Japanese is *chikotsu,* meaning "shameful bones." The character *chi,* which is in *shūchi,* is used in the word *chikotsu.*

62. Guilt and shame are bound together in the ambiguous feeling that the protagonist of *A Dark Night's Passing* has about sex. Kensaku, who is devoid of moralism, "can be most priggish about his own forays into carnality and debauchery. This is the priggishness of a young man prey to temptation but nevertheless forever ashamed of his weakness" (Poulton, p. 29).

63. Some critics have called *Amorphous* "a masterpiece of pornography." The 1987 edition by Kawade Shobō has this description in its blurb. In the same blurb, Kōno Taeko describes the work as Ōba Minako's best. In response to winning the award, Ōba Minako, "Nani ga watashi o ugokashite iru ka" [What Is Propelling Me?], *Chūō Kōronsha* (November 1982): 362–366, had this to say: "Considering the original meaning of the work's title, 'lonely and desolate,' I should say pornography is nothing but that (p. 362)."

64. Ibid.

65. Ibid., pp. 363, 364.

# 3

# Artist as Cultural Critic as Woman

"Unwitting" is the word to describe Minako's "verbal radicalism."[1] She is an unconscious critic in the sense that critiquing and re-visioning have been so much part of her intellectual and emotional life that they are second nature to her. In her deconsructionist, subversive, and paradoxical critique of culture and humankind, on the one hand, and her emancipatory, humanistic approach to reality, on the other, Minako instinctively engages in postmodern-feminist criticism. Skeptical and suspicious of socially constructed and universally accepted notions about reality, she is often drawn into an alliance with postmodernism which seeks to "distance us from and make us skeptical about beliefs concerning truth, knowledge, power, the self, and language that are often taken for granted within and serve as legitimation" for civilization.[2]

Sharing the characteristic element of modern literature which Lionel Trilling calls "a bitter line of hostility to civilization," Minako's work asks "every question that is forbidden in polite society. It asks us if we are content with our marriages, with our family lives, with our professional lives, with our friends."[3] Minako has not actively sought this role of nonconformist and of novelistic gadfly, still uncommon among feminist writers in today's Japan,[4] but she has found the role congenial.

In her quarrel with civilization, the degree of Minako's verbal radicalism varies depending upon the type of writing she is engaged in. While she lowers the intensity of her criticism considerably in interviews and roundtable discussions,[5] she can be very subtle and sarcastic, yet persuasive, in essays. "A Happily Married Couple," one of her early essays published in a collection of 1970–1979 critical writings, begins with a Wildean aphorism: "A happy marriage is a situation which allows you to get a divorce any time, but you have no desire to go ahead with one." She continues:

> A woman who is totally incapable of living without her husband would be a drag on him, and she would become either an object of pity or alienation. A man who is in continual fear that his wife might leave him is usually a very unattractive sort. Keeping in mind that you may have to live alone sooner or later, respecting conditions that allow you to give comfort to each other: that is what makes a happy marriage.[6]

Minako's free-spirited view of marriage extends to the marriage institution itself, which she considers a masculine creation: "When you think about it, it is very strange that just because a man is legally married to a woman, his life is completely bound up with that fact, or that a woman has to live only for the sake of her legally proclaimed husband." She insists that it is not a matter of whether this kind of restrictive gender relationship can possibly exist: "The point is whether the law could make it a viable situation. I say that is absolutely impossible. Whether it is a man or a woman, it is possible to find oneself content with the fetters imposed by one's partner, but it is an entirely different matter once laws come into play."[7]

Minako's radicalism, however, displays an ambivalence that holds her back from taking a more activist role. In her work she straightforwardly articulates thoughts Japanese women have wanted to express but hesitated to state. However, once the stockpile of outrageous ideas, quarrels, and objections is exhausted, she turns elusive. It is as if the writer and her words were two separate entities, although this is not the case. Her strategy is the indirect method often employed by attorneys in a court of law: A defense attorney's (or a prosecutor's) controversial statement or presentation of circumstantial evidence is rejected by the judge, who in turn warns the jurors that the information they have heard is irrelevant and must be ignored. However, it is too late: an idea has been planted in the jurors' minds. Words have the power to influence an outcome.

After pointing out the restrictive and artificial nature of the law on marriage in the above-mentioned essay, Minako reveals what she really wants to say: "Of course, I am aware that the prewar civil laws were crueler than the present laws for women, and that women's position in today's Japan has improved dramatically with the legal guarantee of their rights. But that is not what I am talking about. What I want to say is that the law should not control humans when they *possess the ability to create and critique it*. . . those in power may be able to stop people from expressing their [unconventional] ideas, but they cannot stop the workings of the human brain. When those in power pull the rope too tight, it may choke the neck of the very power which operates it."[8] Minako thus turns the notion of power and authority on its head.

Despite her lack of political involvement, a keen interest in the inherent political implications of sociocultural issues close to her heart is evident in her 1990 work on Tsuda Umeko (1864–1929). The only full-length biography Minako has written (she calls it a "literary biography"), *Tsuda Umeko* is much more than a biography; it is an intimate dialogue between two kindred spirits. In her literary portrayal of the youngest of five girls—who later became the founder of Minako's alma mater, Tsuda College, and who was sent as a child to the United States with the 1871 Iwakura mission—we see Minako the critic, using the familiar strategy of a trial lawyer, highlight many of the problems and contradictions that still plague modern Japanese women.

She instinctively identifies with Umeko, who was very much the product of Japan's modernization and the "contradictions of nineteenth-century feminism in both Japan and the United States."[9] To Umeko's dismay, many of her students later belonged to Japan's first feminist group, called the Seitōsha (Bluestocking Society), whose journal played an active role in the struggle for women's rights.[10] Umeko herself was openly hostile to the political involvement of women yet secretly sympathetic to feminists' discontent with the status quo, and she was heroic in advocating women's economic independence and independent thinking. She believed in influence rather than action.[11] If the Taishō feminists were the logical outcome of Umeko's fierce fight for individual thought, self-reliance, and self-respect,[12] we can say that feminists in today's Japan are the logical consequence of the spirit of Minako's insistence on women's autonomy and gender equality.

There are interesting similarities between the educator Umeko and the writer Minako. Each lived for eleven years in the United States, Umeko from the age of six to the age of seventeen, Minako from the age of twenty-eight to the age of thirty-nine. Umeko was sent as part of the Meiji government's frantic efforts to Westernize Japan and to learn the American way of life, while Minako crossed the Pacific Ocean when her husband was sent by his company to Alaska as part of Japan's postwar reconstruction and reindustrialization efforts. Both women attended all-female colleges. Umeko later returned to the United States to study biology at Bryn Mawr from 1890 to 1892; Minako, as mentioned earlier, is a graduate of Tsuda College, which was founded by Umeko. Both women were thirty-six when their lifelong dreams became reality: in 1900, Umeko raised enough funds to found a private women's school, and in 1968, Minako's short story, "The Three Crabs," appeared in *Gunzō* and won the coveted Akutagawa Prize.

Umeko's sober and critical observations of Japanese and American society are matched in range and force by Minako's interpretations of America, made as a temporary resident, and of Japan made as a returnee. In spite of the sixty-six years separating them, both women share the basic conflicts of the exceptional woman in a male-centered society, which they must face and overcome in order to succeed. Unlike ambitious and successful men, women of authority then as now are haunted by the question of gender. Revealing as much about herself as about Umeko, Minako has this very much in mind as she passionately defends the woman who refused to be domesticated and remained single throughout her life:

> Full of wit and humor, Umeko's writing [i.e., her letters to Mrs. Adeline Lanman, her American mother] sounds straightforward but very suggestive, and is filled with paradox. She had no paranoia about men, nor did she hate them. I can say with absolute certainty that she had a healthy attraction to the opposite sex; she was a woman full of vitality who would captivate any man.
>
> From the breadth of subject matter, the guileless expression, and the emotional sensitivity in her writing, it is also clear that Umeko was not acting the part of a dry, decisive, masculine businessman in his prime. It is conceivable that she was volatile and short-fused, but she was resilient enough to remain rational. More than anything else, she was tuned in to other people. In other words, she was sensitive and imaginative, and had an enormous gift with words. So why did Meiji men ignore a woman of this caliber? It is absolutely beyond me.[13]

In another instance, Minako talks approvingly about Umeko's strategy as a woman striving to make a difference in a male-dominated society: "Umeko's humorous and witty style has the appearance of candidness, and that obviously spurs the reader's imagination. Yet, this same style adheres to the intellectuality and elegance derived from feigned innocence."[14] For all the public posture of indomitability and self-control, Umeko was no saint. She was angry, and she complained, as everyone else did, about injustice, prejudice, and inequality, but Minako chooses to stress Umeko's center-of-the-road approach: "She was not extreme in her combativeness, and if something provoked her to fight back, she tried to enjoy the process of that struggle and look at its bright side."[15] The combative image of the radical feminist does not fit Umeko the pioneer of women's education, whose strategy clearly constitutes the core of Minako's own position as critic and writer.

Writing about Umeko's life was a rite of passage for Minako, an opportunity to reexamine the question of gender. This issue is the central theme of Minako's biography of Umeko, as well as of her critique of modern Japanese society and culture. Nowhere was the gender paradox more clear than in the overwhelming social stacking-of-the-deck that worked against Umeko the returnee. Barbara Rose summarizes it well. Sent by her father, who hoped to "regain some of her family's lost rank and privilege," and by the government anxious to repair the image of Japanese women's low status in the eyes of the West,

> Umeko was groomed . . . for what she assumed would be a position of leadership within the Meiji establishment, a role that she believed would be similar to the influential posts attained by the male students dispatched abroad to study for their nation. Yet the very factor that first made such a prospect possible—her sex—made the same future seemingly impossible: sent abroad to absorb, as a female, what could benefit Japanese women, she was denied any official distinction on her return to Japan because she was female. Umeko was forced to create a role for herself by polishing her image as an authority on the education, both formal and informal, needed by modern middle-class Japanese women.[16]

Yet she continued to believe, as Minako amply shows, that the time will come when women will enjoy equal status with men and a lifestyle of their own choice; that women's education on a par with men's would produce the kind of women who would "be capable of freely exchanging opinions with men and articulating their own views as women; that in mutual support, women would solve problems together with men, and explore the future together."[17] Umeko's job as an educator was to "open women's eyes, provide a workplace, and put them on an equal footing with men."[18]

With a straight face, Minako contrasts this with Umeko's depiction of the ideal woman in Meiji Japan: "From what she could gather, what men called an ideal woman in Japan was a mild-mannered elegant princess whom they could mold into anything they wanted, while the kind of women they preferred to have fun with were entertainers and prostitutes." In other words, for appearances' sake, Japanese men wanted to possess a virgin, for private pleasure, a whore.[19] Modern feminists call this splitting the female self and dividing the female body and mind, a rift which prevents women from gaining a sense of wholeness.[20] Minako both describes and shares Umeko's understanding of the phenomenon: "The majority of women were forced into marriage at such a tender age that they had not even developed a sense of self. Umeko repeatedly complained [to Mrs. Lanman] about the fact that Japanese girls were married off at such a young age against their own will. Some were confined inside the house as the lady of the house; some, less fortunate, were relegated to living only as mothers harassed by their children, or working like slaves day and night."[21]

This critique of the traditional wife-husband relationship in Meiji society by a young Umeko fresh off the boat still remains valid today. Japan's modernization began when the shadows of the samurai class still held power and its dominant "minority" culture "considered [it] unethical for a married couple to enjoy sexual pleasure."[22] Today's Japan has yet to deal with the institutionalization of marriage. Marriage is neither understood nor negotiated as a "relationship between a man and a woman but as the structure within which children are born and raised."[23] The compartmentalization of sexuality and procreation dictated by Confucian-influenced ideology remains intact. Taking the form of *mizushōbai* (sex industry), according to one feminist critic, it ironically contributes to the perpetuation of traditional Japanese marriages: they "remain stable only because of the husband's relationship with women working in the sex industry."[24] Umeko's belief in a logical, natural, commonsensical, and liberating gender relationship is still a dream to the majority of Japanese men and women, almost one hundred years after she inspired early feminists with her independent thinking, self-respect, and self-reliance.

Minako argues further on Umeko's behalf: "Women were not

the only ones involved [in the experimental project of sending the five girls to the United States]. Some Meiji men must have also dreamed about new types of women. . . . Wasn't it why the young Umeko and four other girls were sent to the United States in the first place?"[25] This kind of rhetorical questioning is often used by Minako to couch radical sentiments, in this case, the fact that men are choking their own necks by maintaining a rigid patriarchal system. Suppressing women's individuality and denying women their voices in all areas of human activity hurts men as much as women.

Minako's appreciation of frustrations which Umeko had about women's status in Japanese society is more than the empathy a biographer may develop in the course of writing about his or her subject. Each woman, Umeko at Bryn Mawr and Minako at Tsuda College, experienced firsthand the potential power of women in an environment that freed them from playing a gender role at a site where the idea of equity in every area of human activity was a given. Minako appropriately ends Umeko's literary biography with the famous words of M. Carey Thomas, the dean of Bryn Mawr at the time of Umeko's residency and later its president: "Believe in women." She then links these words to an extraordinary episode taken from an autobiographical sketch written by one of Umeko's students, Hoshino Ai, the president of Tsuda College when Minako was there, an episode which illustrates in a nutshell all the latent power that Minako has thought to awaken in Japanese women:

> [On August 17, 1945] two days after the end of the War I was summoned by the Minister of Education who told me of the impending arrival of U.S. Occupation Forces which would necessitate the temporary closing of the college. . . . Classes finally resumed on the first of October. . . . One day, my lunch was interrupted by Ms. Homma who dashed in to say that U.S. soldiers were loading a truck. I rushed to the scene alone. They were trying to remove basketball equipment from the gym. Desks, chairs, medical instruments, drugs, etc., were heaped on top of the truck. I approached one of the soldiers whom I believed to be an officer. I explained about Tsuda Umeko,

> Bryn Mawr, and Tsuda College, and appealed to his sense of justice, telling him how much my students would suffer without desks and chairs. Listening with perfect composure to what I had to say, he then slowly turned to the soldiers and said quietly, "Boys, I think you had better take them down." I did not detect in the tone of his voice any hint of an officer giving an order. They reluctantly unloaded the cargo and left. The following day we noticed an "Off Limits" sign posted at the school gate and that was the last time we ever had a visit from the Occupation Forces. . . . I do not remember his name, but if my recollection is correct, the officer was a high school art teacher (pp. 267–268).

✱✱✱

The verbal radicalism which Minako blunts in interviews, essays, and biographical writings is given free play in her fiction, particularly in the mouths of her fictional characters. A novel or a short story is the most comfortable and liberating medium for her to work in; here she can dispense with all the inhibitions that polite society imposes. She takes full advantage of the writer's privilege, so to speak, of the fact that writers "are rarely called upon to create policy; unlike cultural critics [by profession], they are not expected to invent strategies that can be actively used and institutionalized." By the same token, it is not only writers but also readers of fiction who have more freedom to "explore the parameters of the social and physical body without explicitly engaging in a discourse of emancipatory praxis."[26]

At the risk of being labeled a "reason-freak" (rikuttsuppoi) in a culture where self-expression is not a particularly endearing act, Minako the novelist is refreshingly verbal, sober, and biting, and through her characters says what is on her mind without mincing words. She spares no person, including herself, and no country, particularly not "criticism-erased Japan."[27]

The earliest work that demonstrates Minako the "artist as cultural critic as woman" is *Garakuta hakubutsukan* (The Junk Museum, 1975), which received the Women's Literature Prize. The result of her therapeutic sojourn in Sitka, the work shows Minako freeing herself from the fetters of the linguistic and cultural imprisonment she retroactively discovered she had experienced in Japan. In her roundtable discussion with Yamamoto Michiko (1936– ), another novelist who accompanied her husband abroad and lived in Australia, Minako attributes the total isolation she had experienced in Japan prior to the Alaskan odyssey, the feeling of not having a language of her own, to her gender[28]: "I realized how different people are in American society from those in Japanese society. In other words, Japan has very little notion of the individual. However, this view may have a lot to do with being a woman, not necessarily with being Japanese. . . . Women in Japan, knowing that they are not allowed to speak out what is really on their mind, give it up even before they think of trying to express it."[29]

This frustration and, in her own words, the *urami* (grudge) she holds against her own society generate the dynamics of *The Junk Museum.* Her individualistic, off-the-wall characters, especially the women, express themselves fully. The dialogues are full of spiteful yet realistic comments about Japanese, Americans, humankind, society, the world, and civilization, delivered with wit and humor; the characters operate collectively as Minako's mouthpiece.[30]

Aya, a "dyed-in-the-wool Japanese" despite her light brown eyes and almost white skin, is an iconoclastic marginal in a liminal world where national identity and cultural labeling hold no sway. Abandoned by a Japanese husband who decides to replace his wife with a more status-enhancing female (a highly intellectual female doctor, the only daughter of a capitalist), Aya later marries an American handyman called Russ who adopts her infant daughter, Chizu. Aya, an abandoned wife, fights back and abandons her home country.[31]

Her first marriage becomes a wake-up call to reexamine the stereotypical Japanese middle-class mentality and the institution of marriage. Her ex-husband, a graduate of Tokyo University, considered the most prestigious university in Japan, "was the type to put down his own wife just because she didn't attend a prestigious women's college, in this case because Aya hadn't attended college at all." In search of a mother-woman, incapable of having flights of imagination, he failed to appreciate Aya's literary mind. "Since he graduated from Tokyo University, he got it into his head that he was an intellectual type, part of the intelligentsia" (p. 74).[32]

The reassessment of her first marriage, a personal matter, also involves a larger issue of a political nature, that of a country willing to embrace certain stereotypes for securing a productive capitalist society to maintain the status quo.[33] Aya's resentment must be rekindled through recollection of the mental and emotional abuse she had to endure in Japan: "Aya resolved to nurture the tiny black seed of resentment inside her, coat it with enough secretion over years of efforts to produce a perfect pearl" (p. 76). To maximize the effect of her biting critique of Japan and to preempt a reactive brush-off from the reader, Minako lets the Sitka residents rather than the omniscient narrator give voice to every unflattering stereotypical image of the Japanese, from their supposed obsequious, antlike nature and women's "domestic power" in the home, to the popularity of cheap pornographic magazines and men's indifference to family life. Aya's response to these comments is even more biting:

> One after another the people [in the tiny Alaskan town] tried to provoke Aya, but she took it all in stride. She never dropped a stitch in her knitting, and said,
>
> "Yes, yes, that exists in Japan, really, after all it's a human society like any other, I'm sure."
>
> Someone popped the question, "Do you like America?"
>
> "There are things I like, things I dislike, but since I've decided to become an American, I just look at things I like."
>
> Another queried, "Do you still love Japan?"
>
> "Not a bit. I think of Japan like an abandoned child trying to remember her parents. Well, I'm sure they had their reasons."
>
> Of course, Aya had no affection for America either, but that was something she kept from the townies. But she declared to Russ decisively, "No matter what happens, I will never die for America, even though I may for you" (pp. 79–80).

It is through Aya's best and only friend, Maria Anrevena, a red-haired Russian refugee who had been ejected from her society in the midst of the Bolshevik Revolution, that Minako articulates her deconstructionist, postmodern views on nationality and power: "Why do you have to be obligated to love your country just because you were born there? I'm convinced that a child has a right to abandon a good-for-nothing parent, and so does a citizen her country. . . . No one chooses one's parents or nation when one is born. . . . Just because you reject your parents or your country, it doesn't mean you're rejecting yourself. . . . If you're tied to the nation of your birth for the rest of your life, I'd say it's a kind of slavery" (p. 95).

Maria, who has left her homeland for political reasons, continues her sober analysis of the power relation of citizen and nation: "A nation never loves those it can't benefit from. Your case is different. You have never protested Japan's way of doing things. You have never rebelled against your own government" (p. 98). In the end Maria the political refugee helps Aya the nonconformist to identify her internalized anger and verbalize her resentment, to name it in her own language:

> "I didn't like those who just went along and cooperated with Japan. Well, what I mean is I was disliked by those Japan liked. I had no use for the country, I was useless, useless in the sense that they were more useful to the nation than I was. That's why I'm saying I have been abandoned by Japan.
>
> It doesn't matter how much I may care about the country. It just doesn't give a damn about me. . . ."
>
> She was getting angrier and angrier. It seemed that all the resentment and grudges she had kept to herself these last ten years, all the complaints she had lodged against Japan exploded in an instant (p. 98)

As is typical of Minako's protagonists, Aya has conflicts that remain unresolved at the end of the story, and she continues to live in the United States.

If Aya represents those Japanese women who are in self-exile abroad, in later works Minako balances her out by creating

Umeko-like characters who return: Keiko the middle-aged widow in *Ōjo no namida* (The Tears of a Princess, 1988), Yukie the twenty-three-year-old expatriate in *Urashimasō* (Urashima Plant, 1977),[34] and Yurie the established novelist in *Birds Crying* (*Naku tori no,* 1985),[35] all of whom return to Japan to confirm their own sense of self, to reintegrate the body and mind. Although Minako is less personal in *Urashimasō* than in *The Junk Museum*, her articulation remains strong, her instinct for comparisons intact.

This time, Minako lets an American male speak out and critique Japanese and American society, through interior monologues. A totally neutral element in the story, Marek is the live-in boyfriend of the protagonist, Yukie, who, unlike Aya, returns to Japan to give the country one last try. The very first line Minako gives to this rather typical American male has no trace of exoticism: " 'Why in the world did I bother to come to Japan, anyway?' He was pissed off" (p. 173).[36] Minako's intention is to present an American perspective on Japan voiced by an astute observer who is visiting Japan for the first time, and who appears to have no vested interest in the matter.[37] Even so, Marek is not especially fond of the country. His relativistic view entails a constant balancing act as he attempts to resist chauvinistic conclusions:

> According to his innate sense of aesthetics, he does not find the Japanese to be a particularly beautiful race. However, a sense of beauty is a strange thing; within the confines of what the norm should be, anything that does not fit the norm is considered not beautiful. Marek thinks Japanese are not beautiful because he is someone brought up in a white culture. On the other hand, people who have not been exposed to whites might find them a bunch of demons.
>
> If a white accidentally pops up in an all-black society which has never seen a white before, he is bound to scare the bejabbers out of the blacks—like the appearance of any ghost would. It is just like food you've been brought up with. A sense of beauty or ugliness, except that part of a person's inner self that seeps out, is nothing but a taste determined by conventions (p. 173).

Falling back on a theory that pits hunting against agricultural cultures, Marek enumerates the stereotypical characteristics of the Japanese, a kind of summary of what Americans know about Japan: They do not like to live alone; they congregate together and all do exactly the same thing; they are always seeking a protector, and if he fails to protect them, they harbor grudges; they demand a lot but are careful not to express their demands; they are patient; they detest the clarity of arguments, and are never in a hurry to reach a conclusion; they are clever at long-term thinking; they refuse to be assertive and possess an ability to get themselves out of jams, that is to say, they never decide for themselves in public whether something is a victory or a defeat; rather they let everyone else decide on their behalf.

However, Marek perceives a contradiction among these group-oriented interdependent Japanese. He wonders out loud: "How is it that these same people have very little civic awareness, when they love to stay together all the time, and once separated from the crowd, look as helpless as mice stranded on a log tossed about on the ocean?" (p. 174). In a system where a tradition is supported by thousands of years of history, Marek reasons, Japanese have learned not to waste energy deconstructing traditions, but to survive by accepting the intricate social networks of their culture and by passively tuning in to each other's motives to make themselves desirable in one another's eyes. "In Japan there is no participation by individuals through their free will; according to the Japanese a society is a place where, whether you like it or not, you are automatically tied down" (p. 174). Minako the cultural critic lets Marek articulate what everyone recognizes in Japan but hesitates to address openly:

> Rather than competing individually in an equal relationship or accepting each other, Japanese kill their egos, build alliances with groups, and in return demand security. Self-assertion means that you have to recognize the other's freedom. Although they are willing to listen to what an individual has to say, they feel they are powerless to do anything or assist that person. What happens in this process is that

> they withhold their opinions and at the same time ignore what the individual is griping about. They are in continual fear of criticism by the community; even when their motives are based on pure egocentricity, their actions appear non-combative and gentle in public.
>
> In the midst of these questionable, egocentric, and intertwined minds, you do not see the spark of creativity in the interactions of people. It seems they have a philosophy that says enlightenment comes strictly in isolated self-examination. They resort to this because they are disgusted with their own passivity, and are in total despair (pp. 174–175).

Employing the techniques of resistance and reason, in this case through the character of Marek, Minako writes what Japanese men do not want to read and would rather ignore: a woman's perspective on social and cultural issues which have been traditionally addressed and universalized by men.

Writing, Minako once made clear, is her way of "refusing to embrace the patriarchal way of thinking."[38] When "half of the human population is female, it's just a law of nature that women and men be given a fifty-fifty chance [in every area] to live out their lives."[39] Unlike other Japanese women and men writers, she never holds back on this score. Kōno Taeko (1926– ), in a roundtable discussion with Minako, stated her admiration of Minako's unwavering spirit: "You have the ability not to let negative responses [from reviewers] bother you. You have a wonderful talent, a career firmly in hand, and a clear sense of self." Kōno implies that no one else could have been as unfazed as Minako under the same circumstances: "You were never crushed but steadily went on to produce *Katachi mo naku* (*Amorphous,* 1982) and *Birds Crying* both of which have given us hours of pleasure." As is typical of Minako, she responded by reconfirming that fiction is her battleground: "Oh, yes, terrible abuse they [the critics and reviewers] heaped on me. People have often told me to respond to those nasty remarks, but I have always replied, 'I'd rather do so in my novels.' . . . I wonder whether I should counterattack [in person]. . . . Well, [I can't.] I guess it's my personality."[40]

In contrast to her noncombative public persona, an assertive

Minako fills the 1976 story entitled "Yamamba no bishō" (The *Yamamba*'s Final Smile) with ammunition, relentlessly satirizing the construction of gender and the institution of marriage in Japanese society. Minako's humorous and witty style, not unlike Umeko's, spurs the reader's imagination with its appearance of candor, its elegant use of feigned innocence. More significantly, beneath the story's narrative surface of vulnerability, cynicism, anarchy, and subversive intent lurks the spirit of playfulness, the ludic, a territory unfamiliar to and often overlooked by Japanese literary critics in discussing Minako's works.

"The *Yamamba*'s Final Smile" is the simple, straightforward story of a folkloric *yamamba,* literally a mountain witch, who spends her entire life in the dwellings of a human settlement, going through the usual rites of passage—childhood, adolescence, marriage, motherhood, old age, and death. The narrator begins the story as if it were a folk tale, focusing on one particular *yamamba* who lived in the form of a human for sixty-two years. According to legend, a *yamamba*-witch is endowed with the uncanny ability to read people's minds and to transform herself into any form that may please men. She is the devouring and castrating woman, ugly and terrifying. The characters in Minako's story are nameless, a subtle indication that the story could refer to the life of any woman on the planet.

A different perception of the *yamamba* emerges as the narrator modulates from the style of an oral tradition to that of fiction. The *yamamba* is transformed into what Virginia Woolf called the "Angel in the House," a self-sacrificing woman who "excelled in the difficult arts of family life . . . [and who] was so constituted that she never had a mind or a wish of her own, but preferred to sympathize always with the minds and wishes of others."[41] In the human world the *yamamba* is never taken seriously and is exploited by everyone around her, the very image of a cursed creature, the embodiment of femaleness in a patriarchal society. At each rite of passage, as a daughter and later as a wife, the *yamamba* deepens her knowledge of humans and perfects the technique of not offending others in interpersonal relationships.

At school she spends an incredible amount of mental energy tuning into everyone else's moods and behavior. In her home, where a father figure is absent for all practical purposes, the young *yamamba* learns not to verbalize what is on her mother's mind and adjusts her own perceptions to meet her mother's needs.

"As things always turn out in life," the narrator tells us, the grown-up *yamamba* "eventually found a mate." In marriage her role-playing techniques become more refined in response to her very demanding husband:

> He was just another stereotypical male, plain and ordinary. His own mother had smothered him with love, and the son never doubted that he had the right to express his every need which would have to be met by the opposite sex no matter how irrational it was. When a man of this type grows up, he automatically assumes that any female who sleeps with him is just a substitute for his mother. He takes it for granted that she is as generous as a mother, as majestic as a goddess, enough of a fool to dote on him with boundless love, yet at the same time possessed of an evil soul, like a vicious dog (p. 342).[42]

Minako thus exaggerates the classic example of the codependent housewife whose sole role is that of reproduction, both procreative and social, and brings out its full irony. The *yamamba* reproduces the next generation and, unwittingly, also perpetuates "sexism, patriarchy, or male supremacy"[43] by performing "mothering" to perfection for her infantile husband and two children. As Nancy Chodorow has written: "[W]omen as wives and mothers reproduce people—physically in their housework and child care, psychologically in their emotional support of husbands and their maternal relations to sons and daughters. . . . Men are socially and psychologically reproduced by women, but women are reproduced largely by themselves . . . the family and women socialize *men* into capitalist society."[44] The further irony of this social task of reproduction is that society encourages it by isolating women in the domestic sphere. In the case of the *yamamba*-woman, what choice does she have but to go along with the institution of family? Her only alternative is to go back to the wilderness. Such an either/or choice is no choice for women.

While a principal theme of the story is renunciation, this parable of a typical Japanese female also masterfully deconstructs the myth of female self-division and a woman's surrender to the split self,[45] the story's real theme. Half-seriously, half-jestingly, the narrator tells us that the *yamamba* suffers from a "powerful tension between aspiration and self-effacement."[46] She often fantasizes in order to console her miserable self. One such fantasy involves the image of her husband "prowling around her hut in a reduced state like a miserable beggar" after she escapes to the wild. What she sees in a mirror is not the face of Snow White, but her own split self of madonna/madwoman: "His voice still ringing in her ears, she would look at her reflection in the spring. Here she was, half her face a benevolent mother with a tranquil smile, the other half an enraged demon. One side of her mouth tore at a man, hungrily devouring his flesh and blood, while the other side showered another man with kisses as he clung to her nipple, suckling like an infant curled up in his mother's caress" (p. 345). Clearly the only way for a woman to identify and display anger is to turn into an enraged demon.

It is, in Alicia Suskin Ostriker's words, "our culture's limited images of feminine personality" that divide the female self, leaving no other possible range of emotions: "[S]elf-division is culturally prescribed, wholeness culturally forbidden."[47] Within this narrowly defined femininity, the gender relationship described in "The *Yamamba*'s Final Smile" is the most stereotypical of all, absurd yet realistic.

Men's convenient use of such words as willpower and insensitivity to describe gender difference (positive traits when associated with men, but negative for women) further erodes the individuality of women. The reduction of men and women to certain qualities overwhelms and isolates the *yamamba:* "She experienced the terrible fear of being among foreigners speaking gibberish; it wasn't only her husband, but most of society that compelled her to feel this way" (pp. 344–345). Ultimately, there is nothing left for the aged *yamamba,* suffering from obesity and a cerebral thrombosis, but to "suffocate herself" so that her death can "unburden" her family. In other words, she happily departs this outrageous human habitat for the wilderness of a *yamamba* world.

Minako's satiric tone turns comical at the end of the story, and the most pitiful, idiotic, and comical character in the story is the husband who stares at the magically rejuvenated body of his dying wife:

> Then she [the *yamamba*] saw her aging husband, woolgathering, standing like a stick beside her. This happy doddering mad old man found himself moved to the core by the loveliness of his wife's naked body. In ecstasy, he stood there transfixed beside her body until the very end, overcome by his own faithfulness and sincerity. What greater human joy than to make others happy. She was content to see him for the last time, a man who had the extraordinary gift of changing any negative situation to his own advantage, and she secretly congratulated him on the happiness he would surely attain in his second life to come (p. 350).

This example of what Minako calls the "absolute irrationality of an unequal treaty" between a man and a woman reminds us of a series of humiliating unequal treaties Japan had to sign with Western nations in the ensuing decades of Japan's modernization. Just as Aya's personal experience in a failed marriage cannot be adequately assessed without the larger question of Japanese middle-class mentality, the *yamamba*'s story, in its totality, is both personal and political: It is, on the one hand, a critique of a "cursed" Japanese woman who allows herself to fall into a life dedicated to reading, deciphering, and assimilating the likes, dislikes, moods, and needs of men, and at the same time she lets society dictate her life. On the other hand, it can also be read as an allegorical tale of Japan's traditional power relationship with the United States. Spending a tremendous amount of energy to incorporate and assimilate Western knowledge and technology, Japan fails to acknowledge the high price its culture pays to hold at bay, in Masao Miyoshi's words, "universalist knowledge, skeptical observation, and individual reflection in order to sustain a close and coherent community inherited from the long past."[48]

While Minako deconstructs male bias and gender inequality with a venom and verbal finesse that "might make a stone weep with rage,"[49] yet in the end she appears cool. Like Virginia Woolf, she seems to subdue her own anger, which is seething just beneath the surface. However, this restraint, almost palpably disturbing, is what arouses such a strong reaction in the reader: one either curses the *yamamba* or laughs with her, or both. In "The *Yamamba*'s Final Smile," and even in works such as *Funakuimushi* (The Ship-Eating Worms, 1969), "The Pale Fox" (*Aoi Kitsune,* 1973), "Candle Fish" (*Rōsoku uo,* 1975), and *Amorphous,* all of which have a surrealistic and magical tone and texture, Minako's critical stance as artist as critic as woman emerges clearly. It is the interplay of lyricism and verbal radicalism, alternately calming and agitating the reader's mind, that sets her apart from other Japanese women and men writers.

## Notes

1. Marsha A. Hewitt, "Illusions of Freedom: The Regressive Implications of 'Postmodernism,' " in *The Socialist Register—1993: Real Problems, False Solutions*, eds. Ralph Miliband and Leo Panitch (London: Merlin Press, 1993), p. 79.

2. Jane Flax, "Postmodernism and Gender Relations in Feminist Theory," chapter 2 in *Feminism/Postmodernism*, ed. Linda J. Nicholson, with introduction (New York and London: Routledge, 1990), p. 41.

3. Lionel Trilling, *Beyond Culture: Essays on Literature and Learning* (New York and London: Harcourt Brace Jovanovich, 1965), pp. 3, 8–9.

4. Among her contemporaries, the feminist writer-critics Saegusa Kazuko (1929– ) and Tomioka Taeko (1935– ) stand out. Like Ōba Minako, Saegusa has aggressively addressed the gender issue and patriarchy, particularly in critical essays. See *Renai shōsetsu no kansei* (Pitfalls of a Romantic Novel) (Seidosha, 1991). Tomioka, also considered as one of the most outspoken feminist writers in Japan, often critiques the family institution in essays and fiction. Some of her critical writings include *Onna kodomo no hanran* (Rebel-

lions by Women and Children) (Chūō Kōronsha, 1981); *Hyōgen no fūkei* (The Scenaries of Expression), (Kōdansha, 1989); and *Fuji no koromo ni asa no fusuma* (Wisteria Garments and Linen Bedding), (Chūō Kōronsha, 1984).

5. For example, a recent collection of Minako's roundtable discussions *(taidan)* with nine Japanese women is entitled *Yawarakai feminizumu e* (Toward Gentle Feminism), (Seidosha, 1992).

6. In Ōba Minako, "Kōfuku no fūfu" in *Onna no dansei-ron* (Discussions on Men by Women) (Chūō Kōronsha, 1982), p. 9.

7. Ibid., p. 12.

8. Ibid., pp. 12–13. Emphasis added.

9. Barbara Rose, *Tsuda Umeko and Women's Education in Japan* (New Haven and London: Yale University Press, 1992), p. xi.

10. Ibid., pp. 146–152.

11. Ibid., pp. 158, 162.

12. Ibid., pp. 126, 162.

13. Ōba Minako, *Tsuda Uemko* (Asahi Shimbunsha, 1990), pp. 168–169.

14. Ibid., p. 146.

15. Ibid., p. 185.

16. Rose, p. 160. See also Yoshiko Furuki, *The White Plum, A Biography of Ume Tsuda: Pioneer in the Higher Education of Japanese Women* (New York: Weatherhill, 1991), pp. xvi-xvii.

17. Ōba Minako, *Tsuda Umeko*, p. 198.

18. Ibid., p. 222.

19. Ibid., p. 197. Furuki also has commented on this: "It was a time when men still boasted of the number of concubines they kept, and when the wives of many government ministers were former geishas" (p. xvi).

20. According to Alicia Suskin Ostriker, *Stealing the Language: The Emergence of Women's Poetry in America* (Boston: Beacon Press, 1986), "The split selves in woman poets are both true, both false—or rather their truth or falsity is not the issue. The issue is the division: that the halves do not combine to a whole, as if a tree had roots and leaves but no trunk" (p. 84).

21. Ōba Minako, *Tsuda Umeko*, p. 197.

22. Matsui Yayori, "Asian Migrant Women in Japan," in Sandra Buckley, *Broken Silence: Japanese Feminism* (Berkeley, CA: University of California Press, 1997), p. 148.

23. Kanazumi Fumiko, "Interview," in Sandra Buckley, p. 80.

24. Matsui Yayori, "Interview," in Sandra Buckley, p. 142.

25. Ōba Minako, *Tsuda Umeko*, p. 194.

26. Sharalyn Orbaugh, "The Body in Contemporary Japanese Women's Fiction," in *The Woman's Hand: Gender and Theory in Japanese Women's Writing,* eds. Paul Gordon Schalow and Janet A. Walker (Stanford, CA: Stanford University Press, 1996), p. 125.

27. Speaking of the "criticism-erased Japan," Masao Miyoshi, *Off Center: Power and Culture Relations Between Japan and the United States* (Cambridge and London: Harvard University Press, 1991), critiques Japan's close-knit codependent literary world: "Paralleling the holy alliance of capital, labor,

and bureaucracy is a powerful consortium of writers (*sakka*), scholars (*gakusha*), reviewers/commentators (*hyōronka*), and publishers (*honya*), all supporting one another in a unified effort to advance their economic interests and power bases. Such a quadrilateral cooperative . . . grows into an unchallenged monopoly . . . the nation's critical consciousness is ill served indeed" (pp. 25, 27).

28. Kōra Rumiko, "An Interview," in Sandra Buckley, a poet and critic, makes a similar point, echoing Minako's frustration: "I felt even as a child that [Japanese] language was not mine, that I existed outside the language that surrounded me, like a foreigner" (p. 104).

29. Ōba Minako and Yamamoto Michiko, "Naze shōsetsu o kakuka—Ikoku de oboeta bungakuteki shōdō" (Why Write Novels?—A Literary Impact We Encountered in Foreign Lands), *Bungakukai* (April 1973): 190.

30. Miki Taku, a writer/critic, "Dokusho teidan" (A Three-Person Roundtable Discussion on Reading Literature), *Bungei* (March 1981): 285), has reluctantly admitted: "I've never heard a voice this candid from any other [Japanese] woman writer."

31. The title of the work comes from Russ's old abandoned ship turned into a junkyard, which the townspeople began to call "the junk museum."

32. The translated passages are from *Garakuta hakubutsukan,* in *Ōba Minako zenshū,* vol. 4 (Kodansha, 1991), pp. 7–174.

33. Kanazumi Fumiko suggests that "what is missing in the modern Japanese family is any real sense of intimacy, any sense of emotion free of obligation or manipulation" (p. 77).

34. For a detailed discussion of *Urashimasō* (Urashima Plant), see chapter 6 in this book.

35. For a detailed discussion of *Naku tori no* (Birds Crying), see chapter 4 in this book.

36. The following passages from *Urashimasō* appear in the 1984 Kōdansha-bunko edition.

37. Minako's description of the insightful comments made by Marek reminds us of Roland Barthes's refreshingly imaginative and somewhat irreverent discourse based upon his two-week stay in Japan in 1970. That was his first visit to the country. He covers everything from Japanese food, packages, and language to people and society. *Empire of Signs*, trans. Richard Howard (New York: Hill and Wang, 1982).

38. "Onna no hyōgen, otoko no hyōgen" (Women's Expression, Men's Expression), an interview in *Waseda bungaku* (November 1985): 10.

39. Ibid., p. 15.

40. Ōba Minako and Kōno Taeko, "Bungaku o gaisuru mono" (Things That Harm Literature), *Bungakukai* (July 1987): 150, 152.

41. Virginia Woolf, "Professions for Women," in *The Death of the Moth and Other Essays* (New York: Harcourt Brace Jovanovich, 1970), p. 237.

42. "The Yamamba's Final Smile" in Ōba Minako, *Ōba Minako zenshū*, vol. 3 (Kōdansha 1991). The following translations in the text are based on this volume. The complete English translation of this story under the title of "The

Smile of a Mountain Witch" is available in *Japanese Women Writers: Twentieth Century Short Fiction*, trans. and eds. Noriko Mizuta Lippit and Kyoko Iriye Selden (New York, Armonk: M. E. Sharpe, 1991), pp. 194–206.

43. Nancy Chodorow, *The Reproduction of Mothering: Psychoanalysis and the Sociology of Gender* (Berkeley: University of California Press, 1978), p. 6.

44. Ibid., pp. 36–37.

45. Ostriker, pp. 77, 78.

46. Ibid., p. 10. Just as the nineteenth-century "genteel ideal of femininity" was embodied in a perfect glass slipper, which stressed the "heart and denied the head" (p. 15), the *yamamba* represents those who are not Cinderella. To borrow the slipper metaphor, the only way for the *yamamba* to fit into the slipper is to shed blood. Besides renouncing her mind-reading ability, she makes a gargantuan effort to feel jealous when she is not, to underrate any man other than her husband, and to pretend to seduce other men.

47. Ibid., pp. 84, 83.

48. Masao Miyoshi, *As We Saw Them: The First Japanese Embassy to the United States (1860)* (Berkeley, CA: University of California Press, 1979), p. 124.

49. Ostriker, p. 126.

# — 4 —

# Becoming and (Un)Becoming: The Female Destiny Reconsidered

In her autobiographical fiction, *Oregon yume jūya* (Ten Nights of Oregon Dreams, 1980), the diarist Ōba Minako, about to depart for the United States, goes through a ritual leave-taking at Narita Airport that seems to last interminably. Against her wishes, her husband accompanies her to the airport. Her friends and acquaintances dutifully gather around her, and a ritual exchange of farewells begins:

> "Abandoning your husband for three months!"
>
> "What will he do while you're gone?"
>
> "He'll be so lonely."
>
> All sorts of people fired questions at me, things that I found totally meaningless. How did I reply?
>
> "He's used to it."
>
> "What do you mean by, What will he do all alone? He's no child. He'll manage by himself, I'm sure. You can't be serious. Would you put the same question to a wife when her husband stays away from home for a long time?" (p. 9).[1]

The typical response in such a social context would go something like this: "I know I'm totally selfish to take off by myself, leaving my husband in the lurch. Please be nice to him and take care of him, if you can. I'd be forever indebted to you. I'll be counting on your good will." This brief abortive exchange illustrates the iconoclastic spirit of Minako's literary imagination, one that introduces a female hero who is "autonomous, intellectual, unwomanly, and ultimately, lovable."[2]

Female readers are often frustrated by women writers who limit themselves to delineating the pain and suffering of woman as married, widowed, kept, or single when they have all the options available, including portraying the relationship of man and woman in its wholeness, a relationship in which love and work do not conflict. The predetermined male view of women that a woman exists only in her relationship to a man, whether father, husband, or son,[3] often binds women into imagining only "a constricted destiny for themselves, allowing the imagination of possibility to be appropriated for the exclusive use of men."[4] In fact, Minako's representative female protagonist is neither the suffering woman nor the loving woman, but the thinking woman, the subversive woman, unrepentant, unapologetic, and undomesticated.

With her series of outrageous replies, Minako undercuts the usual expectation of what parting should involve in Japanese society. In this farewell ritual, she plays on an impulse to deconstruct, to debunk what Japanese call *tatemae* (appearances or rhetoric), an itch that is infectious among her heroines, particularly her autobiographical characters, Yurie in *Kiri no tabi* (A Journey Through the Mist, 1980), and in *Naku tori no* (Birds Crying, 1985). This chapter presents a recursive discussion of the principal themes of these two works.

In both novels, Yurie is a breath of fresh air, clear alternatives to what Carolyn G. Heilbrun calls the "failure of imagination"—a kind of trap into which Western women writers themselves have also fallen:

> Yet women writers (and women politicians, academics, psychoanalysts) have been unable to imagine for other women, fictional or real, the self they have in fact achieved. . . . Women writers, in short, have articulated their pain. But they cannot, or for the most part have not,

> imagined characters moving, as the authors themselves have moved, beyond that pain. Woman's most persistent problem has been to discover for herself an identity not limited by custom or defined by attachment to some man. Remarkably, her search for identity has been even less successful within the world of fiction than outside it, leaving us until very recently with a situation largely unchanged for more than two millennia.[5]

Minako, directly and indirectly, poses these questions shared by women readers: Why cannot we imagine ourselves "as selves, as at once striving and female"? Why not look to literature "not only for the articulation of female despair and constriction, but also for the proclamation of the possibilities of life"? Why not ask women writers to "give us, finally," in Heilbrun's words, "female characters who are complex, whole, and independent—fully human"?[6] In Minako's literary world things are pushed one step further. She has created not only women characters but men as well who are unacceptable, indeed impossible, from the patriarchy's perspective, because, as we shall see, they flaunt unacceptable behavioral patterns.

Perfectly aware that the modern Japanese literary tradition has been dominated by *shishōsetsu* writers, who exhibited their egos, woes, and flaws in painstaking detail,[7] Minako humorously categorizes many of their male protagonists as *darashi no nai otoko*.[8] The adjective, *darashi no nai*, translatable as "pathetic," "slipshod," "out of line," and "unkempt," refers in general to "undisciplined," "lax," or, by extension, "immoral" behavior. What Minako means by *darashi no nai otoko* is a man whose irresponsible behavior is deemed outrageous, but is nevertheless tolerated, and even sanctioned, by male-centered society.

That this tolerance for loose behavior is almost never shown to the other sex is an issue that Minako the literary woman finds pointless even to contest because the double standard is so deeply ingrained in the social system. In a response to critics who find her female characters morally lax, she raises an eyebrow: "It wasn't long ago, was it, when men themselves began to write about *darashi no nai* men. Of course, if female writers do that, male writers get upset. But they still give positive reviews of those written by men. Look at Dan Kazuo (1912–1976) and Shimao Toshio (1917–1986). . . . They must find [the subject of *darashi no nai otoko*] very realistic."[9]

In a similar way, when it comes to depicting "immoral" female characters, Western male writers are masters, Minako argues. How about Flaubert's *Madame Bovary*, or Tolstoy's *Anna Karenina*? Again, Minako's comment reminds us that neither the trickster-like hero of Dan Kazuo nor the pathetic hero of Shimao Toshio meets a tragic ending; they continue a good life, while Madame Bovary and Anna Karenina must kill themselves to end their misery and atone for their "sins." If the reading public and scholars can accept a man writing about a woman or a man who rebels against the established moral codes, surely it is equally acceptable for a woman to write about a man or a woman who is, according to conventional cultural constructs, "immoral."

Minako defends a literary woman's right to imagine a female character in her own way. A literary man, by contrast, has never had to defend his right to imagine a male character any way he sees fit. The "literary patrilineage,"[10] for example, has always regarded the notion of the antihero (especially an amorous one) with a particular sense of reverence, from its beginnings in the picaresque narrative in Europe to its recent revival in the hands of Norman Mailer and Henry Miller, among others.[11] The powerful image of what Sandra M. Gilbert and Susan Gubar call "male intellectual struggle" among strong equals ultimately enables the "male writer to explain his rebelliousness, his 'swerving,' and his 'originality' both to himself and to the world, no matter how many readers think him 'not quite right.' "[12] In other words, society looks upon him merely as a "dissenter," which is not at all a dishonorable term.

Suppose a Japanese woman writer portrayed an antihero or antiheroine of imposing stature? "I can already see," Minako acknowledges facetiously, "a work like this by a woman would be panned by male critics."[13] It was in 1956 that Harada Yasuko (1928– ) introduced a new Japanese female character, Reiko, in

*Banka* (Elegy), a work which won the Women's Literature Award and was enthusiastically received by the public, but which dumbfounded male critics. Harada depicted a twenty-three-year-old woman, a whimsical seducer who wraps a well-established middle-aged man around her little finger. It was unheard of. That is to say, no female writer had ever dared to create such a *darashi no nai* heroine.

Reiko broke taboos on all fronts. The sensational debut of the unknown writer seemed to have succeeded in making a clean break with the stereotypical image of the self-sacrificing and self-effacing Japanese woman. But within less than a year, there was a backlash. The majority of male critics had caught on to Harada's rebellious intent and unleashed their harshest criticism. In their eyes, Reiko became simply a prankster and a spoiled girl, incapable of loving a decent man. Worse yet, she had no principles or morality, and she was an egotist to the core.[14] (Of course, Naomi, the *femme fatale* in Tanizaki Jun'ichiro's *Chijin no ai* [A Fool's Love, 1924; published in an English translation as *Naomi*], did not count as a taboo-breaking heroine. Not only did the male protagonist want her to be that way, but she was the creation of a male author.)

Minako's ambitious novel *A Journey Through the Mist*, which is loosely based on her own life, also became the target of very unhappy male critics. The main part of their criticism was directed at an extramarital affair that the female protagonist, Yurie, has with a Swedish man while she is living in Sweden with her husband. Peter, the boyfriend of a colleague of Yurie's husband, is an aspiring writer of mediocre talent who tutors the couple in Swedish. Eventually Peter seduces Yurie, and the sexual affair continues for a while. One morning Peter invites Yurie to go on an excursion to a lakeside house, and on impulse she accepts; but the experience does not sit well with her, and late that night she returns home by train. Her husband accepts her with no questions asked.

Neither the reader nor Yurie is sure at this point whether the husband is aware of his wife's ongoing affair with Peter. "I was wondering what would happen after it [the excursion]," one critic says, "but what a miserable guy! [meaning the husband]." Another critic responds in disbelief: "This is in no way a realistic portrayal of a man . . . even if he actually exists, I cannot think of him as real."[15]

What they do not say is that Minako should not have written about this kind of relationship, for to do so is too unwomanly.[16] A wife enduring her husband's love affairs in silence (as does Tomo in Enchi Fumiko's *Onna-zaka* [The Woman's Slope, 1957; published in English translation as *The Waiting Years*]) is normative, but the reverse is not. We can safely assume that these same critics would never question the "sincerity" of the egotist Shimamura, who does not think twice about making a plaything of an intelligent, sensitive, and imaginative geisha, Komako, in Kawabata Yasunari's *Snow Country*.[17]

These reviewers of *A Journey Though the Mist* employ the same arguments that Western male critics use to, in Joanna Russ's words, "bury [women's] art, to explain it away, ignore it, downgrade it, in short make it vanish":[18]

> She didn't write it.
>
> She wrote it, but she shouldn't have.
>
> She wrote it, but look what she wrote about.
>
> She wrote it, but "she" isn't really an artist and "it" isn't really serious, of the right genre—i.e., really art.
>
> She wrote it, but she wrote only one of it.
>
> She wrote it, but it's only interesting/included in the canon for one, limited reason.
>
> She wrote it, but there are very few of her.[19]

Yamamoto Michiko (1936– ), a recipient of the Akutagawa Prize for *"Betty-san no niwa"* (Betty's Garden, 1972; published in English translation as "Betty-san"), was labeled a "housewife novelist" (*shufu sakka*) by the media, which trivialized her art by means of a false categorization.[20] The critics reviewing *A Journey Through the Mist* also use the false-categorization ploy. One of them refers to Minako as a "mere woman writer," meaning that she is not to be taken seriously; if she would only break out of her nonpatriarchal mold and realize that pain and frustration are *human* issues, then they could accept her as a "novelist," not a woman writer.[21] In other words, for these critics, as long as a literary woman writes from a woman's perspective, she is not a true artist.[22]

For Minako, their comments are meaningless. Her primary concern is to recount the all-encompassing female experience, a story of woman's free choice and how woman decides to "manage her own destiny when she has no plot, no narrative, no tale [of quest] to guide her." Carolyn Heilbrun's classic study has shown that this lack exists because "in literature and out, through all recorded history, women have lived by a script they did not write. Their destiny was to be married, circulated; to be given by one man, the father, to another, the husband; to become the mothers of men. Theirs has been the marriage plot, the erotic plot, the courtship plot, but never, as for men, the quest plot."[23]

Not unlike female writers in the West, Minako's literary sisters, the Heian women who wrote *Kagero nikki* (The Kagero Diary, ca. 974; two English translations available as The Gossamer Years and *Kagero Nikki*); *Izumi Shikibu nikki* (The Diary of Izumi Shikibu, ca. 1008); and *Sarashina nikki* (The Sarashina Diary, ca. 1060; published in English as *As I Crossed a Bridge of Dreams*) had to live by a script they had no choice but to write themselves, in which they were forever waiting for a man to appear, be he husband or lover. One critic calls the plot of the script they adopted the "visited" and the "read."[24] Does modern Japanese literature offer a comparable fiction, one, for example, in which a woman and a man are on equal terms, affecting each other and adjusting to each other, where a man grows along with the woman he cares for, and allows her to undertake her quest, the "perilous journey to self-development"[25] at her own pace?

In Minako's *Birds Crying* we see a pair that fits the bill quite nicely: Yurie and Shōzō,[26] perhaps the most compatible, equal, independent-minded yet inseparable, and fully human married couple ever portrayed in modern literature. Minako introduced

Yurie and Shōzō for the first time in *A Journey Through the Mist*, covering Yurie's encounter with Shōzō at the age of eleven, her contact with the notorious cousin Fū, the "bad woman"; and her college life, marriage, and move to Sweden because of Shōzō's job. This traditional move made by Yurie, in which a wife follows her husband, is balanced by a role reversal between husband and wife in the sequel, *Birds Crying*. As every film director knows, the creation of a sequel poses a great risk, for it often falls short of the original. But *A Journey Through the Mist* and *Birds Crying* are true equals; they offer a reading as one continuous intertext, or as two separate, independent, permeable texts. Minako establishes here a pattern that is often repeated in subsequent works; that of making her texts resonate with each other.

We might call *A Journey Through the Mist* the narrative of the perilous journey of a young woman to self-development and female self-assertion through words. At this point in her life, Yurie is still in a foggy state of mind, unable to assert her growing self-identity effectively, making the metaphor of mist (*kiri*) most appropriate. The young Yurie gropes her way toward finding her identity as a woman who wants to write but is held back, not by marriage, but by her own ambivalent self. Otherwise put, the narrative is about the labor pains prior to the emergence of Yurie the literary woman.[27]

When the sequel *Birds Crying* opens, Mama Yurie (the unusual surname, Mama, is surely meant as a pun) is a free-spirited, spacey novelist, and Shōzō is a former "salaryman" (salaried white-collar employee) who has retired early from his company in order to enjoy life as a house-husband, secretary, cook, and dependent all in one. Their only child, a daughter Chie, has long since left the nest. Although the couple's intellectual interests do not always mesh—one of them is a writer, the other a trained scientist—they reluctantly admit to each other that the difference keeps boredom at bay and how much they learn from each other.

Presenting a woman's view of the world, society, and human relationships, Minako is, of course, also writing for men, who have "very little understanding of what women really are."[28] Therefore, she creates the character of Shōzō, a man who actually articulates a woman's perspective, openly incorporating a feminist experience of the world into his own.

What is of particular interest in *A Journey Through the Mist* and *Birds Crying* is Minako's emerging sense of self as a woman and a writer, the way she addresses female sexuality,[29] and how she expresses her awakening to new possibilities in middle age. For many women, middle age offers opportunities never before anticipated. At fifty-six Virginia Woolf mustered enough courage to publish *Three Guineas* (1938), on which she had worked for six years, an outspoken indictment of patriarchy that finally unleashed her feminist anger loud and clear. Nine years earlier, at forty-seven, she had written *A Room of One's Own* (1929), but with a more gentle, patient, indirect voice, still hesitant about showing her anger at patriarchy.

Adrienne Rich has not missed this "sense of effort, of pains taken, of dogged tentativeness, in the tone of [*A Room of One's Own*]."

> I had heard it often enough, in myself and in other women. It is the tone of a woman almost in touch with her anger, who is determined not to appear angry, who is *willing* herself to be calm, detached, and even charming in a roomful of men where things have been said which are attacks on her very integrity. Virginia Woolf is addressing an audience of women, but she is acutely conscious—as she always was—of being overheard by men. . . . [S]he was trying to sound as cool as Jane Austen, as Olympian as Shakespeare, because that is the way the men of the culture thought a writer should sound."[30]

Do male writers have a similar concern? Rich answers emphatically in the negative: "No male writer has written primarily or even largely for women, or with the sense of women's criticism as a consideration when he chooses his materials, his theme, his language. But to a lesser or greater extent, every woman writer has written for men even when, like Virginia Woolf, she was supposed to be addressing women." Rich looks forward to the day when women writers will feel secure. "If we have come to the point when this balance might begin to change, when women can stop being haunted, not only by 'convention and propriety' but by internalized fears of being and saying themselves, then it is an extraordinary moment for the woman writer—and reader."[31] Minako is not only unconcerned about being overheard by men in Japan, but openly challenges what she calls their greenhouse "potted plant" nature, through the character of Shōzō.

She had begun *A Journey Through the Mist* at forty-six, and completed it at fifty. Five years later, at fifty-five, she published the sequel, *Birds Crying*. Aging, for her, is never a regression but a blessing, a chance for a second life and empowerment. "To allow oneself at fifty the expression of one's feminism," Carolyn G. Heilbrun notes in describing Woolf's courage in deciding to write *Three Guineas*, distinguishes women fundamentally from men because it "is an experience for which there is no male counterpart, at least for white men in the Western world. If a man is to break into revolt against the system he has, perhaps for his parents' sake, pretended to honor, he will do so at a much younger age. The pattern of men's lives suggests that at fifty they are likelier to reveal their egoism than their hidden ideals or revolutionary hopes."[32]

The plot and the portrayal of the heroine of *A Journey Through the Mist* shows distinct similarities to those of the classic *Bildungsroman* genre. Defined in its pure form as a "novel of all-around development"[33] that is "unremittingly concerned with the *Werden* [becoming] of an individual hero,"[34] this genre found its first major example in Goethe's *Wilhelm Meister's Apprenticeship.* The prototype of the *Bildungsroman* hero "is in many respects a weak and indecisive hero," but he "does have an active mind, and he speaks it often and at length."[35] (As we shall see, Minako's heroine is herself quite garrulous, at least in private.) Defined "in terms of works by, about, and appealing to men,"[36] this classic genre has largely ignored the possibility of a *Bildungsroman* heroine.

> A crude picture of the genre shows an especially rugged or especially sensitive young man, at leisure to mull over some life choices, not so much connected to people or the landscape as encountering or passing through them as "options" or "experiences" en route to a better place. Travel . . . is key, for though the story pulls toward settling the youth—its telos is repose—what it actually recounts is his relentless advance.[37]

The "resisting reader"[38] cannot help but think what a formidable challenge for a woman writer it would be to create a female *Bildungsroman.* After all, simply changing the gender of the hero would not of itself improve the status of literary women, and might even encourage from male critics the scathing accusation that all literary women can do is copy the masculine plot. Minako, unconcerned by such dangers, has happily appropriated the form and its Japanese equivalent, *shishōsetsu*,[39] to put them to her own parodic use.[40]

* * *

For all its outward resemblance to the classic *Bildungsroman* form, *A Journey Through the Mist* is a woman's text, making neither an apology nor grand claims for the legitimacy of telling the story of a female artist growing up. Minako sees no need to neutralize any possible male wrath by belittling Yurie and reminding the reader of her proper duty and position as a woman in society. In other words, the message is not for Yurie to "become," but for her "not to become" the woman required by conventional female destiny. It is not a story of *Werden*, but of unlearning and undoing, of "unbecoming" a woman, and thereby becoming an "unbecoming" woman.[41]

Mobility and individualism, which are pointed out by Susan Fraiman as the two key concepts in the quest/adventure plot of the *Bildungsroman*, play important roles in Yurie's growing-up tale. However, the author's inclusion of options and experiences that do not particularly serve Yurie's self-development can be seen as an intentional, and continual, parody of the genre of the

*Bildungsroman*, while simultaneously playing on the picaresque genre.

*A Journey Through the Mist*, which begins with a fourteen-page prologue of what the reader should expect from Yurie, Minako's fictional alter ego, reveals all the signs of feminist inclinations that are still unformed and unidentified. They persist to the end of the novel, where the young Chie is shown trying in vain to wake Yurie from her state of "hibernation":

> In the dream Chie was gently tugging at me.
> "Mommy sleeps all the time."
> "I can't open my eyes. Can't see a thing. I'll wake up when the mist clears." I mumbled in my sleep (p. 424).[42]

The narrator's not at all misty "doubled" view of women as "agents as well as victims"[43] clearly indicates a strong female desire to place reality in perspective, an attitude shared by many of her contemporaries as well as by older women writers in Japan.[44] Seemingly indecisive and unfocused, Yurie does not excel academically in college, but she is active in the drama club. In Japanese society, she would be called a "juvenile delinquent," for during college she has affairs with two men, gets pregnant by one, and almost ruins her health by having an abortion.

The man she is really after is Shigeru, but her overtures meet with rejection because he is sexually involved with his older brother's wife, Fū. Her sexual conquests stalled at two, Yurie has only one option: to take Shigeru's advice and go to Shōzō, who has somehow never stirred her interest. Rejected by Shigeru, she is relentless in her verbal assault. Her parting words to Shigeru, which take male egoism to task, reveal an independent-minded woman who is willing to take risks and is prepared to begin a long quest of self-development:

> "I thought you were more courageous than that. You are really a coward. You think you're safe by rejecting me, but you've given up what you could have grabbed with your own hands. You're thinking to yourself, 'I've had enough mess in my life. No more.' I'm sure

> you'll play safe for the rest of your life, but never find what you wish you could. But I'm going to find it. . . .
>
> "Nothing scares me. I'll find out in any way I can what men's true colors are. I won't stop watching until my face turns blue. Then I may learn how wonderful men are, or how insignificant, whether there's something I really want from them, or nothing . . ." (p. 123).

During her affair with Peter, Yurie expresses her need for him in the following way: "I've been able to survive so far because men have once in a while cleared away the mist that blocked my way . . . and the mist was also men themselves" (p. 11). Minako avoids the notion of a woman as only the victimized heroine, passively sacrificing her own story to allow a man to tell his. In addition, men in *A Journey Through the Mist* are also portrayed as victims as well as victimizers, both the obstacle and the means by which the "mist" is removed.

There are two circumstances to consider here as we deal with Minako's heroine. First, Yurie is living in a postwar Japan that has been simultaneously crushed and liberated by the United States, its self-esteem and self-identity almost nonexistent. Second, Yurie has attended the most liberal and liberated college in the country, a college based on Minako's alma mater, Tsuda Women's College. These two historical influences help to mold the character of Yurie: she desires to be free from all that convention and propriety dictated to women up to the end of the war and to apply the spirit of her liberal education in her own life, but she is held back by an unawakened, unformed sense of herself as a woman. As a further impediment to Yurie's awakening, the Japanese patriarchal force runs, unchanged and unchanging, beneath the current of political and social liberation by a Western power.

So thick is the mist of her ambiguity that Yurie the college student realizes she needs a "complementary, equal relationship" (p. 113) with a man if she is to find her way through it. But to find such a man in postwar Japan seems next to impossible, and the idea of a conventional marriage as defined by patriarchy never enters her mind. That marriage is not a goal in her life is symbolic of her larger rejection of the female destiny laid out for women by society. Her mother, herself a rather free-spirited soul, nevertheless starts searching for a husband for her daughter in college by sending her photographs of prospective candidates. This is how Yurie rejects one of those marriage proposals, from the son of the owner of a well-known private hospital:

> I never bothered to respond to the young doctor's request for a *miai* [a formal meeting between prospective bride and groom preceding an arranged marriage]. In the meantime, unable to wait any longer, he showed up alone one Sunday morning at the visitors' lounge of my dormitory, where he met a young woman with uncombed hair, no makeup, wearing a sweater inside out and a skirt with holes, and her feet dragging worn-out slippers. He was so flabbergasted that all he could do was to make small talk before he hastily took his leave (p. 156).

What is interesting about *A Journey Through the Mist* is how small a role Shōzō *seems* to play in the process of Yurie's sexual and intellectual awakening. Shōzō, Yurie's future husband, is as unassuming as all other male characters created by early feminist women writers. Like Dorothy Sayers' Lord Peter Wimsey, Lucy Maud Montgomery's Gilbert Blyth, and Louisa May Alcott's Professor Baer,[45] Shōzō gives Yurie what a man in a romanticized courtship fails to recognize: recognition of a woman's need to make a decision on her own terms in her own time.

Shōzō's presence becomes more prominent as the reader becomes aware of the couple's mutual needs. He is the only person who lets Yurie speak her mind. In public, she plays the role of consummate listener. "I always listened, never had a chance to talk about myself" (p. 20). However, there is an advantage in this role for Yurie. As a writer in the making, she can capitalize on the human desire to confess, to complain, and to make up stories in order to go about "collecting" data for her future stories.

Does this mean that Yurie is reticent by nature? On the contrary, she has opinions on everything under the sun, and this is one of the reasons she needs Shōzō. A self-proclaimed misanthrope, he would rather listen to or look at trees, plants, and animals. Yurie the storyteller finds the perfect audience in Shōzō. Although his lines are few and far between, they are crucial, contributing to key moments in the story. For example, here is a "love-scene" that turns into a humorous marriage proposal:

> When we stood up, the beach was shrouded deep in the darkness of dusk.
>
> It so happened we were facing each other as we stood up. He suddenly bit hard into my lips.
>
> I cannot describe it in any other way but to say he bit my lips. They began to swell.
>
> Afraid that they were cut, I gently touched them while he looked at me as if filtering his gaze through a shadow among thick leaves.
>
> "I don't know how to kiss properly. Show me," he said and held me close. . . .
>
> "Stay with me tonight."
>
> He took me to his grandfather's house.
>
> "We may have the same ancestors," he said. I remembered that he had left behind a bouquet of *hamanasu* flowers. "Shall we go back and look for it?"
>
> He shook his head. "I may have to go to a place much further away, further even than Hokkaidō." He suddenly said this in front of his grandfather's house.
>
> "Where?"
>
> "A forestry research center in Sweden."
>
> "For a long time?"
>
> "I don't know. I don't know about the future. Will you come?" . . .
>
> "So, who will keep the house key?" I asked.
>
> "Let's get two. One for each of us." He looked up and laughed (pp. 187–189).

Despite such early signs that there will be a long, happy relationship, Yurie's married life is rather ordinary at the beginning, and she seems not to take advantage of her new position to speak her mind.[46] Words fill her brain, but she cannot find an outlet for them. Peter (Yurie and Shōzō's Swedish-language tutor) clears the mist for her by selecting as a text a book of fairy tales, her favorite type of literature. The routine of the language lesson is that as he reads a story in Swedish, his student is asked to retell it in her own words, which unwittingly encourages the first stirring of a writer's consciousness. Yurie's "fairy tale" affair with Peter has everything to do with his clearing of the mist.

This is a pivotal episode in another way because her sexual relationship with Peter enhances Yurie's power of imagination, and because she comes to understand that Peter is also the mist itself that she must clear away on her own. "[T]he sexual fantasy I had about Peter [before I slept with him] lost its luster, and I had to make every effort to keep it alive" (p. 292). At Peter's urging, the two take off on an impromptu excursion to a lakeside house that belongs to his grandfather.

Although she accepts Peter's invitation, she has no intention of leaving Shōzō for good. She calls him and uses an alibi, to reassure him. When she calls him a second time, Shōzō is clearly upset and says, "You can't even explain to me what's going on. You say you can't come home tonight. And you expect to have a place to come home to tomorrow?" (p. 316). After they spend only one full day together, Peter is ready to assume a more permanent relationship with Yurie.[47] When she insists on returning home that night and tries to start the car engine, she begins to cry "like an animal" (p. 338), her face against the steering wheel.

Yurie tells us, the baffled readers, part of the reason she is crying: "I was not crying to put the blame on Peter. I was struggling with my own incomprehensibility" (p. 338). This sentence does not explain the sense of hopelessness, confusion, wretchedness, and pain that seems to grip her. Is she ashamed of her adultery, or of her own sexual desire? Is she full of remorse for having considered eloping with Peter, as would be the case in a male-inflected text? One thing we know from such texts: If Yurie were a man, she would not experience such a desperate feeling. In the end, Yurie goes back to her husband that night by train and says to him, "I'm sorry" (p. 343).

However, the female text in *A Journey Through the Mist* asserts that she cries for another reason. The outing with Peter makes explicit what Yurie has been vaguely aware of but also fears: the discovery of a female destiny that she has to manage on her own. However briefly, she thinks to herself, it would be fun to be part of the destiny of a man like Peter, and if he has the same aspirations as I do, all the better. In this she shows her unintended complicity with the male-gendered script for women.

But she quickly begins to see Peter as he is: a stereotypically well-meaning male for whom she has to play the stereotypical female, pretending to be captivated by his boyish romantic charm, and suppressing her own ego and creativity. Though she is sick of the lies and pretensions that social decorum force upon her, a life with Peter would be no improvement. Up to now an apparently contented housewife, Yurie is actually, slowly killing herself by not being able to say what is really on her mind. It is this pain, which she is inflicting upon herself, and her willingness to hazard the distasteful, that are incomprehensible to her.

The coincidence of Yurie's becoming pregnant[48] soon after the "aborted" elopement leaves the question of paternity very ambiguous, and it remains so to the end of the narrative. The question is not pursued by Shōzō, nor does it become an issue for Peter, who fails to detect the early transformation of Yurie's body and is not informed of this "accident" before they part. Embracing a perspective that breaks with the norm of a patrilineal society, Minako lets Yurie confide in the reader: "It's neither Peter nor Shōzō I want, but a mere male abstraction, devoid of individuality and personality . . . just the strength of a male who would protect a child" (p. 417).

Her "confession" reflects the collective voice of women, women under a social order that rigidly guards the paternal bloodline, in which female sexuality and desire are secondary to the institution of marriage. "A desire to torment men about their paternity in an eternal pit of suspicion is not just my feeling," Yurie continues in her interior monologue. "It is a force to be reckoned with, the collective will of hundreds of thousands of women, unleashed in one gigantic wave. You men have tormented us about other women. One thing for sure: those children you've had by other women are not mine. But those I've had or your other women have had do not necessarily belong to you" (p. 395).

These unspoken words, precipitated by Yurie's affair with Peter and her pregnancy, are silently acknowledged by Shōzō, who continues to accept her as she is. They put the relationship of Yurie and Shōzō on a new footing. His tacit acknowledgment of Yurie's right to have diverged from the institution of marriage provides an impetus for him to redefine himself as a man who defines manhood not in his separation from the *feminine* or the *womanly*, but in equal partnership with a woman. With Peter as the catalyst, Shōzō emerges as one of those rare male characters in modern literature who allow a woman to have her own destiny apart from his.

Yurie's affair with Peter is more than a sexual seduction; it is a literary seduction as well, an initiation into fiction. Her involvement with Peter opens up a whole new world of fantasy, lies, and secrecy: "We didn't stop seeing each other [even though I had to make every effort to keep the sexual fantasy alive]. We were having lots of fun being frightened of our secret, and lying to each other" (p. 292). Finding herself tangled in a web of fabrication, and seduced by the power of her "lies" and imagination, Yurie finds herself moving closer to her ultimate goal, fiction writing. Her crying at the steering wheel brings to a head the female dilemma of being "forced to choose between the life of a woman or the life of the mind,"[49] and leads in the end to the heroine's decision to mix the two lives, assisted by her husband's active participation in child rearing.

* * *

*Birds Crying*, the sequel to *A Journey Through the Mist*, demonstrates that every so-called happy ending is in fact a new beginning, a new story begging to be told. *Birds Crying* describes the continuation of Yurie's perilous journey to self-development, but this time the heroine is a well-established woman writer, older, more aggressive, and more confident in her self-assertion.

She is also changing and aging in an equal partnership with her husband Shōzō. The middle-aged Yurie settles comfortably into the role of an "unbecoming," unrepentant woman writer, sharing her life with a husband who does not agree that "men can be men only if women are unambiguously women."[50]

The narrative voice in *Birds Crying* often shifts fluidly. Individual chapters are contiguous yet independent. The title of the narrative literally means "of crying birds" (*naku tori no*), and is itself open-ended. The grammatical particle *no* is the classical Japanese subject marker that survives in modern Japanese, and it indicates more to come. The particle frequently ends a phrase in a haiku, inviting another line. Minako explains the symbolic meaning of the carefully chosen title in this way: "[A] fictional world is basically a human world, and in a larger sense it is a universe, within which exists every conceivable kind of space and time. There is no such thing as a state of completion, as the fictional world expands to infinity, yet that world exists at this very moment."[51]

*Birds Crying* offers human life as it is—in Minako's words, *shizen sono mama* ("things just as they are")—not life in an idealized, romanticized, or sanitized form. The author's presentation of Yurie and Shōzō's life offers an unconventional alternative for all married couples, and a broad cross-cultural perspective to challenge the insular Japanese mind. And, even for the jaded reader, it provides a delightful, humorous exchange of opinions and ideas on things that have been considered outrageous by Japanese society. Japanese women have finally found a voice in the character of Yurie, a voice that is unapologetic and uninhibited, full of what Japanese call *honne* (one's true feelings, in contrast to what one is supposed to feel or say).

The story covers a six-month period, beginning in winter, on Mt. Hiei near Kyoto, and ending with the rainy season, in early summer. During these months, different people appear before Yurie and Shōzō, and with each of these visits the reader is entertained anew. We are first introduced to Mizuki, the daughter of Yurie's "notorious" cousin Fū (the young Yurie had had a crush on Fū's lover, Shigeru, who is the younger brother of Fū's husband). Then Fukiko visits, and the reader learns the scandalous story of her husband, Shigeru. But before we can fully engage ourselves in Fukiko's story, Yurie's old friend, Lynn Ann, a Chinese American, appears with her second husband, Henry. Through this couple, we "retrieve the thread of memory" reaching all the way back to Yurie's affair with Peter in *A Journey Through the Mist*.

Next comes Shigeru's son, Tōichiro, followed by the grown-up Chie, Yurie's daughter. The novel closes, for the moment (as Minako might say), with Shigeru's final visit and sudden death, and with the news of Lynn Ann's and Henry's deaths in a car accident. To tell the complex story of these human relationships and interactions, Minako adopts two narrative voices, that of Mizuki and that of the omniscient narrator, interspersed with the interior monologues and the dialogues of the characters.

In other words, *Birds Crying* tells the story of different kinds of "birds," singing and crying out, who visit Yurie and Shōzō and then "fly away," some to return, some never to return. Birds in the wild sing when they feel like singing and cry out when there is danger. The spontaneity of the act, the naturalness of it, is what Minako wishes to capture. Far from being a "caged bird," one of the metaphors most frequently used by Western women writers to describe a woman's emotional and physical confinement,[52] Yurie is a bird flying freely in the wild.

Most strikingly, Minako transcends the mere use of birds as a metaphor for humanity and the status of Yurie and Shōzō as a pair of "rare birds" by intentionally blurring the boundary between the human habitat and the animal kingdom. The two spheres, usually seen in conflict, are blended into a seamless entity through Yurie's vocation as a poet, sometimes a poet with a social message, sometimes a poet of unspoiled nature. For example, retrieving the "thread of memories" all the way back to Alaska, where Yurie and Shōzō once lived, Yurie the nature poet hypnotizes Mizuki with the description of an ocean kingdom:

> Yurie also began to describe the Sea of Alaska with dreamy eyes: the way gigantic sea anemone in full bloom on the ocean bottom flip their tentacles; sea cucumbers resembling monster leeches; intimidating sea urchins; and how abalone, legless and finless, can quickly hop from one rock to another in the water. Yurie, whose arms were now out of the sleeping bag, made flapping movements with her fingers. For a moment, Muzuki had the illusion that Yurie was one of the strange sea creatures in her story.
>
> The dark green of their sleeping bags resembled the color of the ocean, and their body movements underneath, undulations.
>
> There were more. The yellow waves swollen by a large school of herring headed for shore; beaches carpeted by roe; the cries of flapping gulls clamoring after the fish trapped between rocks after spawning, bloodied and dying.
>
> When they spoke of those sea creatures, they ceased to be human. Sometimes they were crabs, other times abalone or herring. One could hear the sound of waves, see the seaweed swaying, the insides of an abalone's suckers, the scintillating white underbelly of a herring (p. 31).

The rapid shifting between descriptions of nature and the human habitat is intentionally repeated, and effectively decenters the narrative. Decentering and disorientation also serve as a means of expressing Minako's "quarrels" with Japanese society. In a battle of wits between, on the one side, the unconventional and "un-Japanese" couple Yurie and Shōzō and, on the other side, Mizuki, an academic professor, the Japanese mother of two adopted children and the wife of a German,[53] Minako critiques the current state of marriage in Japan.

Her choice of Mizuki, not a male character, as a critic of the cosmopolitan couple indicates that it is not just the patriarchal society that imposes the norms for married couples but that women themselves often remain rigid and conventional in their view of marital intimacy.[54] Mizuki is often ambivalent in her response to Yurie and Shōzō, for as much as she wants to criticize them frankly, she also feels the need for diplomacy. It becomes clearer that the poker-faced, taboo-breaking couple are simply beyond Mizuki's conventional imagination. She seems to embrace the collective anxiety of Japanese, for whom a state of being "ambiguously" woman (or man) is unacceptable. The following exchange between Mizuki and Shōzō, one of the most humorous in the story, shows Mizuki as a reflection of Japanese society:

> "Shōzō, Yurie writes anything she damn pleases, doesn't she?"
>
> "It seems what she writes really infuriates men out there. I wonder why. It doesn't upset me at all and I'm her husband."
>
> "They're probably furious about you, too. Like husband, like wife, they'd say." Mizuki tried baiting him. She wanted to see him riled up a bit, but he merely nodded his agreement, completely unruffled.
>
> "I guess so. You might be right. Seiichiro was also like that," he said, changing the subject to Mizuki's father.
>
> "In her novels, Yurie lets her female protagonists do what they damn please with men."
>
> "It looks like my counterparts in her stories are either cuckolded or bovine, or sometimes quack doctors, incompetent scholars, or retirement-age businessmen who have been kicked upstairs."
>
> "Oh, dear, you mean you really enjoy reading that stuff?"
>
> "You never know. There's never a dull moment hanging around a woman like Yurie."
>
> Mizuki was silenced. She could think of no response.
>
> "It must have been the same with Seiichiro," said Shōzō. The subject bounced right back to Mizuki's father.
>
> "Don't you agree with me?" he continued. "He was crazy about Fū. Rumor has it, though, he hit her from time to time."
>
> "All right, all right," Mizuki conceded (pp. 10–11).

Mizuki's reactions and thought patterns reveal deep-seated Japanese cultural biases. Besides being disturbed about the unapologetic female characters Yurie creates, Mizuki finds it difficult to accept that Yurie and Shōzō share a double bed and sleep naked together, that they go everywhere and do everything together, and that Shōzō retired early to help his wife's career. Such phenomena are virtually unheard of on the part of a wife and husband in their early fifties in Japan. It is as though the reader were observing an initiation ritual that Mizuki must undergo: she must first accept the "outrageous" lifestyle of Yurie and Shōzō, and then learn how to be as articulate and self-assertive as they are. Yurie's youngest sister, Momoe, gives Mizuki the best description of their lifestyle and shortly thereafter, the most practical advice:

> "Yurie has lost a marble or two, you know. Be aware of that when you deal with her. It's gotten to Shōzō as well. They're no longer young love-birds, but the way they're glued to each other all year around—I call them goldfish dung. Shōzō just listens with a straight face, enthralled by his wife's selfish ramblings. . . .
>
> "When she's upfront, you've got to be the same" (pp. 7–8).

The self-confident, nonchalant Yurie in *Birds Crying* unintentionally offers mentoring to the still conventional Mizuki, whose sojourn in Japan turns out to be a time of unlearning traditional feminine behavior and of coming to terms with her own past. Shōzō's shopping for fish from a vendor, for example, becomes another assault on Mizuki's unliberated mind.

> Every Tuesday morning, a fish vendor came up the mountain. Mizuki ran into Shōzō this morning. Apparently it was his job to buy fish, and he was eying them with great affection. He was able to tell the freshness of each fish by just looking, and began to show Mizuki which one to choose. "Horse mackerel is in season," he said. He wanted to know where the mackerel came from, and checked the van's license plate number. . . . When he found out that the vendor was from Karasu-chō, he said, "That's good. Close enough to the sea."
>
> After he left with a purchase of eels, the vendor asked Mizuki, "Is he a college professor?"
>
> It must have been very rare for a man to come to buy fish during the day. Finding it a lot of bother to answer, Mizuki just nodded, "Uhm, hum."
>
> He tried again.
>
> "Does he teach or work in an office?"
>
> "Probably both." Mizuki vague reply did not seem to satisfy him. "I think he's doing some research on Mt. Hiei. Working on a book, I gather," she added.

> Residents in this area often held university-related jobs; some were self-employed, among them ceramic artists and painters. Mizuki's answer seemed to have satisfied him and he no longer questioned her. A few housewives nearby were pricking up their ears.
>
> A man in his prime who hangs around at home really sticks out and invites suspicion, Mizuki realized. Loafing around was not accepted by society (pp. 103–104).

Mizuki's observation seems to verify one feminist's remark that the "real myth . . . is the notion that the stereotypes are no longer true" in Japanese society.[55] Time spent abroad by Japanese, or even a series of direct contacts with non-Japanese cultures, often have hardly any impact upon their intellectual development. Mizuki seems to be one of them. Minako leaves her position deliberately ambiguous: we are not sure whether she is siding with the society or simply commenting on the facts of life in Japan. What is clear, however, is that Shōzō's indirect contribution to Yurie's career (in this case, doing grocery shopping) has very little social value. When women do grocery shopping and other domestic tasks, they are simply fulfilling their duties, but if men take care of domestic duties, they are seen as just "loafing around."

What is also revealed in the fish episode is that Mizuki is not prepared to accept the consequences of the vendor's reaction, nor that of the eavesdropping neighborhood wives, if she tells them the truth. Nor does she possess the mischievousness to tease and shock them with the truth by saying, "He's a house-husband!" Afraid of affronting men's and society's sensibilities about gender roles, Mizuki also seems fearful of expanding her definition of woman for fear of what it might require of her regarding her own identity as a woman.

Minako lets Shōzō, rather than the anxious, humorless Mizuki, affirm his status as a house-husband and articulate his view of the female experience. After Carl, Mizuki's husband, finishes comparing the Western diet to that of the Japanese, Shōzō, a man of few words, suddenly interjects:

> "I've been stitching scrub cloths all day today. . . . I used to think, how ridiculous to do anything like that. But now I know it's not really a dumb thing at all. It's a very simple task, not requiring much mental work. That means you can really get into the world of imagination while you stitch. Your mind is completely on something else. The only time you come back to reality is when you have to pay attention to how you're stitching. . . ." (p. 70).

A typical good-natured, patriarchal male, Carl does not know how to respond to this reexamination of the female experience articulated by a man. Henry, Lynn Ann's husband, is an older man who shares some of Carl's prejudices. Serving as a mouthpiece for Western culture, he ridicules Shōzō, but with a certain amount of envy and chagrin.

> "But, you are male, aren't you?" Henry said.
>
> "Huh?"
>
> "You are a man, but you don't let masculine reason dictate your life. You're still in your prime but you quit your job, and now you sit back and absent-mindedly watch what your wife is doing. You certainly are self-secure. I could never do that."
>
> "I may look that way, I may be all bewildered inside, you know. Yurie doesn't like noise, so I watch television with earphones. If I don't, she moves to another room. . . ."
>
> ". . . So you watch television right next to your wife even if you have to use clumsy earphones. What egos! Both of you."
>
> "These days she says the screen bothers her eyes, so she does reading sitting away from the television set."
>
> "I see. I must take my hat off to you. You refuse to turn off the television, you still watch what you want to watch."
>
> "I don't know whether I deserve your praise; a person is the same as a stone in the wilderness. One human being cannot tell another what to do if he or she doesn't want to do it."
>
> "Maybe so, but I would think about smashing the whole earth to get my way. Of course, that's ridiculous. I guess it's a bit like dreaming that I've become the center of the universe, the sun" (pp. 174–175).

Henry reflects the Western concept of rugged individualism and the "relentless advance" to conquer the universe, though he at least shows some signs of self-awareness.

Ironically, the most patriarchal and stereotypically male character in *Birds Crying* is Shigeru, a man Yurie once thought she wanted to share her life with. With hindsight, we could say that she narrowly escaped the tragedy of pursuing the conventional female destiny. Fortunately for her, this is the same man who had detected in Yurie a budding "unbecoming woman" even before she was completely aware of herself, and had rejected her as an unsuitable partner with whom to fulfill his male destiny. As if to highlight Shigeru's own intransigent defense of the masculine plot, Minako brings in his Western counterpart, Carl, and once again inserts Mizuki as a foil:

> "I'm younger than you, Shigeru. That's why I still find women pitiable. I also find women who say things off-the-wall cute." Carl shook his head as he turned toward Mizuki. "But, I'll never let Mizuki climb and work on an electric pole."
>
> "But you certainly have fun watching me pick ginkgo berries, don't you?" Mizuki said.
>
> "I just let you do it because you seem to enjoy it so much, that's all. One of the very few things I don't mind doing is putting frozen fried chicken into the oven."
>
> "Even if there's food already prepared in the fridge, if I have to serve it myself, I'd rather eat out," Shigeru answered curtly (pp. 195–196).

Shigeru's sudden death from a heart attack toward the end of the novel reinforces his image as a stereotypical Japanese male who has fulfilled the male destiny prescribed by the institution of patriarchy in Japan: a loveless marriage but a highly successful climb up the career ladder. That the career is prematurely ended by his death from overwork (*karōshi*),[56] a social phenomenon increasing at an alarming rate among white-collar Japanese, suggests Minako's criticism of the Japanese masculine plot.

Unexpectedly, the entire combined narrative of *A Journey Through the Mist* and *Birds Crying* ultimately rejects the conventional male destiny as well as the female one. Central to Minako's reexamination of the masculine plot and her manipulation of the *Bildungsroman* is her depiction of Shōzō's growing awareness of Yurie's desire to write, an ironic twist on men's stereotypical view of women as manipulative and lying:

> The reason Yurie [while in Sweden] began to think about sending a piece to a literary magazine in Japan was that she could no longer stand not being able to tell anyone what was really on her mind. She had kept it to herself too long.
>
> Every day of the year, without batting an eye, she uttered those things that were not really what she wanted to say. She lied to herself all the time. What almost drove her mad was the fact that people could never discern what was really on her mind; her deception didn't bother them at all (p. 135).

Realizing how necessary writing was to Yurie's well-being, Shōzō reshaped his life to accommodate her needs. This put him in the unconventional position of being a man who makes sacrifices for the sake of his wife's professional and personal fulfillment. He reflects on his role as nurturer of Yurie's talents at the end of the novel:

> He began to feel that what he had been doing for forty years since he met that smart-alecky little kid was indeed the stuff of heroism.
>
> All he wanted was to let her live. He convinced himself that if he could not let her say what was really on her mind, she would die. Why does a parent take care of a crying baby? (p. 311).

Shōzō is also a very unconventional male in his recognition of the endless labor of serving as family cook, work for which women rarely get the credit they deserve. When he decides to prepare a very elaborate dish, his appreciation of the effort it takes to make meals on a regular basis becomes even greater. In one scene, we see Shōzō trying to dress a rather unyielding fish and having a hard time of it, yet "Yurie immediately picked up the knife and, with a few deft strokes, the fish was prepared" (p. 43). Admiration and compliments immediately follow from Shōzō, the novice: "Boy, you're good at that. Well, I shouldn't be surprised, after thirty years of cooking" (p. 43). He later reflects on how his accommodating stance sets him apart from other Japanese men:

> Those men who didn't do what I did, and were highly critical of me—with looks of contempt that said, "What a nuisance to let a wife like that have her own way"—must have taken it for granted that a breakfast of miso soup, grilled fish, eggs, and fresh green tea would be served to them and enjoyed by them every morning. Even this simple breakfast wasn't available to me until I began to assume the role of cook, until Yurie finally switched to the daily routine of getting up early in the morning to write (p. 312).

What a far cry from Shigeru's earlier misogynistic remark about meals!

What makes *Birds Crying* radically different from *A Journey Through the Mist* and at the same time defines the sequel clearly as a feminist work is the role reversal of Yurie and Shōzō, heightened by Minako's success in actually achieving the "reversal of emotions or symbolic value" that rarely accompanies a role reversal in male literature.[57] This she achieves through the mutuality and complementarity of the relationship between Yurie and Shōzō, with all their foibles, rough edges, and contradictions.

Finally freed from the masculine view of the female destiny, *Birds Crying* is a pioneering work in which unconventional male and female plots coexist, each one affecting the other in equal measure. Yurie's long apprenticeship, which offers life options often denied to women, provides a model for a continuing process of unlearning, of unbecoming the woman prescribed by men, and of forging a female destiny imagined and constructed by women.

## Notes

1. The story originally appeared in *Shinchō* (1980), and was published as a book in the same year from Shinchōsa, and in 1984 was reprinted as a Shūeisha paperback. The page number is from the 1984 Shūeisha Bunko edition.
2. Carolyn Heilbrun, "Sayers, Lord Peter, and Harriet Vane at Oxford," *Hamlet's Mother and Other Women* (New York: Ballantine Books, 1990), p. 308.

3. In Tokugawa Japan (1603–1868), the role of women in society was formalized along Confucian lines, to the effect that the lifelong duty of a woman was obedience to parents (usually the father), parents-in-law, husband, and male children. The most representative work of this misogynistic teaching is Kaibara Ekken's *Onna daigaku* (Greater Learning for Women, 1672). For a discussion of the work, see Jennifer Robertson, "The Shingaku Woman," in *Recreating Japanese Women*, ed. Gail Lee Bernstein (Berkeley: University of California Press, 1991), pp. 91–94. Also see an extensive interview of Aoki Yayoi on the subject by Sandra Buckley in *Broken Silence: Voices of Japanese Feminism* (Berkeley, CA: University of California Press, 1997), pp. 1–31.

4. Carolyn Heilbrun, *Reinventing Womanhood* (New York: W. W. Norton, 1979), p. 34.

5. Ibid, pp. 72–73.

6. Ibid.

7. See Chapter 1 of this book.

8. Ōba Minako, "Onna no hyōgen, otoko no hyōgen" (Women's Expression, Men's Expression), *Waseda bungaku* (November 1985): 18.

9. Ibid., p. 13. In his 1975 autobiographical fiction *Kataku no hito* (The Sufferer) (Shinchōsha, 1975), which won the Japanese Literature Grand Award and the Yomiuri Literary Award, Dan Kazuo portrays a slipshod writer who, though the father of several children, is happily (or pathetically) in search of the romantic bohemian life, unable to overcome a taste for booze and women. Shimao Toshio's best novel, *Shi no toge* (The Sting of Death, 1977), translated in English as *The Sting of Death, and Other Stories,* a work of autobiographical fiction that describes the madness of Miho, his wife, between 1954 and 1955, was, like *Kataku no hito*, the recipient of the same two major awards. In the face of Miho's "madness," Toshio, the husband, is helpless, incapable of taking any action, and seems to drive her into madness because he needs an accomplice in a charade of going mad himself. For a feminist reading of the novel, see *Danryu bungaku-ron* (Discussion on Male Literature) by Ueno Chizuko, Ogura Chikako, and Tomioka Taeko (Chikuma Shobō, 1992), pp. 65–132. For an extensive discussion in English of Shimao Toshio and *Shi no toge*, see Van C. Gessel, "The Eternal War: Shimao Toshio," in *The Sting of Life: Four Contemporary Japanese Novelists* (New York: Columbia University Press, 1989), pp. 125–180.

10. The term is that of Sandra M. Gilbert and Susan Gubar, from *No Man's Land: The Place of the Women Writer in the Twentieth Century*, vol. 1, *The War of the Words* (New Haven, CT, and London: Yale University Press, 1988), p. 146.

11. See Michiko Niikuni Wilson, *The Marginal World of Ōe Kenzaburo: A Study in Themes and Techniques* (Armonk, NY: M. E. Sharpe, 1986), particularly chapter 4, "The Image of Embattled Cultural Hero and Picaresque Narrative," pp. 33–47.

12. Sandra M. Gilbert and Susan Gubar, *The Madwoman in the Attic: The Woman Writer and the Nineteenth-Century Literary Imagination* (New Haven, CT: Yale University Press, 1979), p. 74.

13. Ōba Minako, "Onna no hyōgen," p. 13.

14. See Ozaki Hideki, "Sengo besuto serâ monogatari" (The Tale of the Postwar Bestsellers), *Shūkan Jānaru* (7 August, 1966): 37.

15. Miki Taku, "Dokusho teidan" (A Three-Person Roundtable Discussion on Reading Literature), *Bungei* (March 1981): 279. Also quoted in Ōba Minako, "Onna no hyōgen," p. 12.

16. A similar point is made by Ueno Chizuko, a feminist sociologist, who describes a tautological argument used by male critics in Japan: Since feminism is an ideology and "therefore political, anything that is political cannot at the same time be literary." This in turn makes a feminist product (or any writing that demonstrates a feminist perspective) "insidiously political and not to be taken seriously as a literary work. Because it [is] political, it [is] 'masculine' not 'feminine' as it should be." See "The Rise of Feminist Criticism," *Japanese Book News,* no. 2 (1993): 200.

17. It comes as no surprise that Kawabata Yasunari's *Snow Country* is probably the favorite novel among Japanese businessmen and male scholars to take with them abroad. See Kinya Tsuruta, *Kawabata Yasunari no geijutsu: junsui to kyūsai* (Kawabata Yasunari's Art: Purity and Salvation) (Meiji Shoin, 1981), p. 49.

18. Joanna Russ, *How to Suppress Women's Writing* (Austin: University of Texas Press, 1983), p. 17.

19. Ibid., p. 76.

20. In a *taidan* with Nakayama Chinatsu, Yamamoto Michiko describes how the label of "housewife novelist," coined by the male-dominated media, has made her feel denounced by society, as if a married woman's writing were harmful to the maintenance of family life. She once told a male journalist, "If you insist on calling me a "housewife novelist," then why not call a male writer a "husband novelist" (*teishu sakka*)?" Later, she again talks about the unfairness of the situation between literary men and women: "A male writer can work all day, while his wife looks after all his needs. I really envy them." See Yamamoto Michiko and Nakayama Chinatsu, "Kuyashisa no naka kara umareta 'Betty-san no Niwa' " ("Betty-san's Garden" That Was Born out of Chagrin), *Sandê Mainichi* (18 March 1973): 58–92.

21. See also Chieko Ariga's discussion on the subject in "Text Versus Commentary: Struggles over the Cultural Meanings of 'Women,' " in *The Woman's Hand: Gender and Theory in Japanese Women's Writing*, eds. Paul Gordon Schalow and Janet A. Walker (Stanford, CA: Stanford University Press, 1996), pp. 362–363.

22. See Miki Taku, p. 283. Quoted in Ōba Minako, "Onna no hyōgen," p. 11. The most outspoken Japanese woman writer to deplore the frustrating situation of literary assessments, a situation that also affects male writers in Japan, is Kōno Taeko. See Ōba Minako and Kōno Taeko, "Bungaku o gaisuru mono" (Things That Harm Literature), a discussion *(taidan)* with Kōno Taeko, in *Bungakukai* (July 1987): 142–143.

23. Heilbrun, *Hamlet's Mother,* p. 126.

24. The quotation is from Richard Bowring, "The Female Hand in Heian

Japan," in *The Female Autograph: Theory and Practice of Autobiography from the Tenth to the Twentieth Century,* ed. Donna C. Stanton (Chicago: University of Chicago Press, 1987), p. 54. Richard H. Okada takes a much more positive view of the Heian women writers' sociopolitical position in relation to writing: "They were enabled, through their linguistic medium and by their politicocultural space, to speak for themselves and for their men, the latter often existing to be 'read' and written' by women, in a 'feminine hand.' " See *Figures of Resistance: Language, Poetry and Narrating in "The Tale of Genji" and Other Mid-Heian Texts* (Durham, NC: Duke University Press, 1991), p. 163.

25. Heilbrun, *Hamlet's Mother*, p. 307.

26. The name "Shōzō" combines the two Chinese characters used in Minako's maternal grandfather and her father: the character "Yoshi" from "Yoshikazu," and the character "Sabu" from "Saburō." See chapter 1 of this book.

27. Mizuta Noriko, "Mori no sekai: Ōba Minako ni okeru monogaturi no genkei" (The World of a Forest: Ōba minako's Prototype of a Tale), a commentary *(kaisetsu)* on *Ōba Minako zenshū,* vol. 6 (Kōdansha, 1991), pp. 427–436, views *A Journey Through the Mist* as a *kyōyōshōsetsu* (a novel of self-development, the Japanese translation of *Bildungsroman*), a "spiritual history of a woman," but argues that it goes beyond the classic genre as it explores a symbolic cosmic space and the birth of a myth.

28. Ōba Minako, "Onna no hyogen," p. 15.

29. In his discussion of Japanese women writers, Masao Miyoshi, *Off Center: Power and Culture Relations Between Japan and the United States* (Cambridge and London: Harvard University Press, 1991), complains of the absence of serious discussion of sex and gender on the part of Japanese intellectuals: "Whether Confucian or bourgeois in genesis, taciturnity about sexuality—male, female, heterosexual, homosexual, or autoerotic—in intellectual discourse is still prevalent. Its existence is as disturbing as it is puzzling . . ." (pp. 205–206). For the most recent work on these two subjects, sexuality and gender, see a collection of interviews of Japanese feminists conducted by Sandra Buckley, *Broken Silence.*

30. Adrienne Rich, *On Lies, Secrets, and Silence: Selected Prose 1966–1978* (New York: W. W. Norton, 1979), p. 37.

31. Ibid., pp. 37–38.

32. Carolyn Heilbrun, *Writing a Woman's Life* (New York: W. W. Norton, 1988), p. 124.

33. Susan Howe Nobbe, *Wilhelm Meister and His English Kinsmen* (New York: Columbia University Press, 1930), p. 6.

34. Martin Swales, *The German Bildungsroman from Wieland to Hesse* (Princeton: Princeton University Press, 1978), p. 29.

35. Jerome Hamilton Buckley, *Season of Youth: The Bildungsroman from Dickens to Golding* (Cambridge, MA: Harvard University Press, 1974), p. 10. The *Bildungsroman* hero's close relative, the picaresque hero, is helpful to our appreciation of the bumbling heroine in Minako's story. The *Bildungsro-*

*man* hero, by choice, undergoes a series of rites of passage to attain maturity; the picaresque hero is forced by circumstance to fight for his survival by using the only resource available to him, his wits. For further discussion of the picaresque narrative, see Robert B. Heilman, "Variations on the Picaresque (Felix Krull)," *Sewanee Review*, vol. 66 (1958); W. M. Frohock, "The Idea of the Picaresque," *Yearbook of Comparative and General Literature*, vol. 16 (1967); and D. J. Dooley, "Some Uses and Mutations of the Picaresque," *Dalhousie Review*, vol. 37 (1957–1958). One recent work finally focuses on a female version of the picaro: Anne K. Kaler, *The Picara: From Hera to Fantasy Heroine* (Bowling Green, OH: Bowling Green State University Popular Press, 1991).

36. Susan Fraiman, *Unbecoming Women: British Women Writers and the Novel of Development* (New York: Columbia University Press, 1993), p. 3.

37. Ibid., pp. 125–126.

38. The term "resisting reader" is from the title of Judith Fetterley's *The Resisting Reader: A Feminist Approach to American Fiction* (Bloomington: Indiana University Press, 1978).

39. See chapter 2 of this book for the discussion on *shishōsetsu.*

40. Uno Chiyo (1897– ), who "lived the depth and breadth of life—fashion ingenue, magazine editor, kimono designer, celebrated femme fatale," has escaped this potentially damaging criticism by not only copying the masculine plot, but also creating a heroine who has endeared her to Japanese male critics. However, in sharp contrast to what we see in Minako's version of the female *Bildungsroman*, Uno deliberately *misreads* the masculine plot to tell her own story. The male literary establishment unknowingly misreads or overlooks in *Aru hitori no onna no hanashi* (translated into English as *The Story of a Single Woman*, 1971), the blatantly female text of sexual adventures. The autobiographical heroine never loses sight of her own story, the story of a female picaro who survives by her wits. She pretends she is not aware she does anything outrageous, even though she does. She relies on the appearance of humility; after all a word of apology or a gesture of humility, particularly when it comes from a woman, is a powerful weapon against masculine outrage. The female protagonist also constantly smoothes things over to preempt any possible male threat. For a comprehensive biocritical work on Uno, see Rebecca Copeland, *The Sound of the Wind: The Life and Works of Uno Chiyo* (Honolulu, HI: University of Hawaii Press, 1992); the above quote appears on p. vii.

41. I am indebted to Fraiman's study, which prompted me to apply the concept of "unbecoming" to the female *Bildungsroman.* The focus in Fraiman's discussion is how a conventional female destiny eventually harms women, undoing their authority. I use "unbecoming" in two ways: first, in the sense that Yurie must "unlearn" the conventions of what it is to be a woman, and second, in the sense that her refusal to become a conventional woman is inappropriate or "unbecoming." For Yurie, as for the Georgian and Victorian heroines created by British women writers that Fraiman discusses, "the way to womanhood" can be seen "not as a single path to a clear destination but as the

endless negotiation of a crossroads. . . . Thus becoming a woman." In Yurie's case, becoming an unbecoming woman "may be thought of as . . . 'an incessant project, a daily act of reconstruction and interpretation. . . .' It is a lifelong act continuing well past any discrete season of youth. . ." (p. x). Yurie also shares with the British *Bildungsroman* heroines the struggle "unbecoming" women in any culture must face: "a loss of authority" and, although a temporary one, "an abandonment of goals." The story they tell, Fraiman continues, challenges "the myth of courtship as education, railing against the belittlement of women, [and shows them to be] willing to hazard the distasteful and the indecorous" (p. xi). For further discussions on the female *Bildungsroman*, see also Elizabeth Abel, Marianne Hirsch, and Elizabeth Langland, eds., *The Voyage In: Fictions of Female Development* (Hanover, NH: Published for Dartmouth College by University Press of New England, 1983).

42. Page numbers following excerpts from *A Journey Through the Mist* refer to the text of *Kiri no tabi* in *Ōba Minako zenshū,* vol. 6 (Kōdansha, 1991).

43. Fraiman, p. 124.

44. Sharalyn Orbaugh points out the lack of "any overt dichotomization of 'victim' and 'victimizer' in many of the women's texts written between the early 1900s to the present" (p. 127).

45. For the popularity among women readers of these writers and their creations of male and female characters, Elaine Showalter, "Little Women," *Sister's Choice: Tradition and Change in American Women's Writing* (New York: Oxford University Press, 1991), writes that "Alcott's heroine Jo March has become the most influential figure of the independent and creative American woman" (p. 42). See also Carolyn Heilbrun, "Sayers, Lord Peter, and Harriet Vane at Oxford," in *Hamlet's Mother*, 301–310; and Myra Mensh Patner, "Still Crazy About Anne: The Green Gables Novel Going Strong at 83." *Washington Post*, 12 September 1992: C4.

46. The act of speaking one's mind is not as easy as it seems, especially in Japanese culture where stating one's views and position on a certain subject is the equivalent of asserting one's individuality, something to be avoided even by men. It is doubly challenging for women brought up in that society to articulate their thoughts and opinions. The anxiety of Japanese women in such a situation is not quite comparable to that of men because Japanese society allows men to have many other outlets for the assertion of their individuality and gender identity.

47. We see a role reversal here because it is traditionally a woman who assumes that a love affair will lead to marriage. Both Anna Karenina and Madame Bovary assume this, and are disappointed.

48. Mizuta Noriko, viewing Yurie as a *yamamba* (mountain witch), connects the creation of a myth with her procreative power. In the mythical forest of Sweden, Shōzō becomes the gatekeeper who lets Yurie back in regardless of her sexual escapades, and protects her. See Mizuta, "Mori no sekai," pp. 427–436. Saegusa Kazuko, *Sayonara otoko no jidai* (Goodbye, the Era of Men) (Kyōtō: Jinmon shoin, 1984), pp. 177–180, on the other hand, in a short review

of *A Journey Through the Mist*, sees the reversal of male and female roles as a sign of female domination, but clearly it is Minako's intention to avoid a situation in which one gender dominates the other; the relationship between genders should be a dynamic in which the power of each is respected.

49. Gerda Lerner, *The Creation of Feminist Consciousness* (London: Oxford University Press, 1993), p. 30.

50. Deborah Cameron, *Feminism and Linguistic Theory*, 2d ed. (New York: St. Martin's Press, 1992), p. 209.

51. Ōba Minako and Takeda Katsuhiko, "Yojō bungaku towazugatari" (Confessions of Literature's Implicit Feelings), *Chishiki*, vol. 52 (April 1987): 314.

52. See Ellen Moers, *Literary Women: The Great Writers* (New York: Oxford University Press, 1985), pp. 244–251.

53. Like other characters who appear before Yurie and Shōzō to tell their stories, Mizuki has a very unusual tale to share: her mother Fū has often hinted that her uncle, Shigeru, may be her real father. As if to get rid of her, Fū had sent her to America at the age of fourteen. She continued her higher education there and later married Carl, a German, and became the mother of two adopted children, one half-Chicano and half-Chinese, the other a blue-eyed Scot. She and her family normally reside in the United States, but Mizuki is staying in Japan on a sabbatical leave. Mizuki and Fū appear very briefly toward the end of *A Journey Through the Mist*.

54. Aoki Yayoi, "Interview" by Sandra Buckley, points out that the "fundamental nature of the power relations of gender" in a marital relationship is very difficult to break because not only men but women often accept the situation as "normal, even desirable," and that "all too many open-minded radical young men go home to their wives and sit down and wait for their dinner, demand their cigarettes, or shout for anther cup of tea" (p. 7). Kanazumi Fumiko responded to the interviewer Sandra Buckley in the same book: Considering that "less than 30 percent of couples marrying in Japan are 'love couples' in nonarranged marriages," it is not surprising that "too many husbands barely have a sense of their wives as human, much less any sense of their needs or rights" (pp. 72, 75). A lawyer who has handled many divorces in Japan, Kanazumi also talks about the lack of sexual awareness in women: It "is not high enough yet for sexual compatibility to be a major issue in divorce case in Japan" (p. 77).

55. Ida Sachiko, an introduction to the interview by Sandra Buckley, in *Broken Silence*, p. 34.

56. For an excellent discussion of this phenomenon, see also "The Changing Portrait of Japanese Men," by Charles Douglas Lummis and Satomi Nakajima with Kumiko Fujimura-Fanselow and Atsuko Kameda, in *Japanese Women: New Feminist Perspectives on the Past, Present, and Future*, eds. Kumiko Fujimura-Fanselow and Atsuko Kameda (New York: The Feminist Press, 1995), pp. 229–246.

57. Fetterley, p. 72.

# — 5 —

# A Mother-Daughter Plot: An Unsentimental Journey Toward Reintegration

Being an "educating mother," a *kyōiku mama*, in contemporary Japan has been a blessing and a curse for Japanese women. A woman who takes charge of preparing her child for entrance to a prestigious university, managing as well everything connected with household decisions, needs all the skills of a business manager. Yet, a woman's ability and imagination as a manager do not translate outside the home.[1]

In a society which defines the primary roles of a woman as wife and mother and her dominant work site as a home front from which the husband-father is absent most of the time, a Japanese mother's total devotion to her children is almost inevitable. However, as one feminist has pointed out, the fact that the object of her tender loving care is the male child, not the female child, is inherited intact from the Japanese traditional value system.[2] Her overwhelming attention to the male child also defines a markedly ignored site of gender politics, the power relationship between mother and daughter. This aspect of gender issues remains controversial for women and society in Japan, as both collude in reinventing a "sentimentalized image of the perfect mother," which in turn prevents a woman-mother from expressing "her complete psychic reality."[3] Even among American feminists, the reevaluation of the feminine perspective on this intimate subject is a fairly recent intellectual endeavor.[4]

It was Meiji (1868–1911) Japan, in reaction to Western scrutiny, that invented the image of the perfect mother. The government's gender policy "articulated goals for women that included, but were not limited to, the twin ideals of 'Good Wife, Wise Mother' *(ryōsai kenbo),*"[5] ideals that never existed in pre-Meiji Japan. Behind the sudden social rise of women from "breeding mother" to "educating mother" status was a belief and a rationale that without a new sociopolitical construct of the modern woman, Japan would never "become a civilized country equal to the West."[6] The Meiji gender construction that unwittingly "introduced ambiguity into the sexual hierarchy"[7] has persisted, albeit with a different face, into postwar Japan.

Meiji policy-making decisions created a new dilemma for Japanese women: "mother's rights" *(boken)* took precedence over "women's rights" *(joken)* as a sociopolitical issue, and the two issues never really converged.[8] This unfortunate situation, one that delayed and confused the Japanese feminist movement, is rooted in the Edo period ideology of female inferiority, a powerlessness the Meiji leaders had to turn around swiftly in order to join the "civilized" Western nations.

Premodern Japan had regarded women either as sexual commodities or as "borrowed wombs," in either case as persona non grata. The dichotomization was crude and clear-cut: "those with wombs and those with sexual organs."[9] Under the Edo Confucian legal codes a woman was clearly subhuman: in Adrienne Rich's oft-repeated phrase, "something terribly necessary and necessarily terrible."[10] As a wife, the Edo woman was a nonperson: the marriage and divorce law stipulated that it was "only for the sake of perpetuating his lineage [the *ie* institution] that a man takes a wife. Thus, a woman who fails to bear a child must leave."[11] The famous term "borrowed womb" had far-reaching connotations: it literally usurped a woman's right to raise her own child. Child care was a masculine jurisdiction to which women simply lent a hand. Other domestic duties, such as cooking, hosting guests and keeping the family accounts, the tasks now delegated to the modern Japanese homemaker, also belonged to men.

One of the urgent issues Meiji Japan had to face was how to raise women to the level of "mothers," educated and capable of educating children as in the West, particularly in Victorian England. Almost overnight, the Meiji patriarchy, which radically adopted Western ideas and practices in clothing, hairstyle, living quarters, and so on, began to implement the upgrading of women's subhuman status. The result was an idealized image of woman, who could participate in building a strong, civilized nation as an educated, wise mother and a good, faithful wife. Meiji and Taishō (1912–1925) policymakers had no qualms about adopting absolutely alien ideas—the education of women and "sexual egalitarianism"—as long as these fit their political ends.[12] However, the Meiji Civil Code continued to categorize women at the level of children, mentally incompetent and unaccountable under the law.

The complaint lodged by the early Japanese feminists was that, despite these profound changes, women were never clearly recognized as individuals. Since the concept of the individual was foggy at best for a Japan emerging out of the feudal past, it is no wonder that the recognition of women's rights lagged far behind.[13] Given the patriarchal approval of their status as "educating mothers," and provided they remained asexual, devoting their existence to raising their children and to upholding the *ie* institution headed by the emperor, modern Japanese women were still a terribly necessary commodity. But as nonindividuals, women collectively were not a serious threat to the state or to Japanese men. As pointed out by one feminist critic, "these contradictory traditions still cast their shadow over contemporary Japan."[14]

✷ ✷ ✷

For a writer who *seems* afraid of the label "feminist," Minako does not conceal in her tales an unswerving feminist spirit, constantly challenging the structure of motherhood and daughterhood as conceived by a long tradition of patriarchy. Nor, despite the curiously apolitical, nonactivist posture she maintains in interviews, does her literary voice mince words in contesting the stereotypical power relationship central to gender and sexual politics. Well-known for her tough, unsentimental, and biting critique of the cultural contradictions of womanhood and of the magical power invested in women by men, Minako points, in Shari L. Thurer's words, to a "glaring need to restore to mother her own presence, to understand that she is a person, not merely an object for her child, to recognize her subjectivity."[15] Minako's stories taken as a whole demonstrate this painful female restorative process.

In the 1969 narrative *Funakui-mushi* (The Ship-Eating Worms) Minako overtly joined in the pro- and anti-*boseiai* (maternal love) debates which are still ongoing among Japanese feminists. In the course of this story, a male character, a florist, challenges the conventional notion of *boseiai*, which he considers to be nothing more than a way for a mother to bolster her status—and paradoxically, to deny her own subjectivity.

A harsh indictment of the conventional virtues of *seibo* (saintly motherhood) and *boseiai* is spelled out by the florist:[16] "I can't believe it," he says, "an intelligent woman like you doesn't know that a woman looks the ugliest in motherhood. Nothing exposes female egoism more blatantly than when she is a mother. . . . She hangs on to those beautiful words, maternal love, exposing her egoism to the hilt. That's the only way she can feel relaxed, they say" (p. 117).[17]

The florist's argument that a woman exploits motherhood to confirm her own identity because a child is simply the extension of her ego is an ironic corollary of the "anatomy-is-destiny" debate which has been promoted throughout history. Yet clinically speaking, according to the former medical student turned florist, having a child is "a matter of removing those cells no longer needed to create more new cells," the slender pretext whereby a mother "pretends that she has maternal love, dangling from her chest a huge medal which says a saintly mother, trumpeting her way through" (pp. 117–118). Depending on one's point of view, then, a woman can lose her identity by plunging herself into motherhood—or by not plunging into it! The question Minako seems to be provoking the reader to pose is: Can a woman simply be a mother, without being saintly, or unsaintly?

Minako's stories challenge the Freudian view that motherhood brings fulfillment, focusing on women's ancient smoldering patches of anger at the cultural contradictions of motherhood.[18] Women vent anger at their own daughters, daughters at their mothers—refueling societal misogyny and aiming it at themselves. Womenfolk convince themselves that there is no other choice but to compete with one another for the heterosexual gaze, invisible yet physical, that validates their self-identity. Minako exposes the terrible unspoken condition of this power struggle between mothers and daughters whose senses of self clash, often suffocating the little girl within them both.[19]

Theoretically speaking, as members of the same oppressed gender and socially powerless caste, should not mother and daughter unite and fight together for the empowerment of their gender and for their own peace of mind? And if the absence of the mother, often the primary caretaker, is fatal to the girl's future, then does the mother's presence always affect the girl's psychic and emotional development in a positive manner? Minako's early and later stories, including her masterful satire, the oft-quoted "Yamamba no bishō" (A *Yamamba*'s Final Smile, 1976), provide her answer to both questions; she debunks the myth of the good mother and the obedient daughter as efficiently and rationally as any American feminist scholar.[20]

There is no perfect mother nor perfect daughter in Minako's fiction. The mother-daughter dynamic involves despair, anger, self-loathing, madness, self-confidence, and self-determination. Minako presents the relation of mother and daughter like any other power relationship, with its own tangle of lust, violence, manipulation, possession, fear, conscious longing, unconscious hostility, sentimentality, and rationalization.[21]

Yet Minako's "mothers and daughters" try to seek a way out of this sterile situation outside the context of competition between women for men, *first* by demystifying the maternal instinct, maternal desire, and the exclusively female parenting role that confines women's power to the domestic sphere, and *second* by attempting to "construct a voice that can adequately describe female experience."[22] This is Minako's "great unwritten story" (Adrianne Rich's words) of the mother-daughter plot. Hers is the reality of motherhood and daughterhood in a nuclear family under the patriarchal system, a portrayal of an absolutely unsentimental, and even unmotherly, maternal world.

Sandra M. Gilbert's and Susan Gubar's classic rereading of the fairy tale of Snow White illuminates many of the core issues surrounding the mother-daughter plot and is a useful foil for Minako's views. According to the conventional reading, "Snow White" is a "daughter's story," that of an innocent girl who must be rescued from her evil stepmother. The underlying message is that if a woman *behaves*, she will be rewarded with a Prince Charming and socially sanctioned wifehood and motherhood. This one-dimensional reading also regards Snow White as the point of orientation for the narrative's perspective. For Gilbert and Gubar it is not the daughter who is the central character but the Queen, who is a "bad" mother. This second Queen, the protagonist and the storyteller, is "a plotter, a plot-maker, a schemer, a witch, an artist, an impersonator, a woman of almost infinite creative energy, witty, wily, and self-absorbed as all artists traditionally are."[23]

She becomes the sole source of the story's action. Snow White has no mind of her own; she is the art object of the mirror's (heterosexual) gaze and the Queen's gaze, and later becomes the "treasure" of the charming prince: she is the "heroine of a life that *has no story*."[24] The cycle of (female) fate remains intact: "There is . . . no female model for Snow White in this tale except the 'good'(dead) mother and her living avatar the 'bad' mother. . . ." Her choice is between a life of "significant action" which, for a woman, is defined as "a witch's life because it is so monstrous, so unnatural,"[25] by definition an " 'unfeminine' life of stories and story-telling," or the mastery of the "arts of silence either as herself a silent image invented and defined by the magic looking glass of the male-authored text, or as a silent dancer of her own woes, a dancer who enacts rather than articulates."[26]

Seen in this feminist light, "Little Snow White" demonstrates on one level the extraordinary difficulty of female bonding in patriarchy: "women almost inevitably turn against women because the voice of the looking glass sets them against each other,"[27] the "patriarchal voice of judgment" in the mirror (that of the King). But on a deeper level, the story symbolizes one woman's internal hatred of the Angel in the House: "to the extent that Snow White, as her daughter, is a part of herself, she [the Queen] wants to kill the Snow White *in herself*, the angel who would keep deeds and dramas out of her own house."[28] Conversely, to win the prizes that society promises, Snow White must succeed in repressing the assertive Queen in herself.[29]

***

An unsentimental portrayal of the mother-daughter plot is already dominant in Minako's first published story, "The Three Crabs" (1968),[30] that of a housewife, Yuri, who is living abroad with her gynecologist husband and their precocious ten-year-old daughter. Trapped in the transparent coffin of her domestic situation, and pathetically attempting to "repress the assertive Queen" in herself, Yuri wants to kill the Angel in the House and tell a story of her own, but she is unable to break the cycle of female fate, and therefore she begins to hate herself, locked in the dance of anger.

A subtitle for "The Three Crabs" could be "The tale of a mother who is denied her own sexuality and womanhood, and refuses to host a bridge party." Required, in this case, to prepare refreshments for the players, Yuri wants to be somewhere else. Like an unplanned pregnancy, her role as mother, wife, or hostess is an accident, but one she feels she has no choice but to put up with:

> [S]he felt *a faint pain* somewhere deep in her stomach. She cracked eggs and stirred them into the butter *mechanically*, then shook salt and baking powder into the bowl, *feeling a faint nausea like morning sickness* rising in her throat (p. 90).[31]

Like an as-yet-undeclared bad queen, she prepares a cholesterol-ridden cake with, in her husband's words, "the excitement of a poisoner eager to do away with all the bridge party guests."[32] Hers is a hellish kitchen, a transparent enclosure, like Snow White's glass coffin, as remote as possible from the bright image of comfort and nurturance of Yoshimoto Banana's *Kitchen*. By her own admission as well, Yuri's "one wish in baking this cake" is "to fatten Keiko and Sasha like pigs until they'll have heart conditions" (p. 93)[33] and die.

The playful and sarcastic tone of the dialogues between Yuri, her daughter, and her husband in "The Three Crabs" should not distract the intelligent reader from the smoldering patches of deep-burning anger and misery for which Yuri has no outlet. Otherwise, why does she "hold back her tears" when confronted by her husband Takeshi, who shudders at the idea of not having his wife as a hostess at the bridge game? She has no use for her daughter, and Rie reciprocates by challenging and taunting her mother. We witness a perpetual dance of anger between them, as they misdirect the anger against their own sex:

> Rie came in and said, with her hands clasped behind her, in the tone of a female school principal. "You want to look young, don't you, Mommy?"
>
> "That's right. All women do."
>
> "But since everyone knows that I'm your daughter, they won't believe you're under thirty."
>
> "Some women can have a child at sixteen."
>
> "Those kinds of girls aren't nice." . . .
>
> "Why do you keep standing there like that? It's not nice to go around criticizing people. *They don't like it, particularly if you're a girl.*"
>
> "I want to pee. That's why I'm waiting."
>
> "I'm not a boy. I'll just look the other way."

> "That's okay. I'll go later." Rie walked out with a toss of her head.
>
> The way Rie looked at her almost always reminded Yuri of her own mother. She then recalled that she herself had once looked at her own mother in exactly the same way (emphasis added; p. 93).[34]

"The Three Crabs" opens not in the kitchen, but in a dreamlike scene in which Yuri is standing on the beach enveloped by the milky fog of the early morning, in front of a cabin lodge, "The Three Crabs," where she has spent the night. Eschewing a linear unfolding of the story, Minako abruptly introduces the key elements of Yuri's getaway in a flashback. There are no transitional passages or conventional narrative threads. The story ends inconclusively with her on the run, at a time earlier than the beach scene in the chronological sequence of the story, her daughter's brassy, metallic, voice ringing in her ears, "Hmph, nice girls don't do that" (p. 113). As is typical of Minako's narratives, the open-endedness of "The Three Crabs" suggests the unresolved, yet evolving nature of Yuri's entrapment as mother-woman. Her disoriented sense of self is pointedly reflected by the fragmentation and disjointedness of the story's structure.

Before her escape, Yuri observes yet subverts the ritual of a bridge party, as we have seen, even arranging for someone to take her place and giving a not-so-believable excuse for her departure. She also dutifully waits until all the guests have arrived. Her story thus begins not by an act of rebellion, but by a partial rejection of her role, though the "transparent coffin" has a masochistic allure that compels her to keep up appearances, however briefly, in the verbal charade with guests, a mind-numbing repetition of meaningless words.

Aimlessness, indifference, and absentmindedness abound in her getaway. At an amusement park where she parks her car, she is "rescued" by one of the employees, Pink Shirt, when she loses her balance and nearly falls. Her sense of disorientation increases, and she later almost bumps into him "because she wasn't watching where she was going" (p. 106). He again comes to her rescue, this time returning her purse, which she had left behind.

Paired up with a total stranger, riding a roller-coaster with him, Yuri the mother-woman recedes, and a little girl emerges from within:

> When the roller coaster stopped, Yuri found her face buried in the man's shirt. He pulled her to her feet, still holding her, and looked into her face.
>
> "Are you all right?" . . .
>
> "You were huddled there like a dead bird," he said. . . . "Want to try another ride?" he asked, looking down at Yuri. She shook her head.
>
> "Want something to eat?"
>
> Yuri shook her head.
>
> "Something to drink?"
>
> She shook her head.
>
> "A cigarette?"
>
> She again shook her head (p. 109).

Even as Yuri struggles to give birth to herself as a woman, it is also the nurturing of the neglected little girl within that she intuitively craves.

This casual contact with Pink Shirt at the amusement park, and later on the dance floor, brings back Yuri's memories of doing the same things in Tokyo with Takeshi when they were dating. Then, neither the ride nor the dancing was her idea; she simply went along to please Takeshi. Here is a woman without her own voice, without a language.

When Pink Shirt starts making love to her in his car, Minako seems to be reversing sexual politics. It is pointed out that men's sexual relationships with "bad" women "stabilize" marriages in Japan.[35] In this story it is a woman who "abandons" the family and picks up a man to keep a boring marriage intact. However, it is not a simple reversal of "roles." Yuri is totally passive. She *lets* Pink Shirt make love to her: consensual sex without sexual passion or lust. Even while she is physically engaged with a stranger, what occupies her mind betokens the emotional, psychological disengagement she has been experiencing with her husband and daughter: the memory of a female friend in college with whom Yuri once thought she was in love. Yuri says to herself: " 'Even if I returned to Japan, I would have no friends.' . . . [S]he could not think of a single person with whom she felt she could have a pleasant conversation" (p. 113). If there is a common language between herself and Pink Shirt, it is their silence, their indifference about going back to their spouses. The anonymity of the sexual encounter in the end relaxes Yuri: "The man was not starved for sex. He simply enjoyed it. The feeling of emptiness and sadness in him was transmitted to Yuri, and within her it became something gentle and calm" (p. 113).

Yet the tranquility of this chance encounter is short-lived. As her daughter Rie points out, Yuri is one of those girls who are not nice. A nice girl would not run away, make love to a total stranger, or long for a lifestyle outside the transparent enclosure. It is a cruel circle of fate which does not allow Yuri to bond with her daughter or with any of the other women in her life who come and go, "talking of Michelangelo" at her bridge party.

In her 1971 novel, *Tsuga no yume* (The Dream of a Hemlock), Minako again tells the story of a woman in a transparent enclosure, in this case, a typical nuclear family composed of a civil servant husband onto whom the frustrated wife Nobue projects her dreams and fantasies of "significant action," and a son and daughter. Again, the portrayal of the mother-daughter relationship is as gritty, dry, and disturbing as the sand that gets into the shoes of the runaway Yuri in "The Three Crabs."

Nobue exhibits another trait of societal misogyny, child neglect. She has never given a bath to her daughter Sae, not even once when she was a newborn babe. Her breasts remain dry and her husband Ryō bottle-feeds the baby girl: "Of course I had to feed her when Ryō was at work, but left alone on her back, she suckled at the bottle anyway" (p. 29).[36] Ryō sleeps in the same room with Sae and takes over her care until she goes to kindergarten.

Does the mother welcome the role reversal and enjoy her freedom? No, because she considers herself a nuisance to the daughter and thinks Sae is in love with her father. Nobue's attempt to remain sexually attractive (a quality "denied" to a mother) is mocked by Sae, and her attempt to reject motherhood in its nurturing, selfless, self-sacrificing form becomes a source of tremendous guilt inside her. This woman-as-mother, unmothered and unmotherly, has only one option: madness.

The novel ends with Sae running away from home, and the paranoid Nobue becoming verbally abusive and physically violent. Her husband reluctantly leaves her in a mental hospital. She becomes the modern version of the madwoman in the attic, a witch and a *yamamba* all in one, even as Sae becomes a younger version of Yuri, the runaway. As is typical in Minako's stories, the author does not pretend to provide a solution or a conclusion. The final words are given to Nobue's husband, who says to his son: "When the weather gets better, Mom will improve" (p. 281).

In the powerful story "Bōshi" ("A Hat," 1981),[37] Minako uses allegory to illuminate the mother-daughter relationship and women's "odd complicity with their own subjugation."[38] A girl's hat serves as a lid that suppresses her assertiveness, intuition, imagination, intellectuality, and self-identity. The irony of the situation is that the girl's oppressors are her mother and grandmother, who together assist in the molding of the little girl's personality. Accepting the male-identified definition of proper womanhood and femininity, either resignedly or for the sake of convenience, Mayumi's mother and grandmother pass it on to their female children without protest:

> "You're just like Mommy when she was your age," Grandmother said. "She also wore a magical hat just like yours."
>
> Grandmother smelled rancid. But this time Mayumi nuzzled her cheek and whispered sweetly, "I love the way you smell" (p. 83).

"A Hat" explores the ritual process by which women initiate themselves and are initiated by patriarchy and male-identified women into one, and only one, kind of womanhood and motherhood. We see the suppression of the female psyche and those "active, creative impulses" of women that have been viewed by men "as a kind of demonic possession."[39]

Mayumi, a hypersensitive and intuitive little girl, is made to wear a (both real and imaginary) hat all the time because her candid observation of reality around her threatens the canonical process of educating young women. "My, she tells like it is, doesn't she?" says the upset mother. "We've got to make her wear a hat. She couldn't have just left it in her tummy, you know." The grandmother assures her, "Of course, she hasn't left it there" (p. 81).

The little girl, disgusted that her mother always insists on "telling the truth" but does not want to hear the truth, nonetheless begins to be obsessed with her hat. Impressionable, scared, and anxious, she is led to believe in the power of the hat, rather than in the power of her own imagination and her innate ability to commune with the wild kingdom. Her father, like the King in "Snow White," makes no physical appearance in the story, but is the symbol of the complacent voice of patriarchal pronouncement: "Don't worry, you may take it off now," he says to his daughter. "You have another one firmly lodged inside your skull, with your hair covering it. You'll never be able to get rid of it unless you crack your head open" (p. 82) This is the only time we hear his voice. On the one hand he assures her that the metaphorical "hat" which has grown into her flesh pleases him, but on the other he reminds her the "hat" is dangerous because if she tries to remove it, she will die. The education of a young woman, a subtle manipulation of her mind and body, is almost complete.

It is at this point that the significance of the mysterious opening sequence in "A Hat" becomes clear. In the dream a little girl meets a series of grave diggers along the road until she realizes that she has already dug a hole large enough to half-bury herself. The "hat" foreshadows the "death" of the girl who once had "hopes, expectations, fantasies for *herself*."[40] The "hat" immobilizes the grown-up Mayumi, imprisoning her in the transparent enclosures of gender and sexual politics. In spite of her raised consciousness about the oppression of the predominantly male world, she can only grope for self-determination: "If only I had not had that hat on, she was chagrined to reflect" (p. 93). An essentially unchanged Snow White is powerless to truly liberate the assertive, artistic, wily Queen—the major issue raised in Minako's earlier stories.

It is significant, in "A Hat," that Mayumi chooses acting as her profession. The main goal of educating a young woman is to initiate her into a proper role; to step from one role to another becomes Mayumi's livelihood and exacerbates her difficulty in distinguishing between the acting self and the real self. Her primary role in womanhood is to be a desirable woman. She perfects this role to the point that every action or nonaction is automatic and even natural. She flashes a gorgeous smile at a man who happens to compliment her after the performance: "Her body had acted it out even before she thought about it. If she resisted it, her body would turn rigid, then numb" (p. 93). She seems to have no claim to her own mind, body, voice or language.

> She knew the man *assumed* that she loved his gaze. And that was exactly what she gave him. Under the heterosexual gaze, she *had the illusion that her own body craved that attention, a force totally disconnected from what she really wanted.*
>
> Every time a ball bounced into her court, she automatically hit it into his court. After so many returns, the hole she was standing in became deeper and deeper.
>
> She certainly didn't forget what men had to say, either.
>
> Often regretting that they had ever paid attention to the game, they always responded the same way.
>
> "You provoked me."
>
> Mayumi ignored them and deliberately focused on the lovely shape of the balls they handled. If they wanted to, they could have said,
>
> "It just wandered into my court, you know." But, of course, no guy would ever say that.
>
> But on rare occasions one of them, the guy who had no regrets playing the game, would say,
>
> "Why don't you take the initiative once in a while and ask me out?"

> In the end, that drove her to bone up on getting a defective ball to bounce better. Men would look at her in amazement and wonder at her trick; in their minds she had such a wonderful gift. A gift? What gift? (pp. 93–94).

It is the bewitching magical "power," believed to be full of guile, which is invested in women by men. Left alone, a woman is neither "terribly necessary nor necessarily terrible"; her "tricks" and "magic" have nothing to do with her actual nature and everything to do with men's subjective misreading of women. And although it is in the eye of the beholder, in Minako's story women replicate this male misreading by giving birth to daughters who comply with the masculine demand.

Mayumi, the daughter of the new generation, keeps her thoughts to herself, failing to break the relentless cycle of fate; nor is it possible for the mother to "change the cycle of repetitions into which the daughter's lives are being woven."[41] The daughter places blame upon the mother by trying to stay away from her as the latter is dying:

> The mother watched her with such longing as though she had been waiting for her for a long time. The daughter dreamed of the day when she would be free, freed from the mother. Just for the appearance's sake Mayumi pretended to baby her until her mother was completely satisfied.
>
> This, she convinced herself, was the stuff of filial piety. But that was as far as she would go, because she had no interest in getting involved with what the mother was really thinking (p. 95).

This passing of the torch from mother to daughter, a practice the daughter herself would eventually perform without questioning when her own daughter grew up, is depressing and insidious:

> "You've got to have a child. Nobody can escape death, you know," the mother said.
>
> She has heard it before, the same old words. Her body stiffened.
>
> The dying mother's face was now her own, and a baby, who was yet to be, but still hers, took over (p. 95).

The cycle of fate is complete. Mayumi, who is the extension of her mother, is also identified with her own daughter, who in turn will have to struggle with the "hat":

> The little girl looked sadly at Mayumi. She did not want her mother to find out that she had no hat on. She listened hard to what the birds were saying.
>
> The child made a face. How cute she looked! Mayumi wanted to remove the hat for her, but the girl clutched it, pulling at the brim.
>
> "Don't bother. Go ahead and have a baby."
>
> Mayumi had no idea whether the words came from herself or her own dying mother. Her daughter's response was dry as dust.
>
> "A baby? God, Mom, you know you really didn't want me. Why should I want one? She would be just like me" (pp. 95–96).

Here, for the first time, in the rebellion of Mayumi's daughter, is a sign that the cycle of fate can be broken. Mayumi and her mother, however, find the "hat" still binding them together, negative bond though it is, a condition they can share and commiserate about:

> The mother wrinkled up her face like a baby, complaining of pain.
>
> "My head hurts."
>
> "Your hat. It's too tight," Mayumi said. . . .
>
> "You can put mine on your baby, Mayumi. Soon I won't be needing it."
>
> *All she has to do is remove it; then she can relax,* Mayumi said to herself.
>
> She wanted to get it off her head, but here she was crouching beside the mother, unable to remove her own (p. 97).

Having served as a polysemic signifier of female self-denial and self-effacement and of the mastery of the arts of silence, the "hat" has become as well a metaphor for the "essential, distorted, misused"[42] female psychic exchange of energy between mother and daughter. The ambiguous tone of the ending reinforces their disquieting bond: "In the rainy forest, a hat was suspended in midair, not a drop of rain touching it" (p. 97). The "hat" remains untattered and untouched, ready to be passed on to another generation of little girls lost.

Or does the ending suggest that we should expect a day when the "hat" will no longer be the means by which the masculine imagination splits woman into either the Angel in the House or the demonic plotter? If a hat acts as a prop an individual wears either to hide the private self or to improve social performance, regardless of gender, then a woman should have the choice of when to wear it. Minako's stories portray women frustrated at their own inability to control the use and function of the "hat," while her subversive voice says in so many words what women really want but hesitate to say: "Patriarchal man, you created us in the image of what you want to see. It is not the real us, but that's what you say you want and that's what you get. Don't blame women for *your* problems."

Minako is not the only Japanese female writer to express this thought. A diary entry of August 20, 1948, by Miyamoto Yuriko (1989–1951), the author of the autobiographical fiction *Nobuko* and a public figure in socialist struggles in pre- and postwar Japan, shows her frustration at the masculinist image of women. Speaking of Western thinkers such as Nietzsche (1844–1900), Strindberg (1849–1912) and de Montherlant (1896–1972), who were widely read in Japan, Yuriko wrote:

> Their uncontrollable anger toward women may have something to do with their noble mind. Be that as it may, they have made one grave mistake by letting their anger take possession of them. This is very similar to [Natsume] Sōseki's misunderstanding of women. They all find women to be repulsive, yet unavoidable. That alone fuels their outrage. In reality, I know "women" are *nothing like* what men imagine them to be. I also know masculine power and a male-dominated society make women into what they are not. It is a relationship imposed upon them by that society. Men base their own superiority as "male" on the fact that they are not "women," and with this logic treat "women" as their enemy. How could "men" exist without being repulsive themselves in a society where "women" are looked upon as repulsive?"[43]

Another female writer, Kōra Rumiko, is even more blunt about this myth of woman still intact in today's Japan: "The woman that is created in the texts of Japan's male writers is a stranger to me. Those novels make me angry."[44]

Having begun the unsentimental journey of the mother-daughter plot with "The Three Crabs," Minako explores in recent works a journey toward reintegrating the mother-daughter relationship. In her 1985 semiautobiographical narrative, *Naku tori no* (Birds Crying), Yurie the writer and her somewhat neglected daughter Chie learn to respect each other's personhood, accepting their own flaws and foibles, likes and dislikes. And in "A *Yamamba*'s Final Smile," a satire on the devouring and castrating mother, the daughter and the dying mother seem to reach a reconciliation without sacrificing their individuality and womanhood.

This reconciliation and reintegration process also reflects Minako's actual relationship with her mother, Mutsuko. In her two-year correspondence with her own daughter Yū, who was residing in Germany, Minako tried to recreate a letter exchange initiated by Mutsuko during Minako's college years, a practice that lasted until her return from the United States in 1971. "My mother rarely went inside the kitchen, and I have no experience of carrying school luncheons prepared by her," Minako wrote describing the intensity of her memory of the "absent" mother in a rare moment of intimacy with Yū. "If I act mean-spiritedly, it may have something to do with the fact that the person who took care of me really hated my mother."[45]

Minako's attitude toward her mother is summed up by her own choice of words: "You win a few, You lose a few." Imperfection is the stuff of human life. What is most crucial in their relationship is Mutsuko's intellectual and imaginative mind, the stuff of fiction writing. Minako has treasured every word in the letters which Mutsuko never failed to write once a week. She was a reading and writing mother, who insisted that she be accepted as "human" and "woman," with all the complexity of human desires and needs. Someone who would never dream of writing fiction for publication, Mutsuko "said everything she wanted to say through me," Minako wrote to Yū. "I've drawn on the rich bank account of correspondence continually for all these years until not a penny is left."[46] Minako's stories, the sum total of what Mutsuko "made her say," reveal the powerful influence the mother had upon her daughter. Ironically, through this literary influence, the cycle of fate is finally broken for the three generations of women. Minako's mother and daughter have been spared self-annihilation and the glass coffin through her intervention and act of self-liberation.[47]

## Notes

1. Many female critics point out that the so-called domestic power of the modern Japanese housewife is a myth. Aoki Yayoi, "An Interview," in *Broken Silence: Voices of Japanese Feminism,* Sandra Buckley (Berkeley, CA: University of California Press, 1997), writes: "Any power . . . that is delegated to her can be withdrawn. She manages the household but doesn't control it" (p. 5). According to Kanazumi Fumiko, "An Interview," in Sandra Buckley, who is a lawyer, "the practice of the wife controlling the finances is a reflection not of power but of a change in the banking facilities. . . . When it comes down to it, the husband always has the power to stop the deposits or override the wife's financial decisions" (p. 73).

2. Ueno Chizuko, "An Interview," in Sandra Buckley, p. 286.

3. Shari L. Thurer, *The Myth of Motherhood: How Culture Reinvents the Good Mother* (New York: Penguin Books, 1994), pp. xi, 10.

4. For a comprehensive discussion of scholarship on motherhood and daughterhood, see Marianne Hirsch's review essay, "Mothers and Daughters," *Signs: Journal of Women in Culture and Society*, vol. 7, no. 1 (1981): 200–222.

5. Sharon H. Nolte and Sally Ann Hastings, "The Meiji State's Policy Toward Women, 1890–1910," in *Recreating Japanese Women, 1600–1945*, ed. Gail Lee Bernstein (Berkeley, CA: University of California Press, 1991), p. 152. The phrase, "Good Wife, Wise Mother" that "became the guiding aphorism for government policy on women . . . resonates in Japanese society still today" (p. 158).

6. Niwa Akiko, "The Formation of the Myth of Motherhood," *U.S.-Japan Women's Journal*, English Supplement, no. 4 (1993): 74. Also see Nolte and Hastings: "Most important, the [Meiji] laws were part of a systematic state interest in how women and the family system could serve the developing nation" (p. 156).

7. Ibid., p. 75.

8. See "Commentary" in *Feminizumu ryōran: Fuyu no jidai e no hōka* (The Profusion of Feminism: Firing at the Era of Winter), eds. Ogata Akiko and Nagata Michiko (Shakai Hyōronsha, 1990), p. 280; also see pp. 40–41.

9. Matsui Yayori, "Asian Migrant Women in Japan," in Sandra Buckley, p. 148.

10. Adrienne Rich, *Of Woman Born: Motherhood as Experience and Institution* (New York: W. W. Norton, 1976), p. 112.

11. Niwa, p. 72. The Edo woman, the creation of the samurai culture, is in sharp contrast to those women who worked closely with their husbands in the agricultural sector of the Japanese society. See also Kathleen S. Uno's article, "Women and Changes in the Household Division of Labor," in *Recreating Japanese Women,* pp. 17–41.

12. Niwa, p. 74.

13. Aoki Yayoi, " The Anatomy of Dependence and the Family-Emperor System," in Sandra Buckley, p. 28.

14. Ibid.

15. Thurer, p. xii.

16. A former medical student, the florist used to assist a surgeon perform abortions, because women would have died at the hands of the incompetent surgeon, who would botch the operations.

17. Ōba Minako, *Ōba Minako zenshu*, vol. 2 (Kōdansha, 1991).

18. Speaking of this deep-burning female anger, Jane Marcus, "Art and Anger," *Feminist Studies*, vol. 4, no. 1 (February 1978), exposes a male bias toward anger and righteous indignation which she identifies as "the two emotions that provoke the most hostility from the powerful when expressed by the powerless" (p. 69). She continues: "Most women writers have learned to disguise their anger. But their protest never died. . . . Anger signifies strength in the strong, weakness in the weak. An angry mother is out of control; an angry father is exercising his authority. Our culture's ambivalence about anger reflects its defense of the status quo; the terrible swift sword is for fathers and kings, not daughters and subjects" (p. 70).

19. Although the idealized mother and mother love have been a staple literary theme for Japanese male writers, Japanese women writers rarely focus on these subjects with such fervor. As Janice Brown, "Re-writing the Maternal: 'Bad' Mothers in the Writing of Hayashi Fumiko," in *Proceedings of Mothers in Japanese Literature* (University of British Columbia, Department of Asian Studies, 1996), points out, they often break their ties with their mothers, "if not in actuality, then in print" (p. 370). In the case of the mother-daughter relationship, Hayashi Fumiko (1903–1951) is one of the few female writers in Japan who nurtured and was nurtured by her passionate bonding with her mother. This "relationship with the mother was at the core of her lived life" (p. 370).

20. "Yamamba no bishō" is published in English translation as "The Smile of a Mountain Witch," trans. and ed. Noriko Mizuta Lippet and Kyoko Irie Selden (Armonk, NY: M. E. Sharpe, 1991), pp. 194–206.

21. Rich, *Of Woman Born*, p. 56.

22. Sandra Buckley, "Introduction" to Kōra Rumiko's "Interview," Sandra Buckley, p. 102.

23. Sandra M. Gilbert and Susan Gubar, eds., *The Madwoman in the Attic: The Woman Writer and the Nineteenth-Century Literary Imagination* (New Haven, CT: Yale University Press, 1979), p. 39.

24. Ibid.
25. Ibid., p. 24.
26. Ibid., p. 43.
27. Ibid., p. 38.
28. Ibid., p. 39.
29. Ibid., p. 41.
30. "The Three Crabs" originally appeared in *Gunzō*. See chapter 1, note 4.
31. Emphasis added; trans. Yukiko Tanaka and Elizabeth Hanson. The complete translation of this story appears in *This Kind of Women: Ten Stories by Japanese Women Writers, 1960–1976* (Stanford, CA: Stanford University Press, 1982), pp. 87–114.
32. Ibid. I have slightly altered the Tanaka and Hanson translation. Surely, a poisonous "apple pie" would be more appropriate here, but Yuri is not quite aware of her own potential as a wily storyteller.
33. Ibid., p. 93. I have slightly altered the translation.
34. Ibid., p. 93. I have slightly altered the translation.
35. Matsui Yayori, a senior staff editor of Asahi Shimbun, "An Interview," Sandra Buckley, for example, makes a connection between the huge sex industry in Japan and the stability of marriages. See p. 142.
36. The translated passages from *The Dream of a Hemlock* are from the 1971 Kōdansha edition.
37. Ōba Minako, "A Hat," in Bōshino no kiita monogatari (The Stories a Hat Has Heard) (Kōdansha, 1983), pp. 77–97.
38. Thurer, p. 28.
39. Rich, *Of Woman Born,* p. 70.
40. Ibid., p. 166.
41. Ibid., p. 245.
42. Ibid., p. 225.
43. *Miyamoto Yuriko zenshū*, vol. 25 (Shin Nippon Shuppansha, 1981), p. 254. Emphasis added.
44. Kōra Rumiko, "An Interview," Sandra Buckley, p. 105.
45. Ōba Minako and Ōba Yū, *Kaoru ki no uta—haha to musume no ōfuku shokan* (The Poetry of a Fragrant Tree: Correspondence Between Mother and Daughter) (Chūō Kōronsha, 1992).
46. Ibid., p. 166.
47. Perhaps the reader will perhaps indulge me in my wish to cite Luce Irigaray's essay "And the One Doesn't Stir Without the Other," which was translated from French into English in 1981, the same year "Bōshi" was written. It bears uncanny similarity to Minako's treatment of the mother-daughter theme and may well serve as a conclusion. It was published in *Signs: Journal of Women in Culture and Society*, vol. 7, no. 1 (Autumn 1981): 60–67. The translation is by Helen Vivienne Wenzel.

> With your milk, Mother, I swallowed ice. And here I am now, my insides frozen. . . . You flowed into me, and that hot liquid became poison, paralyzing me. . . .
>
> And I can no longer race toward what I love. And the more I love, the

more I become captive, held back by a weightiness that immobilizes me. And I grow angry, I struggle, I scream—I want out of this prison.

But what prison? Where am I cloistered? I see nothing confining me. The prison is within myself, and it is I who am its captive. . . .

With your milk, Mother, you fed me ice. And if I leave, you lose the reflection of life, of your life. And if I remain, am I not the guarantor of your death? . . . .

And when I leave, is it not the perpetuation of your exile? And when it's my turn, of my own disappearance? I, too, a captive when a man holds me in his gaze; I, too, am abducted from myself. Immobilized in the reflection he expects of me. Reduced to the face he fashions for me in which to look at himself. Traveling at the whim of his dreams and mirages. Trapped in a single function—mothering. . . .

But we have never, never spoken to each other. And such an abyss now separates us that I never leave you whole, for I am always held back in your womb. Shrouded in shadow. Captives of our confinement.

And the one doesn't stir without the other. But we do not move together. When the one of us comes into the world, the other goes underground. When the one carries life, the other dies. And what I wanted from you, Mother, was this: that in giving me life, you still remain alive.

# — 6 —

# Marinated in Memory: "Conversations" with Lady Murasaki

Minako's close identification with the celebrated female legacy of tenth- and eleventh-century Heian Japan represents a countercurrent to the universalization of Murasaki Shikibu's *The Tale of Genji* (ca. A.D. 1010); it reclaims the work as an integral part of literature written by women for women.[1] "If I were asked," Minako once wrote, "what single literary work has had the greatest impact on my life since my childhood, I would probably have to say *The Tale of Genji*."[2] However, there is no sentimental bonding involved in Minako's affinity with the rich Heian female tradition, which is not surprising considering Minako's intense dislike of "feminine sentimentality."[3] If, ensconced in "a literary movement apart from but hardly subordinate to the mainstream,"[4] women writers in Japan have suffered for a long time from a kind of identity crisis,[5] *The Tale of Genji* has finally found the right spokeswoman in Minako, who champions this centerpiece of the Japanese classical canon, studied and restudied by critics on a continual basis, as a source of confidence for Japanese women writers.

In a roundtable discussion with a Genji scholar, Akiyama Ken, Minako makes it known that Murasaki Shikibu is the original and recurrent point of her creative process: "I don't really have *The Tale of Genji* clearly on my mind, but when I have the final product before me, I can't help accepting the fact that that's exactly what has influenced my work . . . for example, when I take up a brush, I have no plan to write an 'Evening Face' chapter [from *Genji*], but that's what sometimes happens, and I recognize it with hindsight when I see the completed manuscript."[6]

In other words, Minako is not at all conscious of adopting the flowing, dreamlike prose, the continual and multiple transformation of a narrative voice and subject, or the episodic, indeterminate structure of Heian literature, yet when she stops to think about it, its imprint is everywhere in her own writings. Feminist scholars might call this a process of empowerment afforded to women by the possession of their own literary tradition. Minako tries to identify the Heian female tradition as a collective literary spirit that holds sway over her writing: "I can't write without it [the tradition]. Written words are strange things; It is not me who is putting them down. I somehow feel some mysterious power from the past is letting me do it. . . ."[7]

Minako's first encounter with *The Tale of Genji* reveals much of what she was to cultivate later as a writer: subversive intent. The opportunity to read this masterpiece came with the Pacific War, when the book was suppressed by the authorities because of its allegedly effeminate content. She was twelve or thirteen, and the work already held mysterious power over her. When she crossed the Pacific Ocean with her husband for the first time in 1959, among the few literary books she chose to take with her was a copy of *The Tale of Genji*.[8] The Heian tale became her constant companion for the next eleven years in Sitka, Alaska.

What is it that draws Minako—to use her favorite metaphor—to "retrieve the thread of memories" of one thousand years ago, as she picks up a brush,[9] propelled by the "living spirit" of her great literary ancestors? In her rereading of *The Tale of Genji*, she counters Akiyama Ken with refreshing feminine insight and feminist frankness:

> Everyone says Genji the Shining Prince is the ideal male, but I just can't see it that way. I don't think Murasaki Shikibu meant him to be that way at all. . . . He's after all her own creation, you know, a composite of many historical figures she must have known about. She observes irritating things with such a steady gaze—particularly those things that jar the reader. But she never presents them straightforwardly; she coats them with lovely descriptions. She watches the world around her with absolute calmness and soberness, with an understanding that if Genji or anybody else in that situation were placed within the imperial system, that's how things would happen to him. . . . *Genji* is a dangerous narrative—No, I should say that literature in general is inevitably dangerous because it contains an element of rebellion against what has been established [by the ruling class]. . . .[10]

It is the aesthetics of absence that interests Minako: a purposeful omission of what the author wants to say or wants a character to say. In addition, she finds invaluable the stance and perspective Murasaki Shikibu adopts in her description of the character: her feigned ignorance of what she writes about and her nonchalant attitude toward the impact it might have upon the reader. Rejecting the notion of certain scholars that Fujitsubo, Genji's stepmother and lover, is a divine figure, Minako speculates that Murasaki capitalizes on what was expected in her time and intentionally lets the reader misread Fujitsubo's "sacredness."

This is an example of the indirect combative narrative style Minako prefers: despite the fact that it describes characters who behave in a certain prescribed manner and follow the practical wisdom *(jōshiki)* of the times, it reveals that in actuality they exhibit impudence and insensitivity of every imaginable kind. The cumulative effect of such a "casual" style, Minako observes, is that the reader begins to voluntarily scrutinize the characters' actions with a critical eye.[11] "When I pick up *Genji*," Minako continues, "there are so many things [incidents, schemes, episodes] that are also taking place in our society that I don't really think of myself reading something ancient. Rather, I get the feeling that I'm actually reading a contemporary story."[12]

* * *

As pointed out by Sonja Arntzen, one of Minako's book-length narratives, *Urashimasō* (Urashima Plant, 1977),[13] with its complex interlocked human relationships, reminds the reader of Genji's world, where everyone seems to be related to each other. Another critic has also identified the work as evocative of Murasaki's style.[14] It bears traces as well of the influence of another classic of Heian literature, by Murasaki Shikibu's contemporary, Sei Shōnagon, *The Pillow Book* (ca. 965 A.D.), part collection of jottings, part diary, a work that established the tradition of the essaylike format, *zuihitsu*. In contrast to the retiring, pensive, and scholarly Murasaki, a perfectionist with a "strongly puritanical streak in her make-up,"[15] Sei Shōnagon is an untamed spirit. She is more direct and blunt in her expression, full of combative, witty, and whimsical zest. Minako's affinity with this outspoken, often haphazard, observer of the closed Heian court society, well known for a "worldly approach and promiscuous doings" that shocked many male scholars,[16] is attested by her 1991 translation of *The Pillow Book* into modern Japanese for young people.[17]

*Urashimasō* displays a subtle combination of the writing styles of the two Heian sisters whom Minako most admires: Murasaki Shikibu, with her subversive strategy of couching one's message in character portrayals and dialogues, and Sei Shōnagon who created a distinct female persona to give voice to what was really on her mind in a manner that minced no words. These two contradictory literary formats, one fictional, the other a collection of miscellanies, play with and against each other in *Urashimasō*. Minako successfully delivers a hybrid narrative that synthesizes elements of legend, fairy tale, myth, and satire, in a work as experimental as any postmodern film script or painting. In the hands of a less mature and less accomplished writer, the sheer bulk of the information presented and the issues addressed in *Urashimasō* would have been overwhelming.

One of the most effective devices employed in the narrative is the deliberate omission of direct quotation marks, a practice common in classical Japanese literature,[18] particularly in the dreamy, fluid style of *The Tale of Genji* and *Tales of Ise*[19] (ca. A.D. 904).

Its effect is that Minako's characters resemble the ghost figures in magic realism, capable of going through physical barriers and defying notions of matter and antimatter. The fluidity of narrative voice, coupled with a poetic narrative rhythm that creates a sense of perpetual movement between the present and the past, also marks the strong influence of Murasaki Shikibu. By introducing a diverse group of characters whose points of view alternate with those of the protagonist and an omnipresent narrator through the use of digression and free association, Minako creates a sense of disequilibrium in the continual shifting of voice. This often abrupt transformation of subject and voice is very disorienting, a stumbling block for even the modern Japanese reader, who is now accustomed to the Western definition of the narrative.[20]

Another common feature of *Genji* and *Urashimasō* is the paradigmatic rather than syntagmatic nature of the latter's nonlinear storytelling. According to Minako, the pleasure of reading *Genji* comes from the total sense of freedom it bestows on the reader to open to any chapter, just as in *Tales of Ise* and *The Pillow Book*, without constraints of beginning, middle, climax, and ending. This Minako achieves by eliminating the numbers of the ten chapters of *Urashimasō;* each unnumbered chapter title is based upon a poetic word, or plant, that is central to the self-contained story within the chapter.

❋ ❋ ❋

The disorienting reading experience of *Urashimasō* also derives from Minako's propensity to dig into the past and stir up the depths of memory, which know no boundary or order. What determines the flow and structure of the narrative is not a plot nor a unified action, but rather linked memories that haphazardly highlight a series of observations about life in its most organic and interdependent form. It is what one critic calls "the past marinated in memory, resurrected by the imagination and imbued with meaning."[21]

Linked memories are always the stuff of autobiography, and

*Urashimasō* shares many characteristics of women's literary autobiography. According to Jeanne Braham, it emphasizes revising Oedipal dynamics and shifts its focus from the paternal to the maternal. The stories of three female characters in *Urashimasō* focus on their relationship to mother or daughter. Employing "reflexive strategies of metaphor, memory, and a sense of place (geographic, emotional, cultural)," Minako concentrates on the construction of a "crafted reality," and solicits an active interaction between the author's crafted reality or transcribed life and the reader's empathetic engagement as part of their interdependent and interconnected existence. Also, as in the woman's literary autobiography, Minako activates the reader's "received" response, rather than putting closure on the author's past.[22]

The story of *Urashimasō* derives its power of imagination directly from the memories of two firsthand experiences Minako underwent: her witnessing, as a schoolgirl, of the long procession of A-bomb victims fleeing to Seijō City outside Hiroshima on August 6, 1945,[23] and her eleven-year sojourn in Sitka, Alaska. While the former experience represented humankind's sadomasochistic desire for refined destructiveness and taught Minako the futility of believing in the absolute and the fixed, the latter offered her a dream-come-true opportunity to hone her skills as a sociocultural critic and an observer of U.S.-Japanese relations. The resulting visionary scope of her world view in the narrative, her insightful comparative perspective, the posing of subversive questions on gender and equality, and the creation of a surrealistic narrative voice make *Urashimasō* an erotic parable of humankind and a breathtaking tour de force.

As the title of the narrative indicates, Minako models the twenty-three-year-old female protagonist Yukie after a familiar Japanese folktale, "Urashima Tarō." The eponymous hero rescues a stranded turtle from the harassment by children on a beach and accepts an invitation by the grateful creature, to take him to visit the Dragon Palace in the deep ocean. After a long, enchanting stay at the palace, Urashima Tarō decides to return to his homeland. The Dragon King gives him a *tamatebako* (a

Pandora's box) as a farewell gift, with strict instructions never to open it. Once back on shore, confronted by totally alien surroundings and unable to contain his numbing sense of abandonment, he ignores the king's warning and opens the box. Out comes a puff of curling white smoke, and Urashima Tarō turns into an old man with white hair.

Yukie, Ōba's Japanese Rip Van Winkle as well as her autobiographical self, visiting Japan after an eleven-year stay in the United States, serves as the medium through which the author observes Japan with aesthetic distance and a critical eye. The only nation to experience an atomic bombing, Japan is more than just a homeland for Yukie. By the same token, the bomb which was dropped on Hiroshima is more than an ultrasophisticated weapon. It is also the very real analogue of the *tamatebako*, the unknown, the refined destructiveness of human desire, and the precarious future of humankind.

On another level, *Urashimasō* could be read as a female *Bildungsroman* about a woman searching for her own sense of self by rediscovering her own and Japan's recent historical past. In this personal journey she seeks out her stepbrother, Morito, who in turn brings her into contact with his lover and common-law wife, Reiko. Minako layers together several tales: a tale of "sexual anarchy,"[24] the *ménage à trois* of Reiko, Morito, and Ryū, Reiko's demobilized husband; Reiko's eyewitness account of the Hiroshima holocaust; and the strange relationship between Natsuo, a mixed-blood woman, and Rei, Reiko's and Morito's autistic son. All these characters have bizarre stories to tell. What precipitates their storytelling is always linked memories. In Minako's words, literature seeks out "things hidden from normal social activities—that's why I take them up in literature."[25]

Through three main female characters, Minako explores a vanished life, fragments of life marinated in memory, out of which she tries to spin a story, a revisionist story of female desire and creativity. By focusing on self, gender, and power, she revises Oedipal dynamics and moves her inquiry from the paternal to the maternal. All three women, Natsuo the mixed-blood, Reiko the atomic holocaust victim, and Yukie the unwelcome guest, represent the collective alter ego of the author, who refuses to put closure on her past. She entrusts to each woman a version of Urashima Taro's *tamatebako*: to Yukie, the metaphor of unmapped territory (unopened); to Reiko and Natsuo, the haunted past (opened); and to Natsuo, an alternative lifestyle (both opened and unopened).

These women each overstep the boundaries assigned by society. They are what Victor Turner calls "liminal entities" who are "neither here nor there; they are betwixt and between the positions assigned and arrayed by law, custom, convention, and ceremonial."[26] Although exclusion and outsiderhood are the key components in marginality, according to James Valentine, marginals are "intimately bound up with the mainstream."[27] Just as the concept of the high would not exist without the low, nor the center without the margins, liminal situations imply a "holistic view of the culture and its principal categories."[28] James Valentine points out four types of marginals in Japanese society: people who have foreign blood in them, "that is, [who are] not of 'pure Yamato race' "; those who have had foreign contact; those who are polluted through illness or damage; and criminal or ideological deviants.[29] Minako deals with the first three in *Urashimasō*, stirring the marinated memory to link the personal and the sociopolitical.[30]

Yukie is the second type of marginal. She leaves her homeland for the United States as a high school exchange student because, she feels, Japanese society enforces confinement and obligatory silence for women: "She had left at such an early age because she wanted to run away from Japan, that's what she meant to tell Morito but missed an opportunity [after meeting with him]" (p. 16).[31] She is doubly contaminated by her contact with the foreign: as someone who has chosen a foreign country as her home, and as a woman associated with a foreigner, Marek, her live-in American boyfriend, who joins her during her three-week stay in Japan. Her sense of place—geographical, emotional, and cultural—being fragmented, her return to Japan is fraught with the unexpected, the unpredictable, and the ambivalent. The only certainty is that she has a desire and a curiosity to see her homeland with her own eyes.

Yukie's almost casual homecoming as a curious tourist develops into something she would really prefer not to think about: an examination of her own past and identity. The more curious she gets about her relatives, the further she is dragged into the deep recesses of their psychic worlds. An outsider in her own native land, not quite Japanese, not quite American, Yukie proves to be the indispensable *ur*-listener (the original) of this stories-within-a-story narrative.

Two opposing worlds await her: one represented by Morito, the other by Yōichi, Yukie's and Morito's elder brother, and his bourgeois clan on their father's side. Morito, just like their father, had rejected Yōichi's suffocating upper-middle-class world obsessed with power and status. At the end of the story, Yukie's choice between Morito and Yōichi is clear: "Yukie's thoughts turned to Morito in Tokyo. Through a similar route, they had chosen a lifestyle that was totally unacceptable to their own people in Kambara; they had severed ties, therefore had been cut off from the native community. Yōichi was now a stranger to them, and this fact, separate from the blood tie, bonded Yukie to Morito in solidarity" (p. 251).

Natsuo, who is not of "Yamato" origin, is the most easily identified as marginal. Even her name is an oddity. Literally meaning "born in summer," it is meant for boys. She is the unwanted child of an uneducated but good-natured country girl, a nursemaid hired by Reiko and Morito for their son Rei. The father is a young G.I. who befriended the nursemaid right after the Pacific War. Light-skinned and long-limbed, not quite Japanese, not quite Caucasian, Natsuo is forever labeled with the pejorative *koketsu-jin* (mixed-blood). However, like all marginals, she possesses the power afforded by the position of being partly in the mainstream, partly on the periphery. Unfettered by patriarchal law and custom, capitalizing on her marginality to seek an alternative lifestyle, she goes one step further: she rejects the idea of having a national identity. "I have no nationality. I could fit in with any country. Right now I happen to live in Japan because I like it. Not because I have nowhere else to go, but because I want to stay here. If I chose, I could live anywhere in the world" (p. 74).

It is clear that Natsuo represents Minako's iconoclastic beliefs. Moreover, Natuso recognizes her own image in Yukie, who in turn finds her own unmediated, prototypical self in Natsuo and Rei, an interrelatedness made explicit by the narration. Natsuo confesses to this "visitor from afar," whom she had known only by name: "You're exactly the kind of person I've been looking for. Someone disinterested, but still an insider. I wanted someone like that to hear my story. I mean, this family I've been with—it would be impossible to talk to an outsider about it" (p. 32). Yukie thus plays a marginal among marginals, not quite inside, not quite outside. In Natsuo's mind, her own fascinating story of sexual anarchy with the autistic Rei also becomes Yukie's story: "In all likelihood it's your own story, too, you know." To Yukie's surprise, Natsuo explains: "I mean, a story about you, someone secretly wishing to act out those fantasies which you would never enact in reality" (p. 32). Characters somehow merge, almost losing their individuality as Minako's marinated memory generates a different kind of life apart from reality, a crafted reality.

This story of a crafted reality also applies to Reiko, Natsuo's surrogate mother, who is a marginal not because of mixed blood or self-exile through foreign contact, but because of pollution and madness. Radiation exposure has contaminated her, and the result is an abnormal baby, Rei. Later on, her hair turns white. She also exhibits signs of impending madness. It is Yukie who delivers the diagnosis: " 'You are already mad,' said Yukie [to Reiko]" (p. 94). If Yukie is likened to Urashima Tarō, who finds that a native country of her own imagining vanishes into thin air, Reiko embodies the post-*tamatebako* Urashima Tarō who has inadvertently unleashed the mysterious yet destructive power inherent in human life. Unlike the folktale hero, Reiko does not age physically, but her white hair becomes a metaphor for the *tamatebako*'s "puff of white smoke," the result of humankind's curiosity satisfied at any cost.

❋ ❋ ❋

This dominant physical feature of Reiko, her white hair, is mentioned four times in succession when a jet-lagged and disoriented Yukie sees her for the first time. It seems to symbolize the dual-dimensional orientation of reality and nature: destructive and life-giving, negative and positive, embracing and denying. The mad Reiko, the mother of a mentally retarded son, first appears in a surrealistic scene in which she is reminiscent of a princess in a fairy tale, or an apparition:

> The water splashed and the white otter [Natsuo] was gone, replaced by another woman standing still beside an old tree in the semidarkness. She must have been watching Yukie for some time, but contrary to the radiance of the magnolia spirit [Natsuo], the woman was as fragile as tiny white spirea blossoms.
>
> The hair of the woman standing at the pillar was snow white. The lovely lustrous platinum tresses were coiled into a knot at the back of her head. But she was not old. . . .
>
> This white-haired woman reminded one of the delicate beauty of an Awa doll. . . .
>
> A middle-aged beauty with pure white hair. Not the whiteness that comes with old age, but a rich shimmering platinum that looked as natural as if she had been born with it. But only an albino would have hair of such a light color. . . . Otherwise she looked like a classic Japanese beauty. Only the white hair looked out of place (p. 24).

*Urashimasō* is also a ghost story: What Minako suggests here is that Reiko is not someone of this world, but a ghost figure in an allegory. Among the many variant names given to the "tiny white blossoms of a spirea," Minako specifically uses *yuki-yanagi*, which literally means "white willow tree." In Japanese folktales ghosts are always associated with the willow because that is where the creatures appear at night. Almost always female and legless, they haunt the passerby because of a terrible grudge [urami] they could not resolve prior to their death. The association of suppressed silence and immobility with women is clear.

This ghostlike figure is a fictional reinterpretation of sociocultural and emotional issues that intersect family, gender, self, and sexuality. Reiko's grudges involve the *ie* (family) institution under patriarchy, which refuses to recognize women as persons and confines married women as *yome* (literally brides),[32] a categorization which remains permanent throughout their whole life. A *yome* is nothing more than a possession of the family she marries into. Reiko tells Yukie: "I hated Ryū's [my husband's] family not because they were particularly spiteful. It was because they saddled me with what they irrationally called *yome*'s obligations and kept me indebted. I hated his family because I found those obligations utterly meaningless. With that label of *yome*, I was never on a par with them, not even allowed to reason with them" (p. 72).

As is often the case, the immediate object of her all-consuming hatred is her late mother-in-law, a male-identified woman. In a long tradition of passive collaboration with the masculine social order, she is "entrusted" with the power to re-train and mold the *yome* to fit her husband's *ie* norms. The "women's odd complicity with their own subjugation" seems to be a "problem that has no name."[33]

In the creation of Reiko, Minako again demystifies the image of the stereotypical Japanese woman trapped in convention. She achieves this by letting her speak out, recounting a story of burning anger that has never been told before. Here is a woman who has learned to disguise her anger.[34] Reiko assures Yukie, who listens to her unwritten story, that she never had an open confrontation with Ryū's mother. On the contrary, they were perfectly amiable on the surface. The "battle" of the two women was fought in total silence and finally buried in the ashes of the atomic bombing along with the mother-in-law herself. Yukie makes it possible for Reiko to reenact the battle for the latter's self-preservation.

What is also being reenacted in the portrayal of Reiko is the most basic act of writing, the creation of a crafted reality. In "raw" reality, Reiko has no real voice to articulate her thoughts. The words that are capable of communicating them are locked inside her, frozen and unattainable. In fact, this also applies to the rest of the characters: they find their own voices and words only in the pages of *Urashimasō*.

Interior monologues become the cornerstone of this literary enterprise: Almost everything that Reiko really wants to say but holds back is revealed in them. This stream-of-consciousness technique, which naturally feeds on a character's intuitive and emotional rendering of "felt truth," effectively demonstrates Reiko's preoccupation with self-hatred: she feeds on the energy of this most obsessive form of emotion, which she calls the "resurrection of youth." It nourishes her life and gives it substance, and without it she would not be able to survive. "It excited her. Like the sweet sting of nettles upon the tongue, it was a provocative and sensual intoxication" (p. 60). Reiko the masochistic ghost continues to feed on memories, memories of hatred and anger that are directed against her own sex.

Psychoanalysis notwithstanding, Minako again unabashedly highlights in this narrative the immense difficulty of female bonding in a misogynistic society. In Reiko's interior monologues in *Urashimasō* the reader encounters a biting critique of heterosexual gaze and how it dictates, or how women let it dictate, a woman's psychic life. It is not enough that the *ie* institution pits Reiko against her mother-in-law. Reiko pits herself against every young woman who appears before her as a potential rival, particularly her surrogate stepdaughter Natsuo.

> Men were trapped so easily in those silly spells of hers [Natsuo's]. If only they were strong enough to meet the stupid spells with laughter, I might yet be saved, Reiko told herself. Yet she remembered how she had used the same art to captivate every man around her. She realized that it was because Natsuo was so much like herself in every respect—in action and in speech—that she could not stand the sight of the young woman (pp. 61–62).

If women as wives and mothers intentionally or unintentionally reproduce and socialize family members into society, Minako also appears to feel that women also reproduce—and then become obsessed by—women as seducers, witches, hags, and schemers bent on attracting men's attention. However, as is always true with her critiques, this is only one side of the story. Reiko's female misogyny is bound up with the male projection and gaze, which also "reproduces" stereotypical women:

> If she had not known men, if men did not exist, at least she would not have hated her own sex. Her hatred of young women was generated by a fear that they would divert the heterosexual gaze from her. If men are really as rational as they say they are, if they possess a stronger sense of solidarity than women, it's not only due to their domination of the public space, but also to a female power that enables women to see men more rationally, saving men from their blindness, she silently contested. . . . Isn't it men who have thrust upon women the idea that a young female body is the only marketable commodity? It's men who've trapped me in perpetual anxiety, Reiko decided (pp. 59–60).

The character Reiko thus provides a postmodernist study of "feminine stereotypes,"[35] invented, cherished, mocked, reinvented, and revived by men throughout the centuries.

Minako also parodies many of the conventional feminine attributes.[36] Formlessness (Reiko as a ghost), passivity (silent "acceptance" of her status as *yome*), instability (she is driven insane by haunted memories of the atomic blast), materiality (in contrast to the "masculine alliance with the abstract"[37]), irrationality (associated with her "irrational" hatred of young women), compliance (she is supposedly a masochistic partner in sexual anarchy): if these are what men say women are all about, Reiko's unarticulated opinion implies, why do men hang around women at all?[38] The constraints of gender, family, power, and heterosexuality do not discriminate against only half the population, but implicate both men and women. Minako lets Ryū, who has left Reiko to start a new life, speak up, a point Minako has repeatedly made elsewhere: "Men have tightened the noose around their necks by denying women power. I didn't do it. Our forefathers did it generation after generation. And we descendants are made to pay for it. Here we are straightening out messes they got themselves into" (p. 170).

The critical perspective on gender, power, self, and knowledge in *Urashimasō* is necessarily postmodernist because of the eschatological scale of nuclear power. When the atomic blast leveled Hiroshima and Nagasaki, it also pulverized the humanist notions of human progress and individual autonomy for many who witnessed the holocaust and its victims. Reiko represents this alienated and disoriented group of people. In choosing a strange existence with two men, Reiko subverts the Enlightenment's belief that "human beings are rational, self-conscious subjects with the capacity for autonomous action as agents free to make their own decisions about how to live."[39] In the end Morito and Ryū are accomplices in Reiko's renunciation of autonomy, a thinly disguised act of willfulness and egotism:

> [Morito and Ryū] secretly wanted me to rely on them, so just to please them I played along. But I knew better than that. So I surrendered all my rights and desires as an individual. . . . Morito eventually came around and decided to bring up Rei. Ryū was being selfish and mean-spirited at first, but *realized how comfortable a life with no obligations or individual rights could be. It's not much to dream for, but if life offers no dreams, then you don't have to worry about waking up from them, either* (emphasis added; p. 71).

The postmodern and eschatological outlook of *Urashimasō*, an allegory *cum* ghost story of human desire, psychic fragmentation, and madness, lays bare the refined destructiveness of nuclear power. Hiroshima becomes the center of Urashima Tarō's post-*tamatebako* world: after the gigantic fireball, when tidal waves of scorching smoke incinerated or melted human beings in their path, social order had no relevance. In one split second, Hiroshima became a ghost town. The omniscient narrator takes over from Reiko and speaks on her behalf: "When the world transforms itself in a split second from normalcy to hell . . . , you would first experience a paralyzing terror. However, when this moment is repeated again and again without end, the terror quickly turns into numb despair" (p. 90). Reiko, the storyteller of the eyewitness account of the holocaust, who has seen what the rest of the world has yet to see, knows the futility of communicating such a story: "No matter how much I try, I cannot tell you the story as is. Whatever I say will be a lie. My descriptions of what I saw would never, ever, be as horrible as what actually happened. It was the end of the world" (p. 93).

At the news of the dropping of an ultrasophisticated bomb on Hiroshima, Reiko, out foraging for food for the family in a neighboring town, has one goal in mind when she rushes back to ground zero: confirmation of her mother-in-law's death. In the end she links the refined destructiveness of the nuclear event with a grotesque reorienting of human desire: "It drives you to self-preservation and survival by killing off everyone but yourself. But that very act of survival means something of yourself also perishes with them. I'm the living proof. Can't you see that?" (p. 94). Cackling like a wild bird and sobbing like a little girl, Reiko, a latter-day Lady Macbeth, goes slowly mad as she shoulders her own guilt as well as that engendered by the collective hate and desire of humankind: "See how black the palm of my hands are. The hands of a hag with long crooked fingernails . . . black blood flows through them. I can never wash it away. Listen, it's pumping through my heart, Thump, Thump, Thump" (p. 95).

❋ ❋ ❋

The absence of emancipation evidenced in Reiko's story is counterbalanced by the redemptive voice and action of Natsuo in her tale. Illegitimate and orphaned, Natsuo has been adopted by Morito and Reiko, succeeding her biological mother as nursemaid for the rejected Rei. At the age of twenty-five, she has experienced everything imaginable in Reiko's strange household, but her acceptance of the abnormal circumstances imposed upon her, her resilience in life, and her sensuality place her in sharp contrast to Reiko. The two women are the two sides of the coin of marginality. While Reiko's presence in the narrative defies the dimension of time as she drifts through her memories like a ghost, Natsuo is rooted in the present. Graceful and spirited like a "white otter," voluptuous, exotic, independent, decisive, resourceful, and bilingual (still a rare phenomenon in Japan), Natsuo is unencumbered by any conventional or familial ties. She represents a new kind of woman.

If the ethereal Reiko considers pregnancy and motherhood purely accidental, for the earthy Natsuo these are matters of choice. "I should use Ryū-mother as an object lesson, just as I'm also the evidence of what happened to my mother," Natsuo says to Yukie in breaking the news of her pregnancy by Rei. "I decided long ago that I would of my own free will have a baby. No accidents" (p. 299). It is not only this aspect of motherhood that drives stepmother and stepdaughter apart. Their deep, unspoken animosity arises from the older woman's resentment of her debt to Natsuo, on whom Reiko fobbed off her unwanted child. It is a debt she neither wants to, or is able to, repay.

Natsuo looks forward, Reiko looks back. At one point, Natsuo directly confronts Reiko's obsession with the past: "Humans can't live on stories of the atomic bomb alone" (p. 64). The contrasting portrayal of the two women sharpens in the extreme toward the end of this allegorical tale: Natsuo carries a life inside her while Reiko disappears like a ghost. After a week-long trip to Yukie's birthplace, Kambara, Yukie and Marek, unable to contact Morito by phone, try to visit Reiko's house. Instead, they find a parking lot: "Yukie was dumbfounded. The house had vanished like a puff of smoke" (p. 279).[40]

The character Yukie, situated between Reiko and Natsuo, seems to offer a third type of Japanese woman, one with more alternatives at her disposal. Unlike them, she shows no physical impairment, illness, or racial signs to mark her as an outsider, though in Marek's words, she is a Japanese "who has been shouldered out by her own people." In Japan, as long as she did not associate with foreigners, no one would ever know she had lived in the United States for eleven years. However, those formative years in a host country have been crucial for Yukie's self-development as a woman and a Japanese. They have validated what Japan denied her: individuality and gender equality. Imaginative, articulate, daring, and gifted in reading people's minds, she belongs, according to Marek's friend Larry, who is married to a Japanese, to the type of Japanese woman "American men might find attractive, but Japanese men wouldn't" (p. 127). In a society where individuality is equated with egocentricity, Yukie's belief that "I am what I am, and do openly and freely what is best for me" finds no echo. Yet she passionately tells herself that she "cannot renounce her ego."

What, then, does she want to achieve by staying in Japan? Life should not be a closed book, but an adventure: "Living with Marek has been an adventure"; so is living in a foreign country. "Things have now been reversed," Yukie reveals in one of her interior monologues: "It is Japan that holds the unpredictability of an unknown territory. If she were abandoned in this uncertain and unknown place, would she stop breathing and die on the spot? For a young person, not to meet this challenge would be an acceptance of defeat. She might be able to find some clues to the mystery of this place if she stayed on a little longer" (p. 271).

In less than a month, her status as returnee–tourist–*ur*-listener and her original plan to go back to the United States with Marek undergo a drastic change. She has no more stories to listen to, but one unwritten story, her own, waits to be told: "The *tamatebako* suddenly felt heavy in her hands; a dinosaur's wing slightly raised the lid, revealing condensed time; a wrinkled Adam's apple stood out on the creature's neck. The scales a bluish glimmer, the eyes a brilliant gold" (p. 299). Yukie's real journey of self-rediscovery will continue to follow, not the usual feminine plot of love, courtship, and marriage, but the adventure plot. The fear and lure of human desire and the unknown will propel her story, of which she is no longer a passive observer or listener, but the initiator.

In order to name and act in her own story, she is guided by

Reiko's words, "When I stopped relying on men, I became free for the first time" (p. 71). Central to her decision to leave Marek are the issues of self, knowledge, equality, and power: "When a condition is set, a condition that works for both of them—he can pursue what he wants, ditto for her, cooperating with each other when the need arises—only then would she want to reconsider a long-term relationship with Marek, provided that he would be still interested" (p. 269). If the wish to rethink, reorient and rediscover herself has motivated her to visit Japan, this same wish inspires her to stay.

*Urashimasō* demonstrates in the end how Minako revises the Oedipal dynamics of female desire and creativity in motherhood. It is Natsuo's mothering of Rei and her search for a language to be shared with another human being that shows Yukie an alternative life, freeing her from her distrust of women and motherhood. Natsuo tells her: "Mori-father [Morito] and Rei-mother [Reiko] apparently can't quite understand the way I feel [about having a child by Rei], but as far as I'm concerned, it's them I don't understand, they don't appreciate the fact that I want to bring up a child, someone I would really be able to communicate with" (p. 299).

At the end of the narrative, we see Natsuo make an extremely meaningful gesture toward Yukie: the first physical display of an emotional closeness to another woman. She firmly places her hand over Yukie's; the latter, equally unaccustomed to female friendship, stiffens, not because of hostility, but because of the overwhelming life force that courses through Natsuo's sensuous body, ultimately because of the ambiguities of being female. Three women, three marginals, with vastly different backgrounds, gain knowledge, power, and a sense of self, not from men but from each other. The reader, like Yukie, becomes an integral part of this autobiographical storytelling, an active participant in a literary rite of passage.

## Notes

1. In her paper entitled, "Spiritual Exchange Between a Woman of the Past and a Woman of the Present—Tsuhima Yuko's 'Chased by the Light of the Night' (*Yoru no hikari ni owarete*) and 'Wakefulness at Night' (*Yoru no*

*nezame*)," Shinozuka Sumiko points out the subtle connection between modern Japanese women writers and the classical Japanese literature: ". . . Enchi Fumiko, Ohara Tomie, Setouchi Harumi, Ōba Minako, Kurahashi Yumiko, and others," a group of writers whom we consider thoroughly modern, "are nonetheless drawn at some point in their careers to Heian women's literature and attempt to incorporate something of that literature in their own works." Quoted with permission from a paper presented at the 1996 Annual Meeting of Asian Studies on the Pacific Coast.

2. Ōba Minako, "Without Beginning, Without End," in *The Woman's Hand: Gender and Theory in Japanese Women's Writing,* eds. Paul Gordon Schalow and Janet A. Walker (Stanford, CA: Stanford University Press), p. 33.

3. "Ōba Minako-san ni kiku" (Interviewing Ōba Minako), *Shūkan dokusho-jin,* 7 June 1968.

4. Ellen Moers, *Literary Women: The Great Writers* (New York: Oxford University Press, 1985), p. 42.

5. See an extremely informative article on the issue by Chieko Ariga, "Text Versus Commentary: Struggles over the Cultural Meanings of 'Woman,'" in *The Woman's Hand,* pp. 352–381. Also see her "Who's Afraid of Amino Kiku? Gender Conflict and the Literary Canon in Japanese Literature," *The International Journal of Social Education*, vol. 6, no. 1 (Spring 1991): 95–113. The status of Japanese women writers in relation to the Japanese literary canon is also the topic of Janice Brown's essay, "Reconstructing Female Subject: Japanese Women Writers and the *Shishōsetsu,*" *British Columbia Asian Review,* no. 7 (Winter 1993–1994), p. 19.

6. Ōba Minako and Akiyama Ken, "Monogatari e—Genji monogatari to no ōkan" (To Tales—Traveling Between Now and *The Tale of Genji*), *Kokubungaku* (January 1990): 27.

7. Ibid., p. 23.

8. See Ōba Minako and Akiyama Ken, "Monogatari e," p. 10. See also Ōba Minako, "Genji Monogatari no omoide" (My Memories Concerning *The Tale of Genji*), in *Ōba Minako zenhsu*, vol. 10 (Kōdansha, 1991), pp. 209–211. The reason she took so few literary books with her was that she felt this drastic change in her life would eventually kill her desire to become a writer, and that she would rather not intensify her misery by being reminded of works of literature in her new home abroad.

9. Minako stopped writing in ballpoint pen long ago, preferring the smooth, soft movement of a Chinese brush.

10. Ōba and Akiyama, pp. 13, 15. Another feminist rereading of *Genji,* by Komashaku Kimi, regards the narrative as an indictment of the Heian marriage institution. According to her, the work contains a clear message that Murasaki's women characters rejected marriage. See Komashaku Kimi, *Murasaki Shikibu no messēji* (Murasaki Shikibu's Message) (Asahi Shimbunsha, 1991).

11. Ibid., p. 15.

12. Ibid., p. 17.

13. Sonja Arntzen's comment was made when she was a discussant on a

panel, "Female Gaze/Male Body: Rethinking Female Desire in Ōba Minako's Writings," at the 1996 Annual Meeting of the Association for Asian Studies. *Urashimasō* was originally published by Kōdansha in 1977.

14. Katō Shūichi. Quoted by Akiyama Ken, in p. 8.

15. Richard Bowring, *Murasaki Shikibu: Her Diary and Poetic Memoirs* (Princeton, NJ: Princeton University Press, 1982), p. 12.

16. Ivan Morris, "Introduction" to Sei Shōnagun, *The Pillow Book* (London: Penguin Books, 1967), p. 9.

17. This beautifully illustrated modern Japanese version published by Kōdansha contains major selections of Sei Shōnagon's jottings.

18. The technique is very similar to that used in *The Autumn of the Patriarch* by Gabriel Garciá Márquez, who also completely eliminates quotation marks. The English translation of Márquez's work is by Gregory Rabassa (New York and London: Harper and Row, 1976). This technique is also used by the American novelist Lois Gould, for example, in her *Subject to Change* (New York: Farrar, Straus & Giroux, 1988). Another Japanese woman writer who omits "demarcation between narrative and quoted speech" is Kanai Mieko (1947– ). See Sharalyn Orbaugh, in *The Woman's Hand*, pp. 119–164.

19. Ōba Minako "re-visioned" this classical work and wrote in 1994 a book entitled *Mukashi onnga ita* (Once There Was a Woman). See chapter 7 of this book for a detailed discussion.

20. Minako is very much aware of this criticism from her readers. There are no punctuation marks in *Genji*, making it very difficult to tell when a sentence begins and ends. Although some punctuation marks are used in *Urashimasō*, the reader still must pay close attention to who the speaker is, because modern Japanese does not require the use of personal pronouns and because Minako does not use direct quotation marks. Despite this difficulty, the overall effect of Minako's style is a powerful one.

21. Jean Braham, *Interpreting Contemporary American Literary Autobiographies by Women* (New York: Teachers College Press, 1995), p. 2.

22. Ibid., pp. 2–6.

23. Reiko Tachibana Nemoto, "Hiroshima in Ōba Minako's *Urashimasō:* Desire and Self-Destructiveness," *Journal of the Association of Teachers of Japanese,* vol. 30, no. 1 (April 1996), regards *Urashimasō* as "a centrally important example of the evolution of the postwar *genbaku bungaku* [A-bomb Literature] genre" (p. 18).

24. The term "sexual anarchy" is from a book by Elaine Showalter: *Sexual Anarchy: Gender and Culture at the Fin de Siècle* (New York: Penguin Books, 1990).

25. Ōba Minako, "Onna no hyōgen otoko no hyōgen" (Women's expression, Men's Expression), *Waseda bungaku* (November 1985): 14. See also Ōba Minako and Kōno Taeko, "Bungaku o gaisuru mono" (Things That Harm Literature), *Bungakukai* (July 1987): 140.

26. Victor Turner, *The Ritual Process: Structure and Anti-Structure* (Ithaca, NY: Cornell University Press, 1969), p. 95.

27. James Valentine, "On the Borderlines: The Significance of Marginality

in Japanese Society" in *Unwrapping Japan: Society and Culture in Anthropological Perspective,* eds. Eyal Ben-Ari, Brian Moeran, and James Valentine (Honolulu, HI: University of Hawaii Press, 1990), p. 37.

28. Ibid., p. 37.

29. Ibid., pp. 40–41.

30. Although Ōba Minako seems to shy away from anything that smacks of politics, her writing is certainly not apolitical.

31. All quotations are from *Urashimasō*, trans. Ōba Yū (Sakado-shi, Japan: Center for Inter-Cultural Studies and Education, Josai University, 1995). I have slightly altered the translations throughout this chapter.

32. Japanese men's dread and control of women is demonstrated in the traditional Japanese bridal headgear called *tsunokakushi*, a white silk cloth sack which covers her elaborate coiffure. It means "hiding horns." It was believed that horns would grow from the scalp of jealous women and *tsunokakushi* would either prevent or retard their growth. Even nowadays, men put their hands on both sides of their heads with the index fingers extended straight up to describe that "a woman" is jealous. This horn symbol used against women is not unique to Japanese culture. The horns of the bull, once a Neolithic symbol representing the male, the "benign accompaniment of the New Stone Age goddess and a manifestation of her power," are now considered satanic or evil. See Shari L. Thurer, *The Myth of Motherhood: How Culture Reinvents the Good Mother* (New York: Penguin Books, 1994), p. 19.

33. Thurer, pp. 28, xiv.

34. Jane Marcus, "Art and Anger," *Feminist Studies*, vol.4, no.1 (February 1978): 69.

35. Mary Ellmann, *Thinking About Women* (New York: Harcourt Brace Jovanovich, 1968), p. 57.

36. Ibid., pp. 74–145.

37. Ibid., p. 97.

38. Arguing that "misogyny is not a projection of women who resent men," Adrianne Rich, *Of Woman Born: Motherhood as Experience and Institution* (New York: W. W. Norton, 1976), quotes Eric Neumann, who discusses men's convenient use of woman as either outcast or scapegoat as a mood or a situation calls for: "Only the fact that man cannot exist without woman has prevented the extirpation . . . of this group of 'evil' humans upon whom the dangerousness of the unconscious has been projected" (pp. 114, 111).

39. Marsha A. Hewitt, "Illusions of Freedom: The Regressive Implications of 'Postmodernism,' " in *The Socialist Register 1993—Real Problems, False Solutions,* eds. Ralph Miliband and Leo Panitch (London: Merlin Press, 1993), p. 79.

40. Yukie learns later from Natsuo that Reiko has sold the house, more specifically, the land; in anger Ryū accidently kills his girlfriend whom he was planning to marry; Morito and Reiko do not want to meet anyone because they need time to think about how to help Ryū.

# — 7 —

# Gender Is Fair Game: (Re)Thinking the (Fe)Male

"Gender," along with "sexuality," a recently rediscovered subject for Japanese feminists, has always been an overriding concern for Minako. What energizes her texts is the very nature of gender, which "always adds multiple layers of relational complexity" to a social drama.[1] What her texts decode, as Janice Brown has pointed out, are both "the constructions and constrictions of gender."[2] Gender's power relations not only fascinate Minako but also amuse her because men and women, in different degrees and with different perspectives and motivations, abet one another in constructing it and constricting its full potential.

Many of her stories focus on the private domain of male-female relations as redefined and reinterpreted by women—women who also unabashedly gaze at the male and his body as an intellectual, psychological, and erotic entity. It is in *Mukashi onna ga ita* (Once There Was a Woman, 1994), which is discussed at length later in this chapter, that Minako singles out this issue of the gazing woman. Gazing is the basis of gender politics for Japanese women because the female gaze has a history of a thousand years in Japan: "Oh, Yes, women in my homeland [represented by Michitsuna's Mother, Sei Shōnagon, and Murasaki Shikibu, etc.] have been gazing at men steadily for more than a thousand years, and writing down things they know to be true, things they have seen with their own eyes" (p. 152).[3] In Japanese, the verb *miru* (to see) connotes grave consequences for those who have been seen (*mirareru*).[4] The expression *ashimoto o mirareru* indicates that although you may not detect signs of people noticing anything about you, you are in fact being scrutinized and others are forming certain opinions of you. In other words, it is a warning for the gazee and an indication of the power of knowledge for the gazer.[5] Minako stresses the fact that female gaze does not miss anything it sees. To see is to be empowered, to know things are real, and to record things which cannot be revoked or forgotten.

An early example of the gazing female appears in "The Pale Fox" ("Aoi kitsune," 1973),[6] a surrealistic tale of a woman in a brief relationship with a former lover. The fox, usually the embodiment of the archetypical cunning and mysterious female in Japanese folktales, is in this story a sad, confused, but exhibitionistic male fox in need of someone to praise his lustrous body: "The pale fox believed that he possessed a gorgeous body. One of his favorite pastimes was to walk, very slowly, but straight towards her, body erect and in full view. She knew what he wanted to hear, but thought it too much bother to try to find some words of praise."[7]

The gazing female in "Sea Change" ("Tankō," 1978)[8], something of a freelancer who actively solicits men for a night of fun, makes a point of describing "who envies whom for what body part."[9] Contrary to what most feminists contend about the female gaze, it is anything but passive in this story; it carries with it the power of "action" and "possession" that they tend to describe as an exclusively male prerogative.[10]

Minako skews Freud's notion that men sexualize and objectify women in order to annihilate the threat/dread they entail. She turns the tables, transforming the typical male gaze into a female gaze through a parody firmly centered on the male organ. Clinically, precisely, and without romantic sentiment, Minako disagrees with the centuries-old notion that women are the "*objects* of male theorizing, male desires, male fears and male representations"[11] with their wombs either closed (the celibacy of the nunnery), open (prostitution), or borrowed (motherhood).

The sexual norms of the heterosexual relationship are turned upside down in "Sea Change" in a ménage à trois consisting of two men and a woman. The boundary that distinguishes sexual possession from erotic power in a traditional male gaze is erased, and Minako's playfulness takes over.

> The two male organs thrust alternately before her eyes, now in one form, now in another—how absurd it is, the way they prided themselves on the size and shape of the penises, or got themselves worked up and fell into obsessions and complexes. Sometimes she found the penises beautiful, sometimes pointless and rather frivolous, at another time even ugly; when she thought of how the owners worried themselves to death over them, not knowing what to do with them, or felt them as a source of burgeoning life, she could watch and watch, and could never get enough of them (p. 15). [12]

The woman's unswerving gaze yields a surprising observation: it is not so much that the gazer implicitly wishes to possess the gazee, but that, ironically, men secretly harbor a desire to be gazed at by women. The men are portrayed as if they were artists, anxious and defensive, whose tendency to overestimate their own artwork makes them resentful because they feel it is not appreciated by the appropriate audience, women: "Why, in heaven's name, did this possession of theirs, this smooth, blood-engorged projection, oblige them to boast of it so insistently and at such length, or to explain it away in such apologetic, almost tearful detail? Almost certainly, it was because the most important vital participant, the woman who received its benefits or its evil effects, hardly looked at it, because an idea of subjecting it to a thorough inspection was the furthest thing from her mind" (p. 15).[13] Behind the male gaze and men's self-absorption lurk frustration and insecurity, a belief that women do not take male sexuality seriously. Instead of hostility and competition, Minako suggests, it is just a serious, yet very comical, misunderstanding that fuels the so-called war of the sexes.

The nameless female in the story objectifies and desexualizes the male organ, not to annihilate the threat and dread of men, but to equalize the male-female relationship: "She found them [penises] rather pleasant; it was reassuring, somehow, just to *gaze at* them and *touch* them, but at the same time they were dreadfully inorganic, as insipid as a set of bowling pins lined up, filling up every bit of available space" (p. 15; emphasis added). Minako dismisses the power of the phallus by turning it into an inanimate object, by recasting it as a bit player instead of a lead.

A scene from *Ōjo no namida* (The Tears of a Princess, 1988) illustrates that a woman's gaze is not diluted in male-female relations by the influence of alcohol. The middle-aged widowed protagonist Keiko, vivacious and tipsy after having a gin and tonic with Mr. Smith, unintentionally gives him an opportunity to indulge in a romantic moment: "Keiko found herself having a laughing fit under the magnolia tree. Immediately, though, her lips were covered by Mr. Smith's pressing mouth. While his [fruit-like] thick, meaty, wet tongue continued to suck at her, one of her eyes remained wide open, stealing a peek at the moon bright through the branches of a cassia tree that grew almost on top of the magnolia. His beard pricked her skin like the thorns of a sea urchin" (p. 162).[14] The image of a tropical fruit (Minako uses the word *sarcocarp*) probing a woman's mouth seems to thwart the development of a traditional gender power relation. A piece of fruit (one of the most feminine images) is used in this case to represent a male trying to excite a female! Sexual arousal notwithstanding, Keiko's urge to peep at the night landscape around her with one eye shut, and the minor disturbance caused by the tickling of Mr. Smith's facial hair, seem to extinguish any hope of a romantic moonlit night.[15]

***

*Once There Was a Woman* confronts and parodies questions of gender more than any other work in modern Japanese literature. Shifting the emphasis from gazing to listening, hearing, and speaking, Minako not only "parodically uses and abuses" the conventions of the Japanese literary canon in a postmodern manner, but also "installs and then subverts" the very cultural assumptions of gender she challenges.[16] *Once There Was a Woman* also uses and abuses the formal features of the tenth-century *Tales of Ise*, a collection of 125 brief episodes of prose and poetry that revolve around an archetypical Japanese amorous hero.

Several remarks concerning the classic work's characteristics would be useful as a point of comparison for Minako's rewriting of the work. *Tales of Ise* points to a single historical figure, yet its sequence does not provide a summary of one man's life. Most of the time the man remains nameless, as the opening sentence of every section begins with "mukashi otoko arikeri" "Long ago there was a man," or "Once a man." This is a narrative which poses neither as a biography, a collection of poetry, a diary, nor a memoir, but embraces all of these genres. In Masao Miyoshi's words, the work "seems to invite its reader to deconstruct the notions of biography, fiction, authorship, nature, lyric, originality, poetry, and prose all at once, and to tease the reader into this self-sealed dimension." [17]

Similarly, each episode of *Once There Was a Woman* begins with "Mukashi onna ga ita," a formulaic sentence paraphrasing "Once there was a man" and focuses on nameless women, their memories, experiences, and private thoughts. Although some of the women share similar biographical data, each of the eponymous women is portrayed independently. Many are modeled after Minako herself, others after her mother and her aunts.[18] As in *Tales of Ise*, Minako seems to fuse poetry and prose, "writer and reader, a historically identifiable person and a transparent referentially empty everyman [in her case everywoman] . . . together composing [a] remarkably segmented and unplotted, and yet contiguous and interrelated, story."[19] As we shall see, however, Minako's everywoman, far from being a referentially empty entity, speaks out on every gender issue that Japanese men are reluctant to address.

Seeking an alternative world "through play, through parody, through evasion and illogic,"[20] a world where gender is freed from cultural and social conditioning, *Once There Was a Woman* exercises what postmodernism claims to be all about. Parody, a "perfect postmodern form," serves Minako well because it "paradoxially both incorporates and challenges that which it parodies."[21] She also "asserts and then deliberately undermines such principles as value, order, meaning, control and identity," the basic premises of humanism which she sees as "no longer eternal and unchallengeable.[22]

What she sees as unchallengeable, however, is the historical fact that women's life experience has always been allied with and overlapped men's. As Gerda Lerner has written, women's life "encompasses all that is human; they share—and always have shared—the world equally with men. Equally in the sense that half, at least, of all the world's experience of women has been theirs, half of the world's work and much of its products. In one sense, then, to document the experience of women would mean documenting all of history: they have always been of it, in it, and making it."[23] Everything women have striven for and experienced has also involved men, and thus, any change in gender politics cannot be accomplished without the contributions of both men and women. Minako refuses to "segregate" men from the female experience: she holds men equally accountable for every step women take in life.

In poetic banter, the woman in Episode 13 tries to provoke a man by stating why it is time for men to listen to what women have to say because:

> "My goodness, just to humor men
> Lying, I've been constantly lying—I've had it.
> I want to get everything off my chest,
> tell the truth once in a while" (p. 68).

The man replies that things are not any better for his gender because women are not really serious about what men really want to say:

"The same for men
never saying what we really want to say
constantly keeping women in good humor.
If we ever speak the unvarnished truth, that brief comment
multiplies into ten rocks,
in the end hitting us and killing us all" (p. 68).

The woman then unmasks this as male posturing, the desire to dominate women indiscriminately and be desired by all women:

"Aha, that's why you men
treat women fair and square
ten women who happen to be near you
praise them equally
bless them equally
You're filled with charity, the face of a saint
the object of the nine women's hostility
is what you fear,
so take precautions, and more precautions.
But, you know that would never make you popular
among women, don't you? . . . (pp. 69–70).

What is implicit in Minako's portrayals of the various women characters in these tales is the belief that the majority of women may not be lawmakers and may not openly protest, but they watch, gaze, and observe with clarity, with a critical mind and distance, a fact which men cannot and should not overlook.

The focal point of the female poet's complaint is the pillar of masculine culture, the marriage institution. There is an ambiguity as to whether her logical, and absurd, conclusion is aimed at the man or the woman:

"The marriage institution—
it's a decision to single out and *discriminate* one person, isn't it.
If you want to avoid hostility from other women
If you want to live philanthropically
Do not marry
Do not co-habitate
Do not recognize your children

Do not let them recognize you as their father
passing from one woman to another
All alone until you die, homeless
wifeless, childless, wandering in the wilderness
go and die destitute, I don't care.
Why not say, without lying,
what is really on your mind,
and carry out what your aesthetics dictate to you. . . .

"If you want to live being true to yourself,
Live alone.
Bravo!" (pp. 70–71).

Here Minako parodies masculine authority as a constructed reality, a universalizing facade, which, given the opportunity, men themselves secretly wish to challenge and destroy. She dares them, but as she well knows, they cannot destroy it because at this moment they know of no alternative. The construction of gender and authority "with its insistence on hierarchical dualisms"[24] has been considered the only possible, even natural, system for so long that men are not prepared to question it. The poetic exchange seems to remain one-sided as the female poet issues a challenge: Are you really serious about listening to what I really want to say? Are you really ready for it? Because I can make you very uncomfortable.[25] Minako's woman is in perfect control; she controls the flow of information and the impact of her statement. She has the last word:

"Did you say women should also say
what's really on their minds?
Well, maybe once in a while
we should" (p. 71).

Another "she-says-he-says" poetic exchange, Episode 20, revisits the age-old question which has no answer: Is it better to be born man or woman? The man's answer is predictable and ordinary:

"There are so many things in this world
which don't go my way," the man said to himself.

> "Well, but the idea of being born in the next world
> as a woman does not occur to me either.
> After all, being a man can have advantages,
> in this world," he thought to himself.
> "When questioned by a woman,
> he either keeps his mouth shut,
> or says he doesn't remember.
> He talks off the top of his head
> to take her in, to fend her off" (pp. 112–113).

While the man's poem registers the preferred male position in this world, the woman, after pondering his survival techniques of evasion and manipulation, rejects being a man. The interesting point is that her decision is not based on a judgment of his gender but on the wasteful effort he must exert just being a man:

> "I was not born
> just to be taken in,"
> the woman said to herself, "but,
> in the next world, if I was born a man
> I wouldn't even be able to start thinking
> how to fake my way through."
> What labor it would consume,
> that was enough to turn her off.
> "Either way, it's a world foreign to me,
> to be born a man, it's not my cup of tea,"
> she thought to herself (p. 113).

Here the reader hears pros and cons, but what is missing is any inclusive, dynamic interaction between the man and the woman. It is as if they were reproducing the Heian courtship ritual, from a time when the composition and transmission of a poem was often adequate to express intimacy. Confined in the constructions and constrictions of gender, the man and woman have not found a space to talk to each other.

The absence of such complementary listening and speaking, which is particularly prominent in the average wife-husband relationship in Japan, is the focus in another tale, Episode 9. Tongue firmly in cheek, Minako parodies a domestic life that appears to be determined by the wife and marked by the absence of the husband, who is not given any voice. One day the woman finds a long strand of black hair stuck to the side of the bathtub that her husband has spent a small fortune building; she has never let her hair grow long. In the next several days her meticulous observation yields four more long strands of hair: from the car seat, from the back of a sofa, and from the bedroom floor. She curls them around her finger and keeps them in a matchbox with the date and place of each discovery set down in a journal. When she has collected a total of seven strands, her mind is made up. "Fresh and calm as the wind blowing under a clear sky after a passing shower," she hands the matchbox to her husband and says, "Please put together the divorce papers. It would be too messy to poison each other, I think. Let's leave everything to the attorneys" (p. 24). We never find out what the husband's response is. We are not sure whether it is the wife's obsession with building a case against him or the husband's manipulative mind trying to outwit his wife that is being parodied.

*Once There Was a Woman* also considers how the gender game frustrates both men and woman. The woman poet in Episode 10 rereads one of the most popular premodern performing arts texts from a feminist perspective:[26]

> Once there was a woman.
> At a Kabuki play she found it odd.
> "Women" always take the initiative in Kabuki,
> don't they.
>
> Composed by men
> performed by an all-male cast
> That's why—these plays
> are their dreams, That's right.
> That's what they dream about.
>
> How nice it would be if
> women would woo us.
> They're dreaming, I'm sure.

Real life's
nothing like play.
Men in rage, who'd assault women,
invariably
say in court:
She provoked me.

A woman who's got to have it
her presence alone
a man would read as provocation.
What could she do?

Besides, they would say,
A woman should never woo a man
Wait with patience for his approach—.
But, men are so wishy-washy.
Spring will come and go
before they make up their minds (pp. 55–57).

What the act of gazing takes in and leads to in Minako's parody of *Tales of Ise* goes beyond the *kaimami* (voyeuristic glimpse) idealized in classical Japanese literature. Her female observation and analysis seem to demonstrate what Ursula K. Le Guin calls the "female principle," which "has historically been anarchic": "The domain allotted to women—'the family,' for example—is the area of order without coercion, rule by custom not by force. . . . [T]he two polarities we perceive through our cultural conditioning as male and female are neither, and are in balance: consensus with authority, decentralizing with centralizing, flexible with rigid, circular with linear, hierarchy with network. But it is not a motionless balance, it is wobbling perilously."[27]

Minako understands well this need to balance two opposing, contradictory views. In her self-parody of the woman writer in Episode 26,[28] Minako negotiates this perilously wobbling balance: chaos with order, the amorphous with the organized, the accidental with the deliberate, connectedness with separatedness, the conscious with the unconscious, and life with death:

> Once there was a woman.
>
> Ever since she became aware of right and wrong, she really had to ask herself why she found herself angry at so many things. She more or less concluded that it was all because she was born a woman. She didn't know exactly when, but it had become a habit for her to write down these thoughts, and lo and behold, she became a writer (p. 147).

Being a woman seems an accident; becoming a writer seems also to have happened by chance. "It just happened that way, and as is always the case with such situations, feminists began to discuss the woman's works because naturally they were written from a woman's perspective. Around that time, women throughout the world began to speak up, to charge that they had been unjustly treated; a social movement called feminism spread like wildfire" (p. 147). Central to this rather chaotic, anarchic view of the world is the woman writer's belief that "without our knowing why, certain things change, while other things remain the same."[29]

Minako's writer, her imagination fueled by the fact that she is female, resists everything that is traditionally considered masculine: organization, a goal-oriented life, stability, rationality, control, order, and so on. According to her, writing is simply self-preservation. Speaking and articulating become the central theme in her life:

> However, it did not mean the woman was an activist with any agenda. She just wanted to write down her feelings as they came, and submitted them for publication only because the opportunity arose. It was not the case of "If I can't say what I want to say, I'd rather die," but rather, to live means to speak my mind even though it may endanger my life, the woman decided (p. 148).

Normally carefree and phlegmatic, the woman who "married fairly young, a marriage considered typical in those days," reacts so strongly to one particular incident with such finality that she can no longer write serendipitously. It all begins with her husband's casually uttered remark:

"Do you think you can say what is really on your mind? You'll be in big trouble if you think you can get away with that."

The interaction had none of the usual outbursts of anger that characterize altercations between a wife and husband; he simply reacted to what the woman had said rather offhandedly. The tone of his remark was very mild, so casual that she might have easily let it pass. But his words were like thorns in her side that could never be pulled out.

In the following decades the woman remembered those words, hundreds of times over, with the intensity of fresh blood splattering. Every time that happened, she would say to herself,

"Somehow, some day, I will say goodbye to this man. Until that day, I will show it to the world that I can still survive saying what is on my mind" (pp. 148–149).

Articulation, self-assertion, and the confirmation of one's ego are values the woman writer has taken for granted until now. Her sudden realization that men, through politics, laws, and economy, have told women what to say, what not to say, and what to do even with their bodies throughout history, determines the course of her life. She now has a purpose and a goal in her career other than simple self-preservation. Her relationship to the reader, to the world beyond, becomes an issue for the first time, and she is awakened to a feminist spirit. Things are no longer just accidental, and her approach to writing also becomes deliberate:

In any case, she hoarded the memory of his words in anticipation of the inevitable day when she would have a showdown with that man. Armed with this memory, she would have to figure out how best to articulate her thoughts, how best to capture the readers' attention, and, last but not least, so that she could also survive. This is what she thought about night and day. Well, that was how she began to put things down on paper, and, one day, fiction writing became her profession.

Probably feminism spread in the world because there are lots of women out there who are in pain with a thorn stuck in their bodies, unable to pull it out, just like the woman (p. 149).

To put it another way, the woman writer, through parody, through play, through evasion and illogic, analyzes "how we think, or do not think, or avoid thinking about gender," unmasking the "embeddedness and dependence of the self upon social relations."[30] This episode, mentioned at the beginning of the chapter, discusses over a thousand years of female gazing in Japan, reminding the reader of the "dissatisfactions of real-life people who are neither docile about nor blind to the problems of the society in which they live."[31]

To describe female dissatisfaction, in Episode 7, Minako couches it in the unexpected image of feline indifference, independence, whimsicality, and indolence, in an allegorical tale of the literary woman. Her thinking moves beyond pain and anger, and presents a historical observation of gender power relations:

> Once there was a woman.
>
> She loved to remain horizontal all day, watch absentmindedly the clouds coursing in the sky. It never bored her.
>
> "My ideal is to lounge around like a cat," she declared. . . .
>
> Around that time, the fad was that all women wanted to work outside, to pick up what took men years of sweat to establish at the workplace, to assert their existence on equal terms with men. . . . Back then that was considered acceptable.
>
> The cause of all this goes back to the days when only men worked outside, and by having economic power, they got it into their heads that they were superior to women. The period when men ruled doing whatever they damn pleased lasted too long. Women got angry and stopped relying on them (pp. 39–40).

The woman's gaze and observation miss nothing: the problems of single-parent child care, the increase in the number of women who choose to remain single, the abandonment of children, infanticide, as well as the disadvantages women still face working in male-dominated professions. Now that women must combine domestic duties and a job outside, their workload increases: "However, working conditions were *the same for men*, and in fact they were worse for women" (p. 42), the woman observes. Her unrelenting observation remains detached, like a cat's: "Lying around like a house cat, the woman continued to gaze at these women, as she absentmindedly watched the swiftly drifting clouds" (pp. 42–43). Her detachment is also a contradiction which, she realizes, may invite activist women to label her antifeminist. We see Minako's tolerance for differences, complexities, ambiguity and conflict, as she seeks "to further decenter the world."[32]

The provisionality of Minako's response to human contradictions, as seen in the politics of gender, becomes intensified in the last episode of *Once There Was A Woman*. It appropriately sums up Minako's female principle, describing gender as an interdependent and unstable relationship. The focus shifts back from hearing, listening, and speaking, to gazing and perceiving:

> You call someone who can't see
> a woman clearly for what she is a "man."
> You call someone who can't see
> a man clearly for what he is a "woman."
> No, rather, men are the ones who conjure up women,
> women who don't exist,
> And, women are the ones who conjure up men,
> men who don't exist.
> If you ever claim that you can see everything clearly,
> You're neither woman nor man (pp. 168–169).

Using an approach that is ironic, paradoxical, contradictory, and provisional, Minako, in an almost Zen-like epiphany, both relativizes and essentializes gender relations. Like a postmodern parody, *Once There Was a Woman* reveals "ironic discontinuity, that is revealed at the heart of continuity, difference at the heart of similarity."[33] In Minako's decentered and unstable world, which is in continual flux, the two polarities we perceive through our cultural conditioning as male and female seem to disintegrate and the traditional dichotomy of femininity (*yin*) versus masculinity (*yang*) loses its significance. This gender flexibility and indeterminacy is expressed elsewhere by one of Minako's female protagonists: "I have always liked men. They may disappoint me but I'm never weary of dreaming the impossible about them. This is the way I have survived" (p. 10).[34]

Minako closes this postmodernistic rewriting of the classic masterpiece with her own interpretation of humankind and the world, her conviction of the interrelatedness of life. Using the metaphor of the thread, central to her lyrical production, she presents earth, stars, wind, birds, plants, water, fire, men, women, and sexuality in an interdependent yet unstable relationship. The pondering woman's voice and that of the narrator seem to merge: "Whatever is on one's mind, it is all strung together on an infinitely long thread that is woven into a strange tapestry. It is a lovely patterned tapestry but we're not sure what it really is. It looks like leaves of grass, birds, fish, water or fire, or wind and sand" (p. 162). As in Minako's tenth-century model, *Tales of Ise*, poetry takes over the narrative, in this case as if the contradictions of life can be described only in the flights of poetic imagination:

> A pattern in motion, flowing water
> a thread that has circled the earth once
> still continues
> beyond the earth
> from star to star
> flying though the Milky Way,
> thunderbird, thunderfish, golden sand, platinum rain
> a gyrating vine shooting ever outward.
> Well, that's the landscape
> I see when I think.
>
> Long ago
> overflowing with desire
> the man unconscious of the woman's clear form
> Long ago
> overflowing with desire
> the woman unconscious of the man's clear form
> they were a male god and a female god to each other (pp. 164–165).

Here we see Minako's longing for a return to a prepatriarchal world where dreams and truth are synonymous, where, in another poet's words, "both poetry and politics [as] the territory of human experience . . . should smell of the bodies that have made them, that inhabit them."[35] Toward the end of the poem, Minako drops the words *onna* (woman) and *otoko* (man) and replaces them with *hito*[36] (person), collapsing the gender differentiation.

> Once one is born
> One never dies
> Someone always remembers you,
> and there's someone else
> who remembers the remembered you.
>
> So, you'll never die.
> Besides, even if you're reborn
> as a bird or a flower,
> it's no less fortunate than being reborn human.
>
> Whether you're reborn a star or a rock
> Whether water or fire,
> It's all the same.
> Someone will be there gazing at you.
>
> Once one is born
> One will never fade away.
>
> What we see in the world today
> Is a never-ending pattern
> woven by those from long, long ago
> not a moment lost
> little by little the pattern changing
> but not really changing.
> A strange pattern, it is. (pp. 170–171).

As Minako once wrote about *The Tale of Genji*, the twenty-eight tales in *Once There Was a Woman* are "without beginning and without end," in imitation of the very nature of the world in which we live in. The tales' ending befits Minako's overarching metaphor, the "glittering trail of a broken thread swaying in the breeze."[37]

Postmodernist in her subversive stance, which keeps paradoxes unresolved; feminist in her penetrating "gaze" at gender relations; and individualist in her desire to see individuals freed from sociocultural inhibitions, Minako has opened new doors not only for other Japanese writers, but for all those in search of an alternative vision.

## Notes

1. Ide Sachiko, "Excerpts from *Women's Language, Men's Language: First Person Pronouns,*" in *Broken Silence: Voices of Japanese Feminism,* Sandra Buckley (Berkeley, CA: University of California Press, 1997), p. 50.

2. Janice Brown, "Once There Was a Woman: Revisioning Gender in the Poetic Writings of Ōba Minako." Paper presented at the 1996 Annual Meeting of the Association for Asian Studies, Honolulu, Hawaii. Cited with the author's permission.

3. Ōba Minako, *Mukashi onna ga ita* (Once There Was a Woman) (Shinchōsha, 1994). Unless otherwise noted, all subsequent quotations from this work are from this edition and my translation.

4. This was particularly true for women in classical Japan. Voyeurism, prevalent in classical Japanese literature, is masculine, gazing the signature of a male conquest. Norma Field, *The Splendor of Longing in the Tale of Genji* (Princeton, NJ: Princeton University Press, 1987), explains: "The significance of seeing is also revealed in the form of voyeurism known as the *kaimami*, literally, 'peeping over the fence.' By the Heian period, the visibility of well-born women was extremely restricted. For a woman to allow her face to be seen by a man was tantamout to accepting him as a lover. The romantic literary consequence was the *kaimami*, in which the unseen hero steals a glimpse of a lady through a gap in a fence or an opening in her curtains, a deed that could be termed visual rape" (p. 123).

5. In an interesting contrast to the sexual dominance of the male gaze, gazing and seeing also meant for female characters in *The Tale of Genji* the process of "knowing and understanding the secrets of life," empowering a woman to challenge her confinement and invisiblity by becoming the "noble traveler of the mind." As analyzed extensively by Norma Field, Murasaki's poems reveal her reliance on *me* (eye) or *miru* (seeing or gazing) to describe seeing as knowing, possessing, and at the same time understanding that life brings irrevocable changes, and to explore, in Field's words, "the rupture between seeing and having" (pp. 186, 185). This psychological and intellectual aspect of the female gaze was also explored by Lady Nijō, the author of *Towazugatari* (The Confession of Lady Nijō, 1306 A.D.), and has been a major theme of modern Japanese women's writings.

6. An English translation of "Aoi kitsune" (The Pale Fox), by Stephen W. Kohl, is available *in The Shōwa Anthology: Japanese Short Stories 1924–1984*, eds. Van C. Gessel and Tomone Matsumoto (Tokyo and New York: Kodansha, 1985), pp. 351–361.

7. Ōba Minako, "Aoi kitsune" (The Pale Fox), Ōba Minako zenshū, vol. 2 (Kōdansha 1991), p. 274.

8. *Tankō* literally means "acquaintance" or "casual friendship."

9. Shari L. Thurer, *The Myth of Motherhood: How Culture Reinvents the Good Mother* (New York: Penguin Books, 1994), p. 30.

10. E. Ann Kaplan, "Is the Gaze Male?" in *Powers of Desire: The Politics of Sexuality,* eds. Ann Anitow, Christine Stansell, and Sharon Thomason (New York: Monthly Review Press, 1983), analyzes what she sees as the fundamental difference between men and women: "[M]en do not simply look; their gaze carries with it the power of action and of possession that is lacking in the female gaze. Women receive and return a gaze, but cannot act on it . . . the sexualization and objectification of women is . . . designed to annihilate the threat that woman (as castrated, and possessing a sinister genital organ) poses" (p. 311). Through fetishism (glorification) and voyeurism (disparagement), she continues, men own the desire, and the object of desire—woman as the Other. To "gaze is not necessarily male (literally)," but "to own and activate the gaze, given our language and the structure of the unconscious, is to be in the masculine position" (p. 319). Also see Laura Mulvey's *Visual and Other Pleasures* (Houndmills, Basingstoke, Hampshire: Macmillan, 1989).

11. Susan Rubin Suleiman, "(Re)writing the Body: The Politics and Poetics of Female Eroticism," in *The Female Body in Western Culture: Contemporary Perspectives,* ed. Susan Rubin Suleiman (Cambridge: Harvard University Press, 1986), p. 7.

12. Ōba Minako, "The Sea Change" *(Tankō),* trans. John Bester, in *Japanese Literature Today*, no. 5 (1980): 12–19. I have slightly altered the translation.

13. The translation has been slightly altered.

14. Ōba Minako, *Ōjo no namida* (The Tears of a Princess) (Shinchōsha, 1988).

15. He gets the message and gives up his amorous advances at this moment.

16. Linda Hutcheon, *A Poetics of Postmodernism: History, Theory, Fiction* (New York: Routledge, 1988), pp. 3, 20.

17. See Masao Miyoshi, *Off Center: Power and Culture Relations Between Japan and the United States* (Cambridge and London: Harvard University Press, 1991), pp. 28–30.

18. See chapter 1 of this book.

19. Miyoshi, p. 29.

20. Alicia Suskin Ostriker, *Stealing the Language: The Emergence of Women's Poetry in America* (Boston: Beacon Press, 1986), p. 43.

21. Hutcheon, p. 11.

22. Ibid., p. 13.

23. Gerda Lerner, ed., *The Female Experience*, "Introduction" (New York and Oxford: Oxford University Press, 1977), p. xix.

24. Ibid., p. 46.

25. This is a calculated stance often taken by women writers. In a *taidan* (a two-person roundtable) with Mizuta Noriko, "Onna to hyōgen no kiro" (At the

Crossroads of Women and Articulation: Looking Back at the Last 30 Years), in *New Feminism Review,* vol. 2, *Onna to hyōgen—feminizumu no genzai* (Women's Expression—The Current Situation of Feminism), ed. Mizuta Noriko (Gakuyō Shobō, 1991), Tomioka Taeko talks about a similar strategy: "As far as I'm concerned, when I feel I want to implicate men in a point I'm making . . . I try to say in a language freed from gender things that really ruffle men. Of course, it's important to partially entertain them as readers, but somewhere inside me says that I really want to make them uncomfortable in the end" (p. 18). In her analysis of American women's poetry, Alicia Suskin Ostriker, *Stealing the Language: The Emergence of Women's Poetry in America* (Boston: Beacon Press, 1986), discusses a "humorous exaggeration" of female stereotype: "Do you find me strident? Do I make you uncomfortable? Very well, then, let me make you very uncomfortable. . ." (p. 12).

26. Rereading the literary canon is also attempted by Muriel Rukeyser. In one of her poems, "Myth," which describes the old, blind Oedipus reencountering the Sphinx, Oedipus puts this question to the Sphinx: "Why didn't I recognize my mother?" The Sphinx replies, "You gave the wrong answer." "But that was what made everything possible," said Oedipus. "No," she said. "When I asked, What walks on four legs / in the morning, two at noon and three in / the evening, you answered, Man. You didn't say anything about woman." / "When you say Man," said Oedipus, "you include women too. Everyone knows that." She said, "That's what you think" (This is quoted by Marianne Hirsch in *The Mother/Daughter Plot: Narrative, Psychoanalysis, Feminism* (Bloomington: Indiana University Press, 1989), p. 1. Also, Susan Gubar begins with this same poem a critique of "male-devised stories" which have traditionally offered women readers and writers means of dreaming "through the dreams of men." "Mother, maiden and the marriage of death: Women writers and an ancient myth," *Women's Studies*, vol. 6, no. 3 (1979): 303–316.

27. Ursula K. Le Guin, *Dancing at the Edge of the World: Thoughts on Words, Women, Places* (New York: Harper & Row, 1989), 16.

28. We are fortunate to have a complete English translation of episode 26 by Paul Gordon Schalow, in *The Woman's Hand: Gender and Theory in Japanese Women's Writing,* eds. Paul Gordon Schalow and Janet A. Walker (Stanford, CA: Stanford University Press, 1996), pp. 34–38.

29. This translation is by Paul Gordon Schalow, p. 38.

30. Jane Flax, "Postmodernism and Gender Relations in Feminist Theory," chapter 2 in *Feminism/Postmodernism,* ed. Linda J. Nicholson, with Introduction (New York and London: Routledge, 1990), p. 43.

31. Ōba Minako, *The Woman's Hand*, p. 32.

32. Flax, p. 56.

33. Hutcheon, p. 11.

34. From Ōba Minako, *The Journey Through the Mist.* See the detailed discussion in chapter 4 of this book.

35. Kōra Rumiko, in Sandra Buckley, p. 117.

36. Ursula K. Le Guin, "Is Gender Necessary? Redux," in *Dancing at the Edge of the World,* writes: " 'He' is the generic pronoun, damn it, in English. (I

envy the Japanese, who, I am told, do have a he/she pronoun.)" (p. 15). It is true that a Japanese pronoun, *hito*, refers both to male and female. However, when it comes to a synonym, *ningen* (human being), the same problem that faces American women arises. Like Oedipus, Japanese men take it for granted that *ningen* automatically includes women, when gender is not an issue at all. The best essay on the subject of the word *ningen* is Chieko Ariga's "Text Versus Commentary: Struggles over the Cultural Meanings of 'Women'," in *The Woman's Hand: Gender and Theory in Women's Writing,* eds. Paul Gordon Schalow and Janet A. Wacher. Analyzing a work, *The Lonely Woman* by Takahashi Takako (1932– ), Ariga points out how one male critic disregards gender issues: "[T]he critic uses words such as 'people,' 'inner selves,' and 'human existence,' but the theme throughout the book [*The Lonely Woman*], is the condition of *women*" (p. 363). Jane Flax notes: "Enlightenment philosophers such as Kant did not intend to include women within the population of those capable of attaining freedom from traditional forms of authority" (p. 42).

37. Ōba Minako, "Without Beginning, Without End" (Hajime mo naku, owari mo naku), trans. Paul Gordon Schalow, in *The Woman's Hand,* p. 33. Minako's enigmatic yet hopeful view of humankind, which places an individual life in a larger context of the cosmos, is in sharp contrast to the closing poem of *Tales of Ise*, a "death poem" imbued with a sense of resignation and despair:

> Inevitable—
> About this road I've so often heard
> But how could I know
> My time to be on it would come so soon.

This is a free-style translation of mine. A more erudite version appears in *Tales of Ise: Lyrical Episodes for Tenth-Century Japan*, trans. Helen Craig McCullough, with introduction and notes (Stanford, CA: Stanford University Press, 1968), p. 149.

> This road,
> I have long been told
> Man travels in the end
> Yet I had not thought to go
> Yesterday or today.

# An Interview with Ōba Minako

**Michiko Wilson:** Your work is clearly poetic, but at the same time it contains a socio-cultural perspective, and includes philosophical discussions on humankind in general. Of course, both intellectual and emotional breadth is what makes literature attractive. Yet your work is set apart from that of Tanizaki Junichiro or Kawabata Yasunari, for example.

**Ōba Minako:** In what way is mine different?

**MW:** I think you articulate clearly what you want to say. You once said that you write in a state of unconsciousness. Your work combines the elements of the unconscious and the conscious most effectively.

**OM:** Really! Didn't Tanizaki and Kawabata also say what they really wanted to say?

**MW:** I think those male writers were overtly conscious of adopting the Japanese tradition of leaving things unsaid, of letting the reader read between the lines.

---

I conducted this interview on April 23 and 24, 1994, in Charlottesville, Virginia. Each session lasted approximately one hour and a half. I am most grateful to Noriko Donahue for transcribing the interview. The English translation is mine.

**OM:** Yes, I know what you mean.

**MW:** Your work is more open, more free-spirited, which I find very refreshing.

**OM:** You know, I'm least enlightened when it comes to my own work. I discover something new through readers' comments. They often surprise me.

**MW:** You don't mince words about what you want to say.

**OM:** No, I don't. Except that it's very difficult to say what's really on my mind. I'm never certain whether I'm being successful or not. Overstating something is counterproductive, and getting the writing just right isn't easy.

**MW:** So you're very conscious of it, after all.

**OM:** Sometimes you are required to put down your thoughts effectively. I think I do pay attention to that process. But at the same time, I also know it's best not to think about it too much. To think is a human instinct. Therefore, not to think is more difficult. Although I began to write in my early teens, I did not publish my writings until much later. Early on, I was extremely conscious of what I put down on paper. However, in the last ten years or so I think I have changed quite a bit. I'd rather not think about what I write. All sorts of things are stored in my memory bank, like objects lying on a river bottom. . . . or I should say I let things percolate over a certain period of time in my memory bank. Things then float up to the surface—those things I have not forgotten, things I wanted to forget but couldn't, things that come back to me on their own—these become the material for my fiction.

**MW**: You mean you adopted this approach only ten years ago?

**OM**: It's been probably twenty years since I became conscious of scooping up from my memory hoard only what comes up to the surface. I'm sixty-two now, so it happened when I was a little past forty. I no longer do much research before I write. I mean I'm trying to avoid too much reading and investigating of background data.

**MW**: You used to do a lot of research then.

**OM**: Oh, yes. A lot. A tremendous amount.

**MW**: Could you give us an example in some specific works?

**OM**: All my early works fall into the heavy research category until *Urashimasō*. This book-length work deals with A-bomb issues. At fourteen I had a first-hand experience of the Hiroshima bombing. I have been back to the city many times to collect data. My memory of that experience isn't that good any more, so I've reread many books on the topic to reinforce my memory.

**MW**: How long did you spend on the project?

**OM**: I think at least ten years. *Urashimasō* is my centerpiece. There's a certain time in a writer's life when research becomes necessary. Visiting the actual sites, collecting data, things like that—are necessary in the creative process of a writer. You can't write and bypass it. I was able to produce my core work based on this process. But, for me, that particular stage is over. Nowadays, I'm more interested in writing as if I were singing in a dream, or reciting a poem. My literary journey with poetry started when I was very young. I consider myself a poet. I write prose, but I regard a piece of fiction as a very, very long poem.

**MW**: Would you like to switch to poetry then?

**OM**: I think I *am* writing it, page after page. Many of my readers are poets. They often send me their poems. I'm told that my poetic style and images are attractive, but that these nonetheless positive elements stand in the way because scenes get out of sequence and here are then leaps of logic. I hear that many readers cannot quite follow the plot lines of my stories.

**MW**: Isn't that one of the characteristics of Japanese literature?

**OM**: I think it is; Japan is a land of poetry, after all. Those who say my work is difficult might actually be complimenting me. I do realize, however, that it can be difficult, because I don't adopt any particular line of logic. Images are abundant, but I'm short on logic. Well, I really don't know about myself.

***

**MN**: I read something interesting in one of your autobiographical notes. You were asked in school to write down what you wanted to be as a grownup.

**OM**: I was in elementary school at that time. I wrote down, "Writer." But the teacher told me to put down which school I wanted to enter. It took me totally by surprise.

**MW**: Were you scolded?

**OM**: Probably. The episode remained vivid in my memory; it was the first time I felt that grownups were asking strange things. Why is it that what I wanted to be had anything to do with the name of a school I would attend?

**MW**: Did you feel antagonistic toward the teacher?

**OM**: I just went blank. What a weird thing to say! I don't think I had any sense of hostility. I just felt out of sync.

**MW**: You are very generous.

**OM**: I'm not sure about that. What I learned was that people are different from me, that what they think has nothing to do with what I think.

**MW**: Did that realization increase as you grew older, from girlhood to womanhood? It reminds me of the gripe about Japan that you mentioned in a roundtable discussion with Yamamoto Michiko.

**OM**: I don't remember at all what I said to her.

**MW**: You said, "I couldn't say anything I really wanted to say in Japan."

**OM**: That was true, especially at the time when I left for the United States for the first time. I was in my late twenties. Thirty-odd years ago. My move to the United States gave me a tremendous sense of liberation. After all, I was still recovering from the shock of that teacher.

**MW**: Obviously. The teacher denied you an opinion.

**OM**: Well, I didn't feel I was denied anything at all. I didn't consider it a denial but a difference of opinion. Some people hold entirely different views. From that teacher's perspective, I was a very different child. His utmost concern was which middle school we wanted to go to. That was all he could think of. We were in the fifth or sixth grade.

**MW:** Did the question specifically ask what school?

**OM**: No. The question simply said: What are your future hopes? So I put down, "Writer."

**MW**: Well, it sounds as if your answer was appropriate.

**OM**: Probably so. For me, the question was equivalent to answering, I want to be a mother, a nurse, and in my case I wanted to become a writer. I put down what interested me most.

**MW**: I remember another episode from your autobiographical notes. Toward the end of the Pacific War, mobilized students stationed in an ammunition factory were subject to a government inspection. During an inspector's visit, apparently your mind was elsewhere and your eyes met his. You realized the slip, but it was too late. He flew into a rage. He called you presumptuous and slapped your face. This, and the "writer" episode, really piqued my curiosity.

**OM**: Although we were paid some paltry monthly wage, twenty yen or so, the equivalent of a few hundred dollars nowadays, we were forced laborers. Girls were rarely beaten in those days under military rule, but boys were all year round. I never talked back, but my attitude was bad, they said. I never articulated anything, but when I heard something that was unclear to me, I must have looked blank. So many adults back then said things that didn't make any sense. Instead of maintaining a deferential façade, I probably gave that inspector a funny look.

**MW**: When he raised his hand to you, were you as calm as when you answered that questionnaire and were contradicted?

**OM**: This was different. I was outraged. These men were crazy. A bite from a distempered dog can kill you—that was my wisdom. Don't get involved with people like that. They were insane, I said to myself. I didn't fight back. Instinct, you know. I thought about the physical pain. I didn't want to be beaten up. I just hung my head in silence, hoping he'd go away. I thought he was insane. Stay away from that type. It was the same instinct an animal is born with.

**MW**: Our cat has it. He's no fool.

**OM**: A cat knows when his master is angry or in bad mood. He'll stay away from you. That was the feeling I had. I just stood there stock still. Of course, his type still knows that you dislike him. That knowledge marks you as a defiant child as well.

* * *

**MW**: I understand you had a kind of pre-nuptial agreement to which your husband-to-be consented.

**OM**: It's no big deal now, but in those days, love and work would not mix, we were told, if a woman wrote fiction after marriage. I married in 1955. I didn't think of myself as the marrying type because I wanted to lead a writer's life. The idea of not being able to do what I wanted was distasteful to me—it was in that sense that I felt marriage was not for me. When Toshio proposed to me, I declined his offer because I wanted to write. In the end I compromised and went ahead with it because he said that whatever I wanted to do was fine with him and that he would help in any way he could.

**MW**: There were not many such marriages in the Japan of the 1950s.

**OM**: I wonder. He didn't know anything about literature, nor about a writer. As far as he knew, all I would do is scratch the surface of a piece of paper with a pen. A painter needs costly canvases, a musician requires an expensive instrument, whereas writing is something like making an entry in a diary. My husband was clueless and knew nothing about literature.

**MW**: You certainly had an instinct, though—that this man would not block your future.

**OM**: I still think the marriage was a mistake. It's just not for me.

**MW**: But you've said time and time again that you can't live without a man. Would you elaborate on this?

**OM**: Men and women are physically different, and in one's life a man's strength may be necessary, you know. Of course, a man can say the same thing about a woman. I think it is easier for a woman to have a man around than to live all by herself.

**MW**: And less monotonous.

**OM**: Exactly. In that sense, I find it easier to live with a man. But, I'm terribly selfish. I do whatever I want to do. I'm not really meant for marriage. I talk about divorce every three minutes.

**MN**: Really?

**OM**: Sure, I'm not joking.

**MW**: What is your husband's reaction to that?

**OM**: "There she goes again," I think. He must be so sick of hearing me talk about it.

**MW**: Marriage is really a partnership, a give and take, don't you think?

**OM**: I guess so. For all my bravery, I get terribly lonely. I don't want to be alone. Well, if I got a divorce, I could marry someone else except the second time around might be even worse.

**MW**: How true. One never knows.

**OM**: So, my husband is a very generous person, and the fact that he's not into literature is definitely a saving grace for me.

**MW**: If both of you were the same type, the sensitive type, then you would be clashing all the time.

**OM**: I think so. He thinks entirely differently from me, about things that are totally alien to me. That makes our relationship very interesting. He's into science.

**MW:** In your autobiographical *Ten Nights of Oregon Dreams*, the narrator's husband accompanies her to Narita Airport, where she has to fend off questions from her female friends who have come to see her off. "You'll be gone for three months! What will happen to your husband?" etc. The narrator calmly replies, "So what? He's no child. You mean you'd put the same question to a man who's going away from home for an extended time?" You let characters say totally common-sensical things which in real life would rarely be expressed in Japan.

**OM**: Yes. But I'm not that conscious of what I'm putting down. What was on my mind at the time was, "They ask me the weirdest questions!"

**MW**: I find that frankness to be a very appealing aspect of your work. In American society, you have the choice of saying or not saying things like that. It's different in Japan, and this is where you come in. You have the impudence, the nerve to say things you are not supposed to say. I think it empowers female readers.

**OM**: If my work has that kind of impact upon the reader, it makes me very happy. That's nice. Once I'm in a fictional world, I live there, and the kind of dialogues you mentioned come out of me as if they have always been there. It's as if something that has been sunk to the bottom suddenly surfaces.

**MW**: It's very captivating.

**OM**: This is the era of feminism. Let's say I start thinking about what I should say or not say, as a [feminist] strategy— then I don't think my work would be literature. I'd rather not do it that way. Something spiritual drives me, goads me on to say something, which is the power of literature. A spirit possesses me, and my voice mingles with those of many generations of women. The sum total of the accumulated voices: that's what I want to put down on paper. Anything else would be useless, not effective.

When I put my own personal desire into writing, or put down things just to satisfy my own needs, my writing becomes very superficial. Writing about the resentment and dreams of many generations of women all intertwined in one, putting down what the spirit dictates you to say, I believe that is the power of literature.

**MW**: Do you feel resistant to being characterized as feminist?

**OM**: Well, feminism is not monolithic, and it contains different views and assertions. I'm not too knowledgeable about the movement anyway.

**MW**: I think the sixty-two years of life you've led so far itself exemplifies feminism.

**OB**: I admit that being a woman all my life has resulted in that.

**MW**: I was very much impressed by your use of the word, *futebuteshii* (impudent/unrepentant), in your Rutgers conference paper. Your resiliency—that nothing really affects you one way or another—where does that strength come from?

**OM**: You're probably right about me. It may not be a good thing, though. I'll give you some small example. It seems that I have an autistic side in me. Writers often have it. I've lived with Toshio for nearly forty years. He loves all sorts of sports, particularly baseball. He watches them on TV all the time. But, in spite of being around this man, not a thing about sports has rubbed off on me. I still know nothing about the rules of baseball. One day I saw a pitcher doing something with his hand. I asked Toshio, "Is he a Catholic?" I assumed that he must have been making a sign of the cross so that he could throw a good pitch. My spoken English never really improves and is a perfect example of my closed nature, though. I'm sure I can shop by myself in this country without much trouble. I'm so focused on the world of Japanese language that I probably can't afford to pay attention to anything else. I remember something else vividly from my school days. A teacher asked us every day: How many enemy planes did we shoot down today? It went on every single day. I had absolutely no interest in how many planes were lost, and where, or how many destroyers were sunk. Since I had no interest, I had no figures to report. I'm still like that. I don't read newspapers, and I hardly watch television either.

**MW**: So what happened to you in class?

**OM**: My usual response was, "I don't know."

**MW**: You actually said that? Didn't they box your ears?

**OM**: Luckily, no. But after my answer the teacher was in a foul mood, I can assure you.

**MW**: You didn't let it bother you. Now about your childhood, could you tell me something about your relationship with your mother?

**OM**: A very strange woman, probably like me. She was hysterical. Sometimes she got angry at something I would do, but at other times she showed no interest even if I did the same thing. But she was a very good friend of mine. Very literary, the only friend with whom I could converse about literary matters as an equal.

**MW**: You mean she was an intellectual friend.

**OM**: Right. She was definitely not maternal.

**MW**: Not the doting type.

**OM**: That's right.

**MW**: Did you ever hunger for that type?

**OM**: I used to wish for a mother, simple and stupid. In every other way, though, I should say I was content. It's almost impossible to carry on an intellectual conversation with your own mother. Up till my first publication, she and I were equals in terms of our ability to read literature.

**MW**: Your mother's influence has been very strong, then.

**OM**: Quite so.

**MW**: Does this have anything to do with the fact that you chose literature over drama or painting, both of which you were very gifted in.

**OM**: I think so. But, in drama you have to play *with* someone. I prefer doing things myself. I'm self-centered. I was told time and time again that I had a gift for acting. People really saw my talent in drama, not in writing.

**MW**: Carolyn G. Heilbrun, a former English professor at Columbia University, once wrote that of those women who have accomplished a great deal in male-dominated professions, the majority were raised either in families of all daughters or as the only children, or they attended all-woman colleges.* When I came across that, I somehow thought about you. You went to Tsuda Women's College. Tell me about your experience there.

**OM**: When I went to college, Japan's educational system had undergone a radical change as part of the postwar reforms. Until then, we had no co-educational institutions in Japan. Before the war schools for girls only had five years, while boys went to middle schools which more or less combined junior and senior high schools. Boys could go beyond that. Then overnight, education became co-ed. I went to a girls' school in prewar Japan. I lived in a dorm for almost ten years. High school at that time belonged to the elite, to the sons of the financially well-off. I

***Reinventing Womanhood* (New York: W.W. Norton, 1979), p. 107.

think fewer than 1 percent of children in rural areas could afford education beyond elementary school. The percentage was probably slightly higher in the cities. I was in the third grade when the war ended. As a young woman drawn to the opposite sex, I found the idea of co-education very appealing. However, I continued my education in an all-girls' high school. When I decided to go to college, Tokyo was nothing but burnt fields and was full of danger. Few parents would allow their [female] children to live in an apartment. If you chose a co-ed college, then it was your responsibility to find your own lodging. The homeless were everywhere, and orphans crowded the streets. Food was scarce, rental houses almost nonexistent. College boys could stay in shacks, but parents would not let their daughters do the same. That left me with one option: a women's college. Once you made it in, you were able to live in a dorm, usually two girls sharing a room. If you wanted to go to Tokyo University, you had to rent a room, which was an impossibility at that time. Of course, if your family lived in Tokyo, things were different, but I was in my mother's home town in Niigata Prefecture. That was one of the major reasons why I went to a women's college. Tsuda Women's College was founded by Tsuda Umeko, who studied at Bryn Mawr. The knowledge and experience of American women's colleges was very influential in her life. She saw the lamentable reality of Japanese women's total economic dependence upon their husbands and their inability to speak up as equals of men. She founded the college to educate women for economic independence. That was around 1900. Her spirit was very much part of the education, I think.

**MW**: You knew all that when you entered the college?

**OM**: Yes, to a certain extent. They used to call it Tsuda English Academy, the name my mother was familiar with. My maternal grandfather regarded Tsuda Umeko very highly—a great lady, he used to say. Her father, Tsuda Sen, took up new agricultural methods imported from the West and ran an agricultural school.

Given that he was open to changes and worshipped Tsuda Sen, my grandfather had very little hesitation for me going to a school founded by Sen's daughter. So I went. Co-educational schools were popping up here and there, and many who lived in Tokyo opted for that opportunity. I envied them. I said to myself, How boring, we've got only girls. However, boy- girl interactions were getting more and more acceptable. Hitotsubashi University was nearby, and the Liberal Arts Department of Tokyo University (the former First High School) at Komaba was also close to Tsuda. We did have chances to mix with male students from both universities in study groups, etc. But, of course, it wasn't the same thing as doing things together as peers from the same institution.

With hindsight, I really think that my four years at a women's college were invaluable. Since we couldn't seek men's help, whatever we did, we did all on our own, including saying things on equal terms. A women's college made that all possible. I wasn't aware of that then. Even things we were not cut out for, we just had to go ahead and do. For example, putting on a play requires some carpentry for the scenery and backdrops that at a co-ed institution it's considered a man's job to negotiate with a carpenter. Also, in running organizations, it's taken for granted that male students will take charge. That automatically sends the message to female students to stay away from management responsibilities. It's different at a women's college. Negotiating budgets, setting up extracurricular activities, everything is in the women's domain. Each woman finds her own most appropriate niche. I later learned that once they join the workforce, women's college graduates beat out those from co-ed institutions in discussions and debates. The latter tend to give the floor to men out of respect. I taught at a co-ed university for ten-odd years as a part-time instructor. There was definitely an air of female reserve toward males, and women held themselves back, didn't speak up. My daughter also went to a co-ed university. According to her, female students ended up preparing lunches for club activities throughout the year. Computers had just come out around that time. Again they took it for granted that men were more gifted as far as the new technology was concerned. So men learned the skills, but equally gifted women had no chance to nurture their talent.

You can say the same sort of thing about an all men's school. They still have to do the so-called feminine tasks. Someone has to do it. But, if women were there, making sandwiches would automatically become their task. Inevitably, men lose the opportunity to learn basic culinary skills. But just as women have different talents, so do men, and whether you're man or woman doesn't matter. Some people like cooking, some may possess a talent for managing things. Depending upon the circumstances, each of us may miss the chance to nurture an individual talent. I concluded that it's not a bad idea to live once in our lifetime in an all-men or all-women environment. It took me a while, though, to realize that my Tsuda experience wasn't really a negative one, but a beneficial one.

**MW**: When did you come to realize it?

**OM**: In my forties.

**MW**: When you lived in the United States, then.

**OM**: Yes. From the time I resided here to the time I returned to Japan, I studied at University of Wisconsin and felt exactly the way I described earlier. I was an art student then. Particularly when machines were involved, men took charge of maintaining them, tightening bolts, etc. What interested me, though, was the fact that I was able to witness both masculine and feminine ways of expressing things in a mixed-gender setting, and recognize that there was a gender difference. Co-education didn't present itself negatively then. The possibility that a co-ed institution might stifle women's abilities didn't occur to me. It was only after I returned to Japan that my perspective changed somewhat.

**MW**: Were there male graduate students in the program you taught in in Japan?

**OM**: Oh, yes. The ratio was fifty-fifty, I think. You see quite a few male students in graduate school, even in literature. We read world literature in translation, French, German, and ancient classical works.

**MW**: Did male students speak up more?

**OM**: Not necessarily, but I noticed that there was no engagement between male and female peers; they were extremely courteous to one another. I said to myself, They're so young and full of life, how can they be content with such superficial discussions? My college days were very different. In a poverty-stricken postwar Japan, the only thing we could do was talk. We used to stay up till four or five in the morning every single day. I really think those times together were invaluable to me. Twenty years later, it was my observation of the class I taught that dialogues between men and women were neither deep nor substantial. After the 1980s more and more women began to have full-fledged jobs. My female friends are predominantly scholars and editors. And in this group all-women college graduates really stand out.

**MW**: They're articulate, aren't they.

**OM**: Yes, they certainly are.

**MW**: Are they being courageous or is it that they don't let things bother them? For example, some women tend to fall into this trap: they're overcome by the anxiety that just because men say something one way, women should say it differently, that is, like women.

**OM**: Right. It's not so much that my female friends don't let things bother them, but they aren't aware that they have to say things any differently. Those who have had only co-ed experience know exactly what kind of reaction to expect from men. I think they know almost physically that it's an advantage to say things differently. I must say they do far better at handling the opposite sex than we non-co-ed grads do.

**MW**: Do you think so?

**OM**: I feel it. Women who speak aggressively are almost always women's college graduates. I made that discovery late in my life. I didn't home in on that when I was at Tsuda.

**MW**: Tell me something about the study group you attended with male students from other institutions.

**OM**: It was lots of fun. Opposite sexes attract, you know. There was a sense of liberation, and our postwar generation felt that from then on we didn't have to suppress our voice any more. It was OK to say freely what was on our minds. That played a crucial role in my life. We had to put up with the war and that prohibited us from saying certain things. My painful memories of those war years were still very vivid when I entered Tsuda in 1949. We often talked in the dorm about the horrendous war that had ended only four years earlier.

**MW**: I was pleasantly surprised that Moriyama Mayumi, the first female ever to hold the position of Chief Cabinet Secretary, is also a Tsuda graduate.

**OM**: Ambassador Akamatsu Ryōko who orchestrated the passage of the Equal Opportunity Employment law is also from Tsuda. It passed when she was the director general of the Women's Bureau at the Ministry of Labor. However, the idea for the law was already circulating at the time thanks to Fujita Taki, another Tsuda graduate, who did the ground work for the legislation. She was one of the original Tsuda students taught by Umeko. The passage of the law was to a certain extent a dream come true for Umeko and her followers. Since I came to this country, I've often heard the catch phrase: "People make a difference." In the final analysis, it is people who change things. As the slogan indicates, people's different dreams are superimposed on each other, and although some of the dreams may be slightly off the mark, they connect continuously.

**MW**: When you look back on yours and other women's lives, might you say that women's lives have always been feminist by definition?

**OM**: My main position is that I want to remain natural (*shizentai*). That might be the major characteristic of Japanese culture. The West believes in humanism. Man is the lord of creation, they say. The Western concept of the world doesn't really include trees, animals, rocks, etc. I don't think that's the case with Japanese culture. Japanese have held the notion that every being, every existence, in this world is linked with each other, and as such, humans are just one part of the whole picture. Environmental pollution is being highlighted nowadays, and in my mind it is the by-product of this humanism. What I mean by a wish to remain natural also has something to do with how my genes work, I suppose. They possess the ability to find what's good for me. It seems I'm intuitively faithful to what my genes dictate to me.

**MW**: Ancient Japanese were naturalists like that at the time of *Manyōshu*. The celebration of life was the key.

**OM**: That's right. That's how I've lived so far. I really haven't given much thought to how I live.

**MW**: What do you do, though, if you wish to live naturally, when you encounter all kinds of obstacles along the way?

**OM**: I think I'm so absent-minded that I often don't notice things. I think this has worked for me.

**MW**: On the other hand, your wish to live naturally has given people a lot of opportunity to criticize you.

**OM**: They certainly have, very much so.

**MW**: Has this been true since you were very young?

**OM**: Yes. The situation didn't improve much even after the end of the war. The enormous sense of liberation I felt when I entered Tsuda was a good break for me.

**MW**: After four years of dorm life. . .

**OM**: I got married soon afterward. I met my husband during my first year there. He belonged to a study group of which my Tsuda classmate's brother was also a member. I was one of the first students under the new education system, my husband one of the last of the old system. He went on to Tokyo University. When I met him, he was a junior at the University. He's two years older than me, and we got married seven years after we met.

**MW**: Were you confident that he would provide you a life of "living naturally"?

**OM**: Not really.

**MW**: You were still too young?

**OM**: I felt very insecure about it all. I had lots of doubts about marriage, too. I said to myself, Once in marriage, the man will do and say what he damn well pleases. I wasn't so sure that I could live the way I wanted to live.

**MW**: No more *Manyōshu* spirit; you felt you would be placed in the midst of a samurai culture.

**OM**: Yes. I was a suspicious type, and didn't trust that things would work out in a marriage. As a literary girl I grew up reading only literature. It's my belief that from ancient times, literature has been written to insure human freedom. I never really attribute much importance to common sense.

**MW**: Your parents represented a new type of couple. You had very good role models.

**OM**: At the time I didn't know it. Much, much later I realized that my family was rather eccentric. I don't think they were ordinary people. Japan still has elements of a matrilineal system, where mothers hold power. That means women occupy a powerful position inside the home.

**MW**: On the other hand, Japanese society still incorporates the samurai-based *danson johi* (superiority of men, inferiority of women) that originated in neo-Confucianism. There's ambivalence. Society does not really want to recognize women's power, but has no choice but to do so. That is a saving grace for Japanese women, I think.

**OM**: I see it as a case of *tatemae* (appearance/rhetoric) vs. *honne* (true, private feelings/opinions). What really surprised me when I came to this country in late 1950s was that although the overwhelming majority of American women managed the home, men still controlled the domestic economy. By contrast, it was women in Japan who held economic power inside the home. Wives gave husbands allowances out of their monthly salaries. That was the norm. Wives begging their husbands to get this and that didn't happen in Japan. My discovery that married American women didn't have economic power made sense of the [early twentieth-century] feminist movement, including the subsequent Women's Liberation Movement [in the 1970s]. I can see why the movements gathered strength. I must say that Japanese women were substantially very powerful.

**MW**: Things are still tough for Japanese women in the public domain, though.

**OM**: When I look around, American women look very strong

because they articulate what they have to say.

**MW**: However, there is a machoism in this country that's very different from that of samurai chauvinism.

**OM**: My first impression of the United States was that it's very masculine. When I first came here—I don't know how things are now—men always paid for dining out and shopping. If a couple was eating out, the waiter or waitress always handed the bill to the man. When I returned to Japan and went to a restaurant, I immediately noticed that the bill went straight to the woman as long as the couple was identified as married.

**MW**: How interesting.

**OM**: At department stores, clerks pitch directly to the wives. Husbands just stand around. In Japan, marketing targets women.

**MW**: May I go back to *tatemae* and *honne*? It is often said that Japanese do not say what is really on their minds. In contrast, Americans say things forthrightly.

**OM**: Maybe it was true in the 1950s, but I don't think it's true now. Americans may be more reserved than the Japanese! I sometimes think it's Japanese who expose everything in the end. Americans follow logic, and pick and choose what information to withhold or divulge. In Japan, people operate by a sixth sense. The strategies and approaches may be different, but we aren't that different from each other. Logic-centered Western culture has led to lots of success. I wonder how things will proceed in the future. It appears that so-called Western logic has reached an impasse. The phenomenon is not confined to the United States, it's worldwide. I also think it's an issue for humankind, or rather for the earth. We're all in this together, organic creatures as well as inorganic matter. Ozone and even pebbles. A way out of the impasse can be achieved only by artistic sensitivity—I don't mean just literature. Art is an expression of the cutting edge, expressing sentiments that do not sit well with you, emotions that are unfathomable. Philosophers analyze and synthesize, while literature bypasses that process to speak about things that are weird and painful, things we aren't really sure about. We've talked about being natural. I've stuck by that code. If someone categorizes that way of life as feminist, it's fine with me. Other feminists might find it disconcerting. I recognize different perspectives and different ways of reading a literary text. It's totally up to the reader. I am a living creature, I am what I am, putting down what I feel. This is the way I want to continue writing.

**MW**: I experience this strongly as I read your work. I consider it the central message of your work.

**OM**: Writing is beyond one's small individual effort. Some incomprehensible, intertwined matrix of lives is within me, and glimpses of those lives try to fly out of me, and that's when I start writing. In a way what empowers me to produce has a lot do with the reader response.

Thank you very much.

**MW**: It has been my pleasure.

# Bibliography

Unless otherwise indicated, the place of publication of all Japanese books cited below is Tokyo.

Abel, Elizabeth, Marianne Hirsch, and Elizabeth Langland, eds. *The Voyage In: Fictions of Female Development*. Hanover, NH: Published for Dartmouth College by University Press of New England, 1983.

Aoki Yayoi. "An Interview" and "The Anatomy of Dependence and the Family-Emperor System," in *Broken Silence: Voices of Japanese Feminism*. Sandra Buckley. Berkeley, CA: University of California Press, 1997, pp. 1–28.

Ariga, Chieko. "Text Versus Commentary: Struggles over the Cultural Meanings of 'Woman'" in *The Woman's Hand: Gender and Theory in Japanese Women's Writing*, eds. Paul Gordon Schalow and Janet A. Walker. Stanford, CA: Stanford University Press, 1996, pp. 352–381.

———. "Who's Afraid of Amino Kiku? Gender Conflict and the Literary Canon in Japanese Literature," *International Journal of Social Education*, vol. 6, no. 1 (Spring 1991): 95–113.

Barthes, Roland. *Empire of Signs,* trans. Richard Howard. New York: Hill and Wang, 1982.

Ben-Ari, Eyal, Brian Moeran, and James Valentine, eds. *Unwrapping Japan: Society and Culture in Anthropological Perspective*. Honolulu: University of Hawaii Press, 1990.

Bowring, Richard. "The Female Hand in Heian Japan," in *The Female Autograph: Theory and Practice of Autobiography from the Tenth to the Twentieth Century*, ed. Donna C. Stanton. Chicago: University of Chicago Press, 1987.

———. *Murasaki Shikibu: Her Diary and Poetic Memoirs*. Princeton, NJ: Princeton University Press, 1982.

Braham, Jean. *Interpreting Contemporary American Literary Autobiographies by Women*. New York: Teachers College Press, 1995.

Brown, Janice. *Hayashi Fumiko: I Saw a Pale Horse and Selected Poems from Diary of a Vagabond*, trans. and with Introduction. Ithaca, NY: The Cornell East Asia Series, 1997.

———. "Once There Was a Woman: Revisioning Gender in the Poetic Writings of Ōba Minako." Paper presented at the 1996 Annual Meeting of the Association for Asian Studies, Honolulu, Hawaii.

———. "Reconstructing the Female Subject: Japanese Women Writers and the *Shishōsetsu*," *British Columbia Asian Review*, no. 7 (Winter 1993–1994): 16–35.

———. "Re-Writing the Maternal: 'Bad' Mothers in Writing of Hayashi Fumiko." *Proceedings of Mothers in Japanese Literature*. University of British Columbia, Department of Asian Studies, 1996, pp. 369–396.

Buckley, Jerome Hamilton. *Season of Youth: The Bildungsroman from Dickens to Golding*. Cambridge, MA: Harvard University Press, 1974.

Buckley, Sandra. *Broken Silence: Voices of Japanese Feminism*. Berkeley, CA: University of California Press, 1997.

Cameron, Deborah. *Feminism and Linguistic Theory*, 2d ed. New York: St. Martin's Press, 1992.

Chan, Wing-Tsuit. *A Source Book in Chinese Philosophy*, translated and compiled. Princeton, NJ: Princeton University Press, 1969.

Chodorow, Nancy. *The Reproduction of Mothering: Psychoanalysis and the Sociology of Gender*. Berkeley, CA: University of California Press, 1978.

Copeland, Rebecca. *The Sound of the Wind: The Life and Works of Uno Chiyo*. Honolulu: University of Hawaii Press, 1992.

Dan Kazuo. *Kataku no hito* (The Sufferer). Shinchōsha, 1975.

de Bary, Brett. "Introduction" to *Origins of Modern Japanese Literature* by Karatani Kōjin, ed. and trans. Brett de Bary. Durham, NC, and London: Duke University Press, 1993.

Dooley, D. J. "Some Uses and Mutations of the Picaresque," in *Dalhousie Review*, vol. 37 (1957–1958): 363–377.

Egusa, Mitsuko, and Urushida Kazuyo, eds. *Onna ga yomu Nihon kindai bungaku* (Women Reading the Modern Japanese Literature). Shin'yōsha, 1992.

Ellmann, Mary. *Thinking About Women*. New York: Harcourt Brace Jovanovich, 1968.

Fetterley, Judith. *The Resisting Reader: A Feminist Approach to American Fiction*. Bloomington, IN: Indiana University Press, 1978.

Field, Norma. *The Splendor of Longing in the Tale of Genji*. Princeton, NJ: Princeton University Press, 1987.

Flax, Jane. "Postmodernism and Gender Relations in Feminist Theory," chapter 2 in *Feminism/Postmodernism*, ed. Linda J. Nicholson, with Introduction. New York and London: Routledge, 1990.

Fowler, Edward. *The Rhetoric of Confession: Shishōsetsu in Early Twentieth-Century Japanese Fiction*. Berkeley, CA: University of California Press, 1988.

Fraiman, Susan. *Unbecoming Women: British Women Writers and the Novel of Development*. New York: Columbia University Press, 1993.

Frohock, W. M. "The Idea of the Picaresque," *Yearbook of Comparative and General Literature*, vol. 16 (1967).

Fujii, James. *Complicit Fictions: The Subject in the Modern Japanese Prose Narrative*. Berkeley, CA: University of California Press, 1993.

Furuki Yoshiko. *The White Plum, A Biography of Ume Tsuda: Pioneer in the Higher Education of Japanese Women*. New York: Weatherhill, 1991.

Gessel, Van C. *The Sting of Life: Four Contemporary Japanese Novelists*. New York: Columbia University Press, 1989.

Gilbert, Sandra M., and Susan Gubar, eds. *The Madwoman in the Attic: The Women Writer and the Nineteenth-Century Literary Imagination*. New Haven, CT: Yale University Press, 1979.

———. *No Man's Land: The Place of the Women Writer in the Twentieth Century*, vol. 1, *The War of the Words*. New Haven, CT: Yale University Press, 1988.

———. *No Man's Land: The Place of the Woman Writer in the Twentieth Century*, vol. 2, *Sexchanges*. New Haven, CT: Yale University Press, 1989.

Gould, Lois. *Subject to Change*. New York: Farrar, Straus & Gioux, 1988.

Guber, Susan. "Mother, maiden and the marriage of death: Women writers and an ancient myth" (lower-case letters in the original title). *Women's Studies*, vol. 6, no. 3 (1979): 303–316.

Hayashi Fumiko. Hōrōki (The Diary of a Vagabond). *Hayashi Fumiko zenshū,* vol. 2. Shinchōsha, 1951.

Heilbrun, Carolyn. *Reinventing Womanhood*. New York: W. W. Norton, 1979.

———. "Sayers, Lord Peter, and Harriet Vane at Oxford" in *Hamlet's Mother and Other Women*. New York: Ballantine Books, 1990, pp. 301–310.

———. *Writing a Woman's Life*. New York: W. W. Norton, 1988.

Heilman, Robert B. "Variations on the Picaresque (Felix Drull)," *Sewanee Review*, vol. 66 (1958).

Hewitt, Marsha A. "Illusions of Freedom: The Regressive Implications of 'Postmodernism,'" in *The Socialist Register 1993—Real Problems, False Solutions*, eds. Ralph Miliband and Leo Panitch. London: Merlin Press, 1993.

Hirsch, Marianne. "Mothers and Daughters," a review essay, *Signs: Journal of Women in Culture and Society*, vol. 7, no. 1, (1981): 200–222

———. *The Mother/Daughter Plot: Narrative, Psychoanalysis, Feminism*. Bloomington, IN: Indiana University Press, 1989.

Hodgson, Godfrey. "Mysteries, Sacred and Profane," a review of *Dorothy Sayers: Her Life and Soul*, by Barbara Reynolds London (Sydney and Auckland: Hodder & Stoughton, 1993). *Washington Post Book World*, August 22, 1993.

Hutcheon, Linda. *A Poetics of Postmodernism: History, Theory, Fiction*. New York: Routledge, 1988.

Ide Sachiko. "Excerpts from *Women's Language, Men's Language: First Person Pronouns*," *in Broken Silence: Voices of Japanese Feminism*, Sandra Buckley. Berkeley, CA: University of California Press, 1997, pp. 48–50.

Imai Yasuko. "The Emergence of the Japanese *Shufu*: Why a *Shufu* Is More Than a 'Housewife,'" *U.S.-Japan Women's Journal*, English Supplement, no. 6 (1994): 44–65

Irigaray, Luce. "And the One Doesn't Stir Without the Other," *Signs: Journal of Women in Culture and Society*, vol. 7, no. 1 (Autumn 1981): 60–67.

Iwao, Sumiko. *The Japanese Woman: Traditional Image and Changing Reality*. Cambridge, MA.: Harvard University Press, 1993.

Kaler, Anne K. *The Picara: From Hera to Fantasy Heroine*. Bowling Green, OH: Bowling Green State University Popular Press, 1991.

Kanazumi Fumiko. "An Interview," in *Broken Silence: Voices of Japanese Feminism*, Sandra Buckley. Berkeley, CA: University of California Press, 1997, pp. 70–81.

Kaplan, E. Ann. "Is the Gaze Male?" in *Powers of Desire: The Politics of Sexuality*, eds. Ann Anitow, Christine Stansell, and Sharon Thompson. New York: Monthly Review Press, 1983, pp. 309–327.

Karatani Kōjin. *Origins of Modern Japanese Literature*, ed. and trans. Brett de Bary, with Introduction. Durham, NC and London: Duke University Press, 1993.

Kitada Sachie. "Contemporary Japanese Feminist Literary Criticism," *U.S.-Japan Women's Journal*, English Supplement, no. 7 (1994): 72–97.

Komashaku Kimi. *Murasaki Shikibu no Messēji* (Murasaki Shikibu's Message). Asahi Shimbunsha, 1991.

Kōra Rumiko. "An Interview," in *Broken Silence: Voices of Japanese Feminism*, Sandra Buckley. Berkeley, CA: University of California Press, 1997, pp. 104–119.

Le Guin, Ursula K. *Dancing at the Edge of the World: Thoughts on Words, Women, Places.* New York: Harper & Row, 1989.

Lerner, Gerda. *The Creation of Feminist Consciousness.* New York: Oxford University Press, 1993.

———. *The Creation of Patriarchy.* New York: Oxford University Press, 1986.

———, ed. Introduction in *The Female Experience.* New York: Oxford University Press, 1977.

Lummis, Charles Douglas, and Satomi Nakajima with Kumiko Fujimura-Fanselow and Atsuko Kameda, "The Changing Portrait of Japanese Men," in *Japanese Women: New Feminist Perspectives on the Past, Present, and Future*, eds. Kumiko Fujimura-Fanselow and Atsuko Kameda. New York: The Feminist Press, 1995, pp. 229–246.

Marcus, Jane. "Art and Anger," *Feminist Studies*, vol. 4, no. 1 (February 1978): 69–98.

Marcus, Marvin. *Paragons of the Ordinary: The Biographical Literature of Mori Ōgai.* Honolulu: University of Hawaii Press, 1993.

Márquez, Gabriel Garciá. *The Autumn of the Patriarch*, trans. Gregory Rabassa. New York and London: Harper & Row, 1976.

Matsui Yayori. "Asian Migrant Women in Japan," in *Broken Silence: Voices of Japanese Feminism*, Sandra Buckley. Berkeley, CA: University of California Press, 1977, pp. 143–155.

Miki Taku. "Dokusho teidan" (A Three-Person Roundtable Discussion on Reading Literature), *Bungei* (March 1981): 272–286.

Miyoshi, Masao. *As We Saw Them: The First Japanese Embassy to the United States (1860).* Berkeley, CA: University of California Press, 1979.

———. *Off Center: Power and Culture Relations between Japan and the United States.* Cambridge and London: Harvard University Press, 1991.

———. "Women's Short Stories in Japan," *Mānoa: A Pacific Journal of International Writing*, vol. 3, no. 2 (Fall 1991): 33–39.

Mizuta Noriko. "Mori no sekai: Ōba Minako ni okeru monogatari no genkei" (The World of a Forest: Ōba Minako's Prototype of a Tale),

Commentary (*kaisetsu*) to *Ōba Minako zenshū*, vol. 6., Kōdansha, 1991, pp. 427–436.

Monnet, Livia. "Jealousy: Tsushima Yūko's 'The Chrysanthemum Beetle,'" in *The Woman's Hand: Gender and Theory in Japanese Women's Writing*, eds. Paul Gordon Schalow and Janet A. Walker. Stanford, CA: Stanford University Press, 1996, pp. 382–424.

———. "The Politics of Miscegenation: The Discourse of Fantansy in 'Fusehime,'" *Japan Forum*, vol. 5, no. 1 (April 1993): 53–74.

Moers, Ellen. *Literary Women: The Great Writers*. New York: Oxford University Press, 1985.

Mossberg, Barbara Ann Clarke. "Reconstruction in the House of Art: Emily Dickinson's 'I Never Had a Mother,'" in *The Lost Tradition: Mothers and Daughters in Literature*, eds. Cathy N. Davidson and E. M. Broner. New York: Frederick Ungar Publishing Co., 1980.

Mulvey, Laura. *Visual and Other Pleasures*. Houndmills, Basingstoke, Hampshire: Macmillan, 1989.

Munich, Adrienne. "Notorious Signs, Feminist Criticism and Literary Tradition," in *Making a Difference: Feminist Literary Criticism*, eds. Gayle Greene and Coppelia Kahn. London: Routledge, 1988.

Nemoto, Tachibana Reiko. "Hiroshima in Ōba Minako's *Urashimasō*: Desire and Self-Destructiveness," *Journal of the Association of Teachers of Japanese*, vol. 30, no. 1 (April 1996): 1–21.

Niwa Akiko. "The Formation of the Myth of Motherhood," *U.S.-Japan Women's Journal*, English Supplement, no. 4 (1993): 70–82.

Niwa Fumio. "Annoucement of the 1982 Tanizaki Junichirō Prize," *Chūō Kōronsha* (November 1982): 359–360.

Nobbe, Susan Howe. *Wilhelm Meister and His English Kinsmen*. New York: Columbia University Press, 1930.

Nolte, Sharon H., and Sally Ann Hastings. "The Meiji State's Policy Toward Women, 1890–1910," in *Recreating Japanese Women, 1600–1945*, ed. Gail Lee Bernstein. Berkeley, CA: University of California Press, 1991, pp. 151–174.

Ōba Minako. "Akai mangetsu" (A Blood-Red Moon), in *Shinchō* (June 1996): 198–205.

———. *Akutagawa-shō zenshū* (Collected Works on Akutagawa Prize), vol. 8. *Bungei Shunjū*, 1982, pp. 573–578.

———. "Bōshi" (A Hat) in *Bōshi no kiita hanashi* (The Stories a Hat Has Heard). Kōdansha, 1983.

———. "Candle Fish" (Rōsoku uo) in *Unmapped Territories*, trans. Yukiko Tanaka. Seattle, WA: *Women in Translation*, 1991, pp. 18–38.

———. "Dansei-tachi hotta haka-ana" (A Grave Men Have Dug for Themselves) in *Ōba Minako zenshū*, vol. 10. Kōdansha, 1991, pp. 407–410.

———. *Funakui-mushi* (The Ship-Eating Worms) in *Ōba Minako zenshū*, vol. 2, Kōdansha, 1991.

———. *Garakuta hakubutsukan* (A Junk Museum) in *Ōba Minako zenshū*, vol. 4. Kōdansha, 1991.

———. "Genji Monogatari no omoide" (My Memories Concerning *The Tale of Genji*," in *Ōba Minako zenshū*, vol. 10. Kōdansha, 1991, pp. 209–211.

———. *Katachi mo naku* (Amorphous). Kawade Shobō, 1982.

———. *Kiri no tabi* (A Journey Through the Mist). *Ōba Minako zenshū*, vol. 6. Kōdansha, 1991.

———. "Kōfuku no fūfu" (A Happily Married Couple). *Onna no dansei-ron* (Discussion on Men by Women). Chūō Kōronsha, 1982.

———. *Mai e, mai e, katatsumuri* (Dance, Snail, Dance, into the Sky). Fukube Shoten, 1984.

———. *Mukashi onna ga ita* (Once There Was a Woman), chapter 26, trans. Paul Gordon Schalow, in *The Woman's Hand: Gender and Theory in Japanese Women's Writing,* eds. Paul Gordon Schalow and Janet A. Walker. Stanford, CA: Stanford University Press, 1996, pp. 34–38.

———. *Mukashi onna ga ita* (Once There Was a Woman). Shinchōsha, 1994.

———. *Naku tori no* (Birds Crying). Kōdansha, 1985. Partial tranlsation of chapter 1, trans. Michiko Niikuni Wilson and Michael K. Wilson, in *Chicago Review*, vol. 39, no. 3 and 4 (1993): 186–195.

———. "Nani ga watashi o ugokashite iru ka" (What Is Propelling Me?), *Chūō Kōronsha*, (November 1982): 362–366.

———. *Ōba Minako zenshū* (Complete Works of Ōba Minako). 10 vols. Kōdansha, 1990–1991.

———. "Ōba Minako-san ni kiku" (Interviewing Ōba Minako). *Shūkan dokusho-jin* (7 June 1968).

———. *Ōjo no namida* (The Tears of a Princess). Shinchōsha, 1988.

———. *Onna no dansei-ron* (Discussions on Men by Women). Chūō Kōronsha, 1982.

———. "Onna no hyōgen, otoko no hyōgen" (Women's Expression, Men's Expression). *Waseda bungaku* (November 1985): 8–18.

———. *Oregon yumejūya* (Ten Nights of Oregon Dreams). Shūeisha-bunko, 1984.

———. "The Pale Fox" (Aoi Kitsune), trans. Stephen W. Kohl, in *The Shōwa Anthology: Modern Japanese Short Stories 1924–1984,* eds. Van C. Gessel and Tomone Matsumoto. New York: Kōdansha, 1985.

———. "The Sea Change" (Tankō), trans. John Bester. *Japanese Literature Today*, no. 5 (1980): 12–19.

———. "The Smile of a Mountain Witch" (Yamamba no bishō), in *Japanese Women Writers: Twentieth Century Short Fiction*, trans. and eds. Noriko Mizuta Lippit and Kyoko Iriye Selden. Armonk, NY: M. E. Sharpe, 1991, pp. 194–206.

———. "The Three Crabs" (Sanbiki no kani), trans. and eds. Yukiko Tanaka and Elizabeth Hanson, in *This Kind of Women: Ten Stories by Japanese Women Writers, 1960–1976*. Stanford, CA: Stanford University Press, 1982, pp. 87–114.

———. *Tsuda Umeko*. Asahi Shimbunsha, 1990.

———. *Tsuga no yume* (The Dream of a Hemlock). Bungei Shunjū, 1971.

———. "Umi ni yuragu ito," in *Umi ni yuragu ito* (A Thread Swaying in the Sea). Kōdansha, 1989), pp. 137–164.

———. *Urashimasō* (Urashima Plant). 2 vols. Kōdansha-bunko, 1984.

———. *Urashimasō* (Urashima Plant), trans. Ōba Yū. Sakado-shi, Japan: Center for Inter-Cultural Studies and Education, Josai University, 1995.

———. "*Urashimasō* ni yosete" (Concerning Urashimasō). *Ōba Minako zenshū*, vol. 10. Kōdansha, 1991, pp. 102–104.

———. "Yamamba no bishō" (The *Yamamba*'s Final Smile). *Ōba Minako zenshū*, vol. 3. Kōdansha, 1991.

———. *Yawarakai feminizumu e* (Toward Gentle Feminism), a collection of interviews with nine Japanese women, ed. Oba Minako. Seidosha, 1992.

———. *Yōbaidō monogatari* (Tales of Yōbaidō). Chūō Kōronsha, 1984.

———. "Without Beginning, Without End" (Hajime mo naku, owari mo naku), trans. Paul Gordon Schalow, in *The Woman's Hand: Gender and Theory in Japanese Women's Writing*, eds. Paul Gordon Schalow and Janet A. Walker. Stanford, CA: Stanford University Press, 1996, pp. 19–40.

Ōba Minako and Akiyama Ken. "Monogatari e—Genji monogatari to no ōkan" (Two Tales: Traveling Between Now and *The Tale of Genji*). *Kokubungaku* (January 1990): 138–158.

Ōba Minako and Kōno Taeko. "Bungaku o gaisuru mono" (Things That Harm Literature). *Bungakukai* (July 1987): 138–158.

Ōba Minako and Ōba Yū. *Kaoru ki no uta-haha to musume no ōfuku shokan* (The Poetry of a Fragrant Tree: Correspondence Between Mother and Daughter). Chūō Kōronsha, 1992.

Ōba Minako and Takeda Katsuhiko. "Yojō bungaku towazugatari" (Confessions of Literature's Implicit Feelings). *Chishiki*, vol. 52 (April 1987): 314–321.

Ōba Minako and Yamamoto Michiko. "Naze shōsetsu o kakuka—Ikoku de oboeta bungakuteki shōdō" (Why Write Novels? A Literary Impact

We've Encountered in Foreign Lands) *Bungakukai* (April 1973): 186–204.

Ogata Akiko and Nagata Michiko, eds. *Feminizumu ryōran: fuyu no jidai e no hōka* (The Profusion of Feminism: Firing at the Era of Winter). Shakai Hyōronsha, 1990.

Okada, Richard H. *Figures of Resistance: Language, Poetry and Narrating in The Tale of Genji and Other Mid-Heian Texts*. Durham, NC: Duke University Press, 1991.

Orbaugh, Sharalyn. "The Body in Contemporary Japanese Women's Fiction," in *The Woman's Hand: Gender and Theory in Japanese Women's Writing*, eds. Paul Gordon Schalow and Janet A. Walker. Stanford, CA: Stanford University Press, 1996, pp. 119–164.

Ostriker, Alicia Suskin. *Stealing the Language: The Emergence of Women's Poetry in America*. Boston: Beacon Press, 1986.

Ozaki Hideki, "Sengo besuto serā monogatari" (The Tale of the Postwar Bestsellers), *Shūkan Jānaru* (7 August 1966): 35–39.

Patner, Myra Mensh. "Still Crazy About Anne: The Green Gables Novel Going Strong at 83." *Washington Post*, 12 September 1992: C4.

Rich, Adrienne. *Of Woman Born*: *Motherhood as Experience and Institution*. New York: W. W. Norton, 1976.

———. *On Lies, Secrets, and Silence: Selected Prose 1966–1978*. New York: W. W. Norton, 1979.

———. *What Is Found There: Notebooks on Poetry and Politics*. New York: W. W. Norton, 1993.

Robertson, Jennifer. "The Shingaku Woman," in *Recreating Japanese Women*, ed. Gail Lee Bernstein. Berkeley, CA: University of California Press, 1991, pp. 88–107.

Rowbotham, Shelia. "The Trouble with 'Patriarchy' " in *The Woman Question: Readings on the Subordination of Women*, ed. May Evans. Oxford, England: Fontana, 1982, pp. 73–79.

Rose, Barbara. *Tsuda Umeko and Women's Education in Japan*. New Haven, CT, and London: Yale University Press, 1992.

Rukeyser, Muriel. "Myth," quoted by Marianne Hirsch in *The Mother/Daughter Plot: Narrative, Psychoanalysis, Feminism*. Bloomington, IN: Indiana University Press, 1989, p.1.

Russ, Joanna. *How to Suppress Women's Writing*. Austin, TX: University of Texas Press, 1983.

———. *To Write Like a Woman: Essays in Feminism and Science Fiction*. Bloomington: Indiana University Press, 1995.

Saegusa Kazuko. *Ren'ai shōsetsu no kansei* (Pitfalls of a Romantic Novel). Seidosha, 1991.

———. *Sayonara otoko no jidai* (Goodbye, the Era of Man). Jinmon Shoin, 1984.

Schalow, Paul Gordon, and Janet A. Walker, eds. *The Woman's Hand: Gender and Theory in Japanese Women's Writing*. Stanford, CA: Stanford University Press, 1996.

Shimao Toshio. *The Sting of Death and Other Stories*, trans. Kathryn Sparling. Ann Arbor, MI: Center for Japanese Studies, 1985.

Shinozuka Sumiko. "Spiritual Exchange Between a Woman of the Past and a Woman of the Present—Tsuhima Yūko's 'Chased by the Light of the Night' (Yoru no hikari ni owarete) and 'Wakefulness at Night' (Yoru no nezame)." Paper presented at the 1996 Annual Meeting of the Association for Asian Studies on the Pacific Coast.

Showalter, Elaine. "Little Women: The American Female Myth," in *Sister's Choice: Tradition and Change in American Women's Writing*. New York and London: Oxford University Press, 1991, pp. 42–64.

———. *Sexual Anarchy: Gender and Culture at the Fin de Siècle*. New York: Penguin Books, 1990.

Smith, Sidonie. *A Poetics of Women's Autobiography: Marginality and the Fictions of Self-Representation*. Bloomington, IN: Indiana University Press, 1987.

———. *Subjectivity, Identity, And the Body: Women's Autobiographical Practices in the Tweneith Century*. Bloomington, IN: Indiana University Press, 1993.

Suleiman, Susan Rubin. "(Re)Writing the Body: The Politics and Poetics of Female Eroticism," in *The Female Body in Western Culture: Contemporary Perspectives*, ed. Susan Rubin Suleiman. Cambridge, MA: Harvard University Press, 1986.

Suzuki, Tomi. *Narrating the Self: Fictions of Japanese Modernity*. Stanford, CA: Stanford University Press, 1996.

Swales, Martin. *The German Bildungsroman from Wieland to Hesse* Princeton, NJ: Princeton University Press, 1978.

Tajima Yōko. "A Rereading of *Snow Country* from Komako's Point of View," *U.S.-Japan Women's Journal*, English Supplement, no. 4 (January 1993): 26–48. The original Japanese version in Egusa Mitsuko and Urushida, eds. *Onna ga yomu Nihon kindai bungaku* (Women Reading the Modern Japanese Literature). (Shin'yōsha, 1992), pp. 149–180.

Taki Kōji. *Tennō nō shōzō* (The Portrait of the Emperor). Iwanami Shinsho, 1988.

*Tales of Ise: Lyrical Episodes from Tenth-Century Japan*, trans. Helen Craig McCullough, with Introduction and notes. Stanford, CA: Stanford University Press, 1968.

*The Tao of the Tao Te Ching*, trans. Michael LaFargue, with commentary. New York: State University of New York, 1992.

Thurer, Shari L. *The Myth of Motherhood: How Culture Reinvents the Good Mother*. New York: Penguin Books, 1994.

Tomioka Taeko. *Fuji no koromo ni asa no fusuma* (Wisteria Garments and Linen Bedding). Chūō Kōrōnsha, 1984.

———. *Hyōgen no fūkei* (The Scenaries of Expression). Kōdansha, 1989.

———. *Onna kodomo no hanran* (Rebellions by Women and Children). Chūō Kōronsha, 1981.

Tomioka Taeko and Mizuta Noriko. "Onna to hyōgen no kiro" (At the Crossroads of Women and Articulation), in *New Feminism Review*, vol. 2, *Onna to hyōgen—feminizumu no genzai* (Women's Expression: The Current Situation of Feminism), ed. Mizuta Noriko. Gakuyo Shobō, 1991, pp. 5–29.

Trilling, Lionel. *Beyond Culture: Essays on Literature and Learning*. New York and London: Harcourt Brace Jovanovich, 1965.

Tsuruta, Kinya. *Kawabata Yasunari no geijutsu: junsui to kyūsai* (Kawabata Yasunari's Art: Purity and Salvation). Meiji Shoin, 1981.

———, ed. *Shiga Naoya's a Dark Night's Passing*. Singapore: Department of Asian Studies, National University of Singapore, 1996.

Turner, Victor. *The Ritual Process: Structure and Anti-Structure*. Ithaca, NY: Cornell University Press, 1969.

Ueno Chizuko. "Are the Japanese Feminine? Some Problems of Japanese Feminism in Its Cultural Context," in *Broken Silence: Voices of Japanese Feminism*, Sandra Buckley. Berkeley, CA: University of California Press, 1997, pp. 293–301.

———. "The Rise of Feminist Criticism," *Japanese Book News*, no. 2 (1993): 5, 20.

Ueno Chizuko, Ogura Chikako, and Tomioka Taeko, eds. *Danryū bungaku-ron* (Discussions on Male Literature). Chikuma Shobō, 1992.

Uno, Kathleen S. "Women and Changes in the Household Division of Labor," in *Recreating Japanese Women*, 1600–1945, ed. Gail Lee Bernstein. Berkeley, CA: University of California Press, 1991, pp. 17–41.

Valentine, James. "On the Borderlines: The Significance of Marginality in Japnese Society" in *Unwrapping Japan: Society and Culture in Anthropological Perspective*, eds. Eyal Ben-Ari, Brian Moeran, and James Valentine. Honolulu: University of Hawaii Press, 1990, pp. 36–57.

Vernon, Victoria V. *Daughters of the Moon: Wish, Will, and Special constraint in Fiction by Modern Japanese Women*. Berkeley, CA: Institute of East Asian Studies, University of California, 1988.

Walker, Janet A. "A Naturalist Quest for the Sexual Self," *in Shiga Naoya's A Dark Night's Passing*, ed. Kinya Tsuruta. Singapore: Department of

Japanese Studies, National University of Singapore, 1996, pp. 157–196.

Wilson, Michiko Niikuni. *The Marginal World of Ōe Kenzaburo: A Study in Themes and Techniques*. Armonk, NY: M. E. Sharpe, 1986.

———. "Re-Visioning Japanese Literary Studies Through a Feminist Perspective," in *Revisionism in Japanese Literary Studies*, *PMAJLS* (Proceedings of the Midwest Association for Japanese Literary Studies), vol. 2 (Summer 1996): 119–137.

Woolf, Virginia. "Professions for Women," in *The Death of the Moth and Other Essays*. New York: Harcourt Brace Jovanovich, 1970, pp. 235–242.

Yamamoto Michiko and Nakayama Chinatsu. "Kuyashisa no naka kara umareta 'Betty-san no Niwa'" ("Betty-san's Garden" That Was Born Out Of Chagrin). *Sandē Mainichi* (18 March 1973): 58–92.

# Index

**Michiko Niikuni Wilson**, born and raised in Japan, studied in the United States for her B.A. in English, and her M.A. and Ph.D. in comparative literature. She is the author of *The Marginal World of Ōe Kenzaburo: A Study in Themes and Techniques*, the first book-length critical work on the 1994 Nobel Laureate. She is also the translator of his 1976 "fantastic" narrative *The Pinch Runner Memorandum*. In addition to her interest in Ōba Minako, Ms. Wilson has written an article on another Japanese female writer, Miyamoto Yuriko, that appeared in *U.S.-Japan Women's Journal*. She has completed an English translation of *Naku tori no* (Birds Crying) by Ōba Minako. The first chapter appeared in *Chicago Review* (1993). She teaches Japanese language, literature, and culture at the University of Virginia.